BIO-YOUNG

BIO-YOUNG

BIO-YOUNG

*Get Younger at a Cellular
and Hormonal Level*

ROXY DILLON, BSc, MSc

ATRIA PAPERBACK

NEW YORK · LONDON · TORONTO · SYDNEY · NEW DELHI

ATRIA PAPERBACK

An Imprint of Simon & Schuster, Inc.
1230 Avenue of the Americas
New York, NY 10020

First Atria Paperback edition February 2017

ATRIA PAPERBACK and colophon are trademarks of Simon & Schuster, Inc.

For information about special discounts for bulk purchases, please contact
Simon & Schuster Special Sales at 1-866-506-1949
or business@simonandschuster.com.

The Simon & Schuster Speakers Bureau can bring authors to your
live event. For more information or to book an event, contact the
Simon & Schuster Speakers Bureau at 1-866-248-3049
or visit our website at www.simonspeakers.com.

Interior design by Paul Dippolito

Manufactured in the United States of America

10   9   8   7   6   5   4   3   2

The Library of Congress has cataloged the hardcover edition as follows:

Names: Dillon, Roxy.
Title: Bio-young: get younger at a cellular and hormonal level / Roxy
Dillon, BSc, MSc.
Description: First Atria Books hardcover edition. | New York : Atria
Books, 2015.
Identifiers: LCCN 2015014733
Subjects: LCSH: Aging--Prevention. | Longevity. | Aging--Nutritional
aspects.
   | Dietary supplements. | Hormone therapy. | BISAC: SELF-HELP / Aging. |
   HEALTH & FITNESS / Beauty & Grooming.
Classification: LCC RA776.75 .D55 2015 | DDC 613.2--dc23 LC record
available at http://lccn.loc.gov/2015014733

ISBN 978-1-4767-9681-9
ISBN 978-1-4767-9684-0 (pbk)
ISBN 978-1-4767-9685-7 (ebook)

DISCLAIMER

The information given in this book is intended as information and is not a substitute for medical advice. If you suffer from any medical condition or if there is any possibility of pregnancy, please consult an appropriate physician for advice before implementing any of the suggestions made in this book. Before using any topical treatment, please test it on the inside of your wrist and wait twenty-four hours. If any redness, rash, or irritation develops, find an alternative from the list of suggestions applicable to the condition you wish to treat. Do not use any substance you are allergic to.

The treatments included in this book are only for adult use.

For my children, for Matilda, and for MK

CONTENTS

Contents

PART III · THE *BIO-YOUNG* PROGRAMS

Youth is wasted on the young.

—Oscar Wilde

So stay young with *Bio-Young*!

—Roxy Dillon

BIO-YOUNG

Redefine What It Means to "Age Naturally"

My love for nature and its potential to heal and support the body—from vitamins, tinctures, and supplements to food, herbs, and botany—began very young. A dear family friend, a dermatologist, encouraged me at just three years old to enjoy half a lemon and a handful of vitamin C tablets every day. This became my favorite snack and was intended to ward off colds and flu at the time and keep my skin supple as I aged. I was so fascinated with the idea that vitamins could help our bodies function and thrive that I often recited a vitamin alphabet for fun—vitamin A, vitamin E, and vitamin C—the way other kids sang their regular ABCs. I memorized their dosages by age six, and around the same time, I became fascinated with plants and flowers, too. I grew up in Slovakia. Sometimes I rode the train for almost two hours to simply visit a meadow where a deep purple orchid called *Epipactis atrorubens* grew. When I couldn't get there, I'd pull out a card I'd bought with a dried silver edelweiss pressed onto it. I'd lift the cellophane that protected the flower's starlike shape and touch its small, downy petals. To me, nature was a source of beauty, fascination, usefulness, and wonder.

I bought my first book on DIY beauty treatments, *Natural Beauty Secrets* by Deborah Rutledge, when I was thirteen and began concocting my own face, hair, and body preparations. The first one I made was a lanolin-based cleansing lotion—I was so impressed when it quickly washed ink stains from my fingers! A cultivated interest in nature transitioned into a greater passion for science and biology on an academic scale. I studied neuropsychology and neuroscience in college, and after graduation, counseled clients on nutrition and herbal treatments. I earned a master's degree in biochemical pharmacology, with postgraduate research on nutrition, serotonin and depression, and the sodium, potassium, and calcium channels in neurons. Throughout, I was fascinated with how our cellular and hormonal functioning affects how we age—a field that's grown rapidly in the last fifteen years. In an ideal marriage of my personal passions and scientific research and discovery, I've used natural substances to restore and reverse the aging process in thousands of clients ever since.

In my practice, I treat various aspects of what we call aging—from heart disease, to diabetes, to cancer. People turn to me when they feel there's "nothing the doctors can do," which makes success with natural therapies all the more gratifying. As a result, I've always been at the forefront of this field. For instance, I recommended gou qi zi—or "goji"—berries for kidney and eye health more than a decade before they were known as a mainstream superfood; I advised the topical use of Vitasorb C, which is a preparation for internal use, years before the first serum appeared on the market to treat wrinkles; and I recommended that my patients use flax oil and healthy fats at a time when doctors insisted that fat and cholesterol were bad for their health, and now the latest research shows that many are not.

In my own life, I love trying out new treatments on myself based on exciting scientific findings that ultimately form the basis of what I believe, study, and practice. My own anti-aging routine varies according to what I need that day or week, but I assure you that I've used every suggestion in this book. My goal is always to activate anti-aging pathways, and to keep cellular and hormonal function at a youthful level. If my hair needs a boost, I'll use rosemary and eucalyptus, or maybe lard or lanolin; if my skin looks tired, I'll go for avocado oil and licorice; and if it's sagging, I'll concentrate on an almond oil and dill essential oil mix to increase elastin. At its simplest, I take fenugreek powder and fennel powder every day by adding it to a liquid. I take boron and vitamin E and eat whole-wheat pasta and soy yogurt every day. I use estrogenic herbs on my face, hair, and body—including licorice, which I extract and then add to an avocado oil base, plus a fennel, aniseed, ylang-ylang, and dill essential oil combination blended with a cocoa butter or avocado oil base. To make it easy for you, the specific plan I lean on most is at the end of this book, in chapter 12. And as a result of all my anti-aging efforts, at the age of fifty-eight I'm frequently thought to be in my thirties—no matter what age you are now, you can look significantly younger with the *Bio-Young* program!

I find this work to be very rewarding. I recently helped a forty-year-old client who was desperately unhappy, because shortly after having a hysterectomy for health reasons, she began to see rapid signs of aging—bad wrinkles, sagging skin. I told her not to worry and gave her one of my preparations—a cocoa butter and olive oil base with fennel and ylang-ylang essential oils—and just three days later, her face had become smoother and suppler. She was thrilled! Then there's my thirty-six-year-old client whose friend recently mistook her for sixteen (yes, sixteen!), and another who's sixty and was told she had the body of a twenty-five-year-old! This last one had been using a breast cream I made for her from olive oil and fenugreek powder, and a cocoa butter cream made with avocado oil plus fennel, ylang-ylang, dill, and aniseed essential oils. The preparation increased her breast size, firmness, volume, roundness, and heaviness. They also lifted, and wrinkles between her breasts vanished—

all this, over ten years after having her last child. Is that incredible or what?

Going Biologically Au Naturel

The central message of *Bio-Young* and what makes it so unique and revolutionary is that by following the plans outlined here a woman can actually *become* biologically younger. This book is not about appearing to look or seem young via cosmetic or superficial means. Looking and feeling younger here is the result of *actual* biological anti-aging in your body, and *actual* younger cellular and hormonal function. And best of all, you will use safe and incredibly effective natural substances to achieve this.

Three great perks come to mind when I think about why it's so wonderful to use natural treatments for age-related concerns. First, natural remedies don't just make you look young—they can turn back the clock. Estrogen levels are restored, skin becomes more pliable and resilient. The second benefit comes from the biological fact that our bodies respond to natural and complex herbs, foods, and supplements very quickly, because the approach is both gentle and in harmony with our biology. The third benefit is safety, which is paramount to many people. The natural substances that I recommend to my clients and in this book are very safe. I have used them myself for decades, and my clients have also used them with confidence and without any detrimental side effects. Unfortunately, that cannot be said of conventional hormone therapy or many aging-related prescriptions and creams.

My program is culled from cutting-edge science, client success stories, and my own experiences with natural herbs, foods, and supplements that have been in existence for thousands of years. What's more, science is providing exciting validation that gentle, natural substances produce astonishing anti-aging effects in the human body; researchers have been classifying and naming the active compounds found in herbs, foods, and other natural sources for the greater public. For instance, chamomile is an herb, but allantoin is a compound isolated from chamomile and thus has been named a "cosmeceutical." Quercetin, found in onions, has been termed a "nutraceutical." And all of these compounds are known as "bioceuticals." How the compound is used determines its name, so allantoin, which is used externally or cosmetically on the skin, is a cosmeceutical, whereas quercetin in pill form, intended for internal use, is a nutraceutical. For ease of understanding, you'll hear me refer to the whole lot of these as "natural substances," but trust me when I say they all have very scientific legs.

The prime of your life, when everything in your body works best, is thirty years old. After that, cellular and hormonal function declines rapidly, and this is aging. So the aim of *Bio-Young*'s program is to return cellular and hormonal function to that of a thirty-year-old. I'll show you how to bring your prime back in real ways by activating biochemical mechanisms and reversing damage.

Why Youthful Cellular and Hormonal Function Is Ideal

In this book, you'll often hear me refer to two levels at which our bodies age, because it is necessary to treat both to achieve youthful results. First, there's cellular aging. This involves the slowing down of cellular function. Here the components in every cell carry out their tasks with less efficiency and much less speed than they do in a young body. Cellular aging therefore leads to genetic changes, which can result in a disease like cancer, as well as changes in the synthesis of essential structural components such as collagen and elastin, which leads to the formation of wrinkles. Cellular aging affects the basic, moment-to-moment cellular activity of the body, resulting in decreased production of many components. One of the major ones is ATP, or adenosine triphosphate—this is the energy source of a cell that makes life possible. Without it, the cells of the body and, thus, the body itself would not function. Put another way, the body cannot survive without this cellular function.

Hormonal aging refers to the decrease of essential hormones that occurs with age and can negatively impact our appearance, energy, and sex drive. I consider decreased sex hormones to be particularly detrimental to how we look and feel, but other hormones also decrease with age, such as human growth hormone, which supports muscle and bone mass, as well as melatonin, which influences how much we sleep and our energy the next day. The hormonal system is slower than the activity within the cell. It has a "macro" field of action, influencing the overall functioning of organs.

The two systems have unique areas of influence—cellular activity happens within cells and hormonal activity governs organs. This means that natural substances, like green tea, can affect cellular activity and prevent genetic changes from occurring and offer substantial cancer protection. Hormones affect cells, too, but in more general though extremely powerful ways; without a hormonal component, the full impact of aging cannot be prevented or reversed. So to use green tea as an example here, it protects against sun damage, but it cannot rebuild skin thickness. Sex hormones are needed for that, particularly estrogen in women, and estrogen and testosterone in men. This is why this program is so powerful and unique. Both these vitally important biological areas are addressed.

Cellular aging and hormonal aging don't happen at separate times or affect different body systems. Everything in the body happens all at once, all the time. I am always treating both at the same time, but for ease of understanding, I separate them when discussing specific mechanisms. It is difficult to comprehend, but right now, trillions of biochemical reactions are taking place in your body. Synthesis and breaking down—two opposing mechanisms—take place almost simultaneously. Cellular mechanisms are affected by hormones, and aging cells in your hormone-producing organs result in lower levels of hormones. But when improvement happens, it happens all at once, too, and continues to occur, as long as you support them in the best way.

Some improvements are visible before others, and that's because some body systems repair themselves more quickly. So skin, for instance, is one of the first systems to show improvement, because skin cells have a fast turnover. Hair takes longer to show improved growth, since hair growth is much slower than skin cell turnover. In this respect, it's important to note that purely cellular approaches to certain anti-aging efforts are less effective than a cellular and hormonal approach. So using hair as our example, if you simply applied caffeine to affect it on a cellular level, it would be far less effective than using the cellular and hormonal approach in this book that utilizes rosemary, eucalyptus, fennel, and ylang-ylang essential oils to improve your hair on both levels. The same is true of all anti-aging treatments. If these treatments only improve cellular function, they will produce only limited improvements.

When I treat age-related concerns, the medical and aesthetic goal is one and the same. What is visible in the face as the disappearance of wrinkles and folds is the result of fewer changes to the genetic code, more accurate structural protein synthesis, and a more youthful hormonal status. This also means that the risk of heart disease, cancer, diabetes, and other age-related medical conditions has been lowered.

Walking, Talking, Anti-Aging Proof

Though I consider myself a scientist, some of the most compelling "data" I've encountered are actually my clients' success stories. I think of Janet, a woman in her fifties who was a lifelong smoker and heavy drinker, which contributed to pucker lines around her mouth. This made her lipstick bleed and produced a marked loss of firmness in that area, which made her lips look sunken. She'd tried many expensive treatments and creams before seeing me. I suggested she use topical application of Vitasorb C, a skin-friendly preparation of vitamin C. Not only did her lips improve, but the skin on her face gained an even, glowing tone with no side effects!

Aging also affects people's hair and scalps. I remember when my client Sandra was in her late forties and shocked to discover she'd developed two bald spots on either side of her head, just above her temples. The part in her hair had also become worryingly wide— she could hardly collect hair at the nape of her neck for a small bun! I advised Sandra to rub rosemary and eucalyptus essential oils into her scalp, paying special attention to the thinning areas. Two weeks later, her hair began to grow back in her part, and it only took a total of eight months to see new growth, improved thickness, texture, and weight that actually swings around her shoulders when she moves.

Of course, not all aging concerns are aesthetic; many are functional and can affect your confidence in a way that bleeds into every corner of your life. For instance, my client Carol was in her mid-fifties when she saw me for severe vaginal atrophy, which is the thinning, drying, and inflammation of the vaginal walls due to having less estrogen in your body. As you can imagine, this affected Carol's sex life and self-assurance. She felt so bad about herself, she avoided sex for two years, even with OTC lubrication! She turned to me as a last resort, and boy, was she happy she did. I suggested a cocoa butter and avocado cream with a small amount of fennel essential oil to avoid irritating the delicate vaginal tissues. She also took a genistein supplement and fenugreek powder to improve her hormone levels. Her body responded within days and her vagina returned to a youthful state—thicker walls, increased lubrication, and a longer vagina. Because the vaginal walls are composed of mucous membranes, the treatment was easily absorbed into her body and her entire being benefited. Her skin glowed, her joints felt more flexible, and her stomach pouch shrank. The only side effect? She had more confidence and heightened libido, and she initiated sex with her husband!

How to Use This Book

Bio-Young is divided into three parts that show you how to reverse cellular and hormonal function in the aging body, with programs to use at various times in your life, depending on your specific needs. The chapters transition from focusing on a more basic, cell-based system, to more complex systems, while we also move from simpler concepts mostly based on cellular function, such as cell protection and collagen/elastin synthesis, to more hormonal concepts that affect the body, emotions, and psychological parameters. In every chapter, I'll discuss concepts and natural substances that drive toward a handful of treatments at the end of each one. Experiment with these and feel free to integrate your favorites into a program in the final section. *Bio-Young* is also structured in a way that begins with basic skin mechanisms and then progresses to more complex mechanisms. Some chapters do involve more of one area, say cellular, or of the other, hormonal, but remember, cellular and hormonal events are in constant interaction. It is not possible to separate them in a strict, categorical, black-and-white manner. Biology is far more complex than that. So even though it may seem that there is more cellular or hormonal function at any point occurring, this can change within a chapter. By the time you get to chapter 10 on menopause, you will see that some of the treatments are hormonal, some are cellular, and some strongly affect both. If I may quote a rather well-known maxim: "The knee bone is connected to the thigh bone . . ." In other words, biology is very complex.

I'd also like you to keep a few guidelines in mind as you try preparations:

Mind your dosages. Most doses are given in the form of capsules, tablespoons, or tincture drops. One capsule of herb is equivalent to one gram of that herb. If a supplement's directions specify nine capsules, then take nine grams or two teaspoons (not both) of loose powder instead.

Be a selective shopper. For all natural substances, organic is your gold standard, but if this is not available or is out of your price range, that's okay, too. For supplements, I like vegetarian capsules; "citrate" forms of minerals are fine, and vitamin E and beta-carotene must be in their natural form. Look for essential oils from companies that specialize in essential and carrier oils. These don't have to be organic, but it's better if they're available in that form.

Don't worry about availability. Most of the substances here are easily available all over the world. In the event that your local health food store does not carry a product mentioned here, ask them to order it. If this is not possible, check Amazon. I purchase everything I recommend via Amazon.

Be safe. Do not store any treatments you make in glass containers, because they can break should you find yourself using them in various rooms and toting them around when you're on the go. Also, when making your own preparations, never leave oils or fats unattended on the cooker, and never heat beyond a gentle simmer. Allow all hot liquids to cool to a safe temperature before handling.

By the end of this book, you should feel empowered to know that your age is not a number. It's a function of your cellular and hormonal activity. And with *Bio-Young*, I will show you how to become younger as your cellular and hormonal function returns to working at a youthful level using safe, natural substances. On a tangible level, you should experience improved brain function, more energy, a youthful optimism, improved sleep, rejuvenated skin, hair, and bones, and an increased libido. It will help your limbs to become taut, your stomach to lose its paunch, and help your jowls to vanish.

With *Bio-Young*, you have access, for the very first time, to a unique and revolutionary anti-aging program. Make the most of it! Take advantage of how your cellular and hormonal function can be stimulated to make you young, at any age, at any time. Celebrate the fact that aging is not inevitable, and that the aging process can be slowed down and, in many cases, reversed. Living a healthy, long life and looking much younger than your years are entirely within your grasp.

Part I

YOUNGER CELLS, YOUNGER YOU

CHAPTER I

Super Sirtuins! Or, How to Look Great on Your 256th Birthday

ANTI-AGING MECHANISM: Longevity gene activation

USE: Increasing lifespan and energy

STARRING: Berries, green tea, garlic, ginseng, gotu kola

For centuries, nearly every culture has searched for a way to slow and even reverse the aging process. Greek writers pursued the Fountain of Youth as far back as the fifth century BCE. India still recognizes the ancient science of longevity called Ayurveda, which is believed to add years to your life by nourishing and detoxing the body. My favorite success story of all, however, is that of a Chinese herbalist named Li Ching-Yuen, who, according to some records, was born in 1677 and died 256 years later. Regardless of whether you believe Master Li's story is myth, reality, or a little of both, you have to admit there's a part of you that when you hear this thinks, "I'll have what he's having."

Cut to the twenty-first century, and we're just as focused on discovering the mechanisms that prevent and reverse aging as our global ancestors were. In fact, one of the most studied proteins in the past ten years that's been found to aid the anti-aging process is called sirtuin, or silent information regulator. Sirtuins control the rate at which we age, and the length of our lifespan. They've been dubbed "longevity genes," which is also why I thought it would be a great place to begin our anti-aging program. Stimulate your sirtuins, the thinking goes, and you'll live longer and look younger.

One of the most studied sirtuins is called SIRT1. Among other sources, it's found in garlic, Panax ginseng, and *Polygonum multiflorum,* an herb grown in China that research has shown demonstrates anti-aging properties that activate a variety of biological processes in the body. There has been some controversy recently regarding possible liver damage resulting from the internal use of *Polygonum multiflorum,* and for that reason I do not recommend that you use it.

But guess what? These three herbs were an integral part of Master Li's regimen, switching on his SIRT1 when he used them! Even if he lived half the years that sources claim, it's still an impressive number and one that supports the longevity-enhancing properties of herbs, in a time long before science showed us how.

In this chapter, I'd like to first explain how the body ages and reinforce the importance of addressing anti-aging solutions on cellular and hormonal levels. Then I'll discuss the power of modern-day sirtuin activators that you can add to your daily routine to help you look and feel young.

Aging Is More Than Skin Deep

Aging affects every part of your body—how you look, feel, and function. It affects your hair, face, and body in more ways than you probably realize. In *Bio-Young,* you will learn what Master Li seems to have known, too—that you can extend and even reverse your years using natural remedies. Some of the substances that do this are EGCG (found in green tea), turmeric, red grape juice, coffee, hawthorn, ginkgo, hops, fennel, fenugreek, red palm oil, as well as supplements like nicotinamide adenine dinucleotide (NAD), R-alpha-lipoic acid, ubiquinol and CoQ10, vitamins, minerals, and numerous other compounds that have the power to make a real impact on how long you live and how young you look. We will show you how to use these elements and others to improve cellular function and increase hormonal levels to stop and reverse deep changes, at every level of your body, right down to the bones.

We tend to think of aging as an effect on the skin—wrinkles, creases, and sags as far as the eye can see. But as you age, every layer of older skin is depleted and disorganized, from the outermost epidermis to the supporting muscle and the deepest fat layers. Topical preparations, particularly vitamin A derivatives and natural vitamin E, can repair and plump up the epidermis, the top layer of the skin, and make the surface look smoother and less wrinkled. This is very welcome, of course.

But aging does not stop at the upper skin layers. It profoundly depletes the deeper layers, leading to unmistakable signs that no makeup can disguise and only anti-aging at both the cellular and hormonal levels can repair. Not even cosmetic surgery can correct some of these consequences, like pallor due to the loss of capillaries or the loss of youthful lip, eye, complexion, and hair color due to the loss of pigment-producing cells called melanocytes. In *Bio-Young* you will learn how to repair even these seemingly irreversible changes by using safe, natural substances.

Although using natural substances can help make you look decades younger, please keep in mind that the exciting science that explains the mechanisms that underlie their actions is very young and fresh. The bulk of our knowledge about what happens as we age comes from studies that have appeared in the last ten years and have only been available, for the most part, in scientific journals.

The Ultimate One-Two Punch:
Cellular + Hormonal Function

To achieve true anti-aging, you must activate cellular mechanisms, plus biochemical and hormonal anti-aging pathways, and restore them to youthful functioning. So it's important to understand how the combination of certain herbs, foods, and supplements can promote deep and long-lasting effects.

Why this approach? When you improve cellular function, every one of your cells operates better, and this yields great results. When you improve cellular function through natural means, you reverse your age in a real, biological sense. Your cells are younger, and you look younger.

But cellular improvement isn't enough. Take the power of vitamin C. Applying this to your face as a serum can increase collagen levels there. Taking it internally will help rejuvenate mitochondrial function in your skin and heart. Cellular function acts on the level of every cell, improving energy production, repair, and clearing of cellular debris. All of these mechanisms become slower and less efficient as we age. Improved cellular function very effectively reverses this decline, making you biologically younger at the cellular level. This is visible on the outside! Because there are many changes that aging causes in your body, some are not corrected, or reversed, by only optimizing your cellular mechanisms. Think of it this way: a healthy thirty-year-old has great cellular function *and* hormones working at peak performance. So to look truly young past thirty, and to continue doing so, you must rejuvenate at cellular and hormonal levels. And since vitamin C can only increase the muscle and fat atrophy that shrivels our skin as we get older, we have to add hormones to the picture for deep, and highly visible, anti-aging results.

Varicose veins are a great example of an aging concern caused by cellular and hormonal factors and should be addressed that way, as well. With age, your leg muscles atrophy, skin thins, and your blood vessel walls become weaker. Hormonal factors play a part, since women, particularly during pregnancy, are more likely to develop this condition. So thickening the skin, strengthening the muscles, and increasing elastin in the blood vessel walls bring about great improvement. But how do we do this naturally? Bioflavonoids such as lemon peel and bilberry are very helpful, as they work on a cellular level by strengthening the blood vessel walls. But many people do not experience varicose vein relief with bioflavonoids alone—you must cure this at the hormonal level by increasing elastin directly in the vein through the use of dill seed essential oil. Because dill is estrogenic, it produces the beneficial effects of this hormone in your body and is known to tighten saggy areas, too.

As you will read in later chapters, dill seed essential oil is just one natural substance that has a positive estrogenic effect on the body, which can also protect you from certain cancers and heart disease. Raising your hormones with safe, natural means can lead to truly astonishing, visible results, because estrogen is a dominant hormone in a woman's body. As we age, more and more effects of declining estrogen appear, including the decline of elastin, collagen, muscle, and fat. Even the sudden appearance of dry skin after age thirty is due to declining estrogen, which causes a decrease in ceramides and hyaluronic acid, substances responsible for keeping skin moist, supple, and hydrated.

A Note About Hormone-Affecting Substances

It's obvious that male hormones should be kept low when women are trying to restore their youthful, girly curves and glow. At the same time, raising your female hormones, particularly those in the estrogen family, will not lead to concerns about hormonally sensitive cancers. By using the safe methods outlined in *Bio-Young*, you can rest assured that your risk will not be increased.

However, some of the most well-known hormonally active and oft-suggested remedies can actually harm your hormone function. One of these remedies is soy, which has been touted as a cure-all for women of a certain age. The problem is that soy has been shown to lower certain estrogens and can produce detrimental effects, particularly when a woman has reached menopause. Soy also lowers thyroid function, leading to weight gain and a dramatic loss of energy.

Wild yam is another hormone-affecting herb known for producing contradictory effects in women. Wild yam, or *Dioscorea villosa*, is not related to the yams, or sweet potatoes, that you buy at the grocery store. *Dioscorea villosa* is thought to work by raising progesterone, though there is a good deal of controversy surrounding this idea, since it's unclear how the human body could convert diosgenin, the compound found in wild yam, to progesterone.

The interesting thing is that any negative effects are entirely absent when other sources of diosgenin, such as fenugreek or sarsaparilla, are used instead of wild yam. Creams that contain pharmaceutical doses of estrogens, such as estradiol, have been shown to produce visible anti-aging effects in as little as one week. But most women are wary of using pharmaceutical estrogens, as some of the estrogen from the cream will be absorbed by the body, which may result in undesirable side effects like nausea, bloating, breast lumps, headaches, unusual vaginal bleeding, and increased blood clotting, which can lead to strokes. How amazing, then, that these results can be obtained using certain fragrant essential oils that act in a very similar way, but without any of the health concerns.

Finally, bio-identical hormones on the market also come with a degree of risk. Both the more commonly used hormonal replacement preparations and the newer, bio-identical hormones are manufactured in a laboratory and possess marked hormonal activity. Bio-identical hormones resemble the hormones found in your body more closely than the pharmaceutical ones regularly dispensed by doctors, but because they are equally powerful, they can also cause pronounced imbalances in the body that are negative. Supplying your body with hormones leads to reduced glandular function and gland atrophy, and this applies to all hormone-producing glands, including the ovaries and the testes.

When Natural Choices Are Full of Good Surprises

All that said, when it comes to aging, natural substances are the way to go. They stimulate the beneficial processes that help you look and feel young, while preventing DNA damage and disease. The results can even surprise you in the best way.

The most remarkable example of this occurs in the treatment of blood pressure through natural means—and a stable blood pressure in many ways is essential to healthy aging. Panax ginseng, for example, has been shown to both raise and lower blood pressure, depending on the individual's needs. In other words, if you take Panax ginseng and your blood pressure is too high, it can help lower it. If your blood pressure is too low, ginseng can help raise it. In each case, blood pressure will be normalized and brought into a normal, healthy range. This kind of effect can only be achieved if the mechanisms that led to the imbalance in blood pressure, whether high or low, are corrected. Drugs cannot do this, because their pharmaceutical actions are highly specific and unidirectional. They will either raise blood pressure, and do this in all people, at all times, or they will lower blood pressure, and, again, do this regardless of the starting blood pressure of the person who takes the drug, lowering it even if the person's blood pressure is already too low, and resulting in dangerous side effects.

Another remedy for lowering blood pressure will have an effect both while you take it and after you've stopped the supplement. This is not the case with most pharmaceuticals. This plant is called hawthorn and has this effect, in part, by inhibiting angiotensin-converting enzyme (ACE). This mechanism is the basis of drugs used to lower blood pressure, the ACE inhibitors. But one of the unfortunate side effects of ACE inhibitor drugs is kidney damage, a side effect completely absent when using natural hawthorn. I should also mention that natural hawthorn clears your arteries, strengthens the heart muscle, offers antioxidant protection, and prevents your body's tendency to lay down fat stores. Not bad for side effects, right?

Many Actions, Many Pathways

Researchers estimate that there are more than one hundred fifty anti-aging pathways active in the human body. It is then necessary to focus on the most effective mechanisms that deliver the most visible results. It is important to remember that every natural substance has many actions, often influencing several anti-aging pathways at the same time, in various beneficial ways. Just as there are so many anti-aging pathways, so there are hundreds of natural substances that affect them. There isn't one superfood or one herb that can do it all, no matter how effective it is.

Because nothing in your body occurs in isolation, activating life-enhancing sirtuins will help produce beneficial effects on many other anti-aging pathways. For example, in a lab model of breast cancer, resveratrol has been shown to activate SIRT1 and, at the same time, inhibit a protein called survivin, in this way preventing the growth of breast cancer cells. Inhibition or disruption of the survivin pathway suppresses tumor growth, so we see that stimulating SIRT1 produces a very beneficial effect on another pathway that plays a role in remaining youthful and disease-free.

Remember Master Li's sirtuins—aka our "longevity genes," which control the rate at which we age, and the length of our life span? A part of that anti-aging includes anti-cancer effects, brain protection, and younger skin and hair. Adding sirtuin activators to your healthy diet and beauty regimen also gives you the type of expanded lifespan that researchers have seen with landmark concepts like calorie restriction (CR), which was the first means ever found to prolong life across a variety of species, including rats, yeast, fish, mice, dogs, and even monkeys. That being said, there have been no human studies on calorie restriction, and there are a few reasons for that. First, it's not possible to restrict human calorie intake for a reasonable length of time under experimental conditions, even though we have data concerning oxidative stress, metabolic rate, insulin sensitivity, endocrine and sympathetic nervous system function, and these point strongly to an anti-aging effect of calorie restriction in humans. In addition, we have "negative" data, that is, data from overfed, obese individuals, which show accelerated aging in all aspects of this process. Second, there are obvious ethical problems with restricting calories from infancy or childhood, or during adulthood, under experimental conditions for a significant length of time. Good thing sirtuins mimic the effects of calorie restriction without producing any negative effects at all!

Eat Your Way to Sirtuin Stimulation

So far, seven sirtuin proteins have been identified in the human body, each one with a slightly different mode of action. An easy way to activate your sirtuins every day is to choose foods from the following list. All of these contain compounds that can help stimulate your sirtuin longevity pathways.

Foods	Sirtuin-Activating Compounds
red grape juice	resveratrol
blueberries	resveratrol
cranberries	resveratrol
pomegranate juice	resveratrol
cocoa powder	resveratrol
tart cherry powder	resveratrol
green tea	epigallocatechin-3-gallate
turmeric	curcumin
onions, especially red	quercetin
apple juice	quercetin
tomato paste	chalcones
strawberries	fisetin
garlic	allicin

Eating these foods, drinking the juices, and using concentrated freeze-dried powders or other concentrated products will provide you with a much higher concentration of sirtuin-activating compounds than the fresh fruit or vegetable, and do wonders for how young you look, how great you feel, and how long you live. These complex plant sources have been shown to activate not only a variety of the magnificent seven sirtuins, but many of the other one hundred fifty anti-aging pathways so far discovered. This is the cellular function revolution at its best. By eating a variety of specially chosen, concentrated supplements, you can achieve a level of mitochondrial rejuvenation that truly helps to reverse the effects of aging.

I'd now like to focus on three sirtuin activators that pack a noticeable punch and illustrate the power of this naturally occur-ring science—resveratrol, green tea, and garlic. You can enjoy them naturally or consume them as supplements, as I suggest at the chap-ter's end.

1. Radical Resveratrol

Resveratrol is a sirtuin-activating compound that's found in red wine and may provide an explanation for what's known as the "French paradox"—that is, the finding that the French, who eat a diet full of saturated fat, have surprisingly low levels of heart disease. Resver-atrol, one of the most potent sirtuin activators discovered so far, is found in red wine. In March 2013, Harvard researchers found that resveratrol is capable of slowing aging. This has important implica-tions for human longevity.

Resveratrol, or trans-3, 5, 4'-trihydroxystilbene, is an antioxidant found in the skin of many fruits, including blueberries, peanuts, and, when eaten with the thin, papery red skin, even rhubarb. It is partic-ularly found in the red grape, and in the red wine made from these grapes. Levels of resveratrol in red wine vary according to grape type and country of origin. The highest levels are found in wines from cooler countries, with the highest being from Bordeaux, and lower levels found in red wines from California. The pinot noir grape produces the highest levels of resveratrol, but cabernet sauvignon from the cooler regions and Italian sangiovese are also very high in this compound.

Resveratrol activates the sirtuin anti-aging pathway. This path-way is a chain of biochemical reactions, which, when activated, ac-tually slows down aging. This stimulation is complex and appears to require resveratrol in its natural state, with many cofactors intact—as it's found in plants. It is far less active in its chemically purified form. What's more, every one of your cells contains an energy-producing factory called a mitochondrion (plural, mitochondria), and optimal mitochondrial function is essential to long life, energy, and a youthful appearance—and sure enough, resveratrol stimulates the sirtuin that affects aging mitochondria.

But there is a big problem here: alcohol is aging. It damages your body on every level, from your liver, to your skin, to your brain. It's wonderful to learn that resveratrol is found in the glass of red wine you might occasionally have to relax, but it's not an everyday option. Nor can you safely indulge in large enough quantities if you want to achieve dramatic anti-aging effects. Fortunately, resveratrol is found in a whole range of other tasty, easily accessible foods and herbs, all of which are safe to eat every day in effective quantities that give you the anti-aging benefits of sirtuins.

Since sirtuins have such powerful and far-reaching anti-aging effects, and because resveratrol is so highly effective at activating these amazing enzymes, there is, as you would expect, an ongoing and feverish hunt for the most effective resveratrol-type drug. Scientists estimate that the effect of such a drug would be an increase in the normal, healthy human lifespan to one hundred fifty years!

And while sirtuin activators have become one of the hottest topics in cosmeceuticals, which are cosmetic products with biological ingredients so highly active they require a special category to themselves, purified resveratrol results have been disappointing. One of the problems with resveratrol is that it degrades very rapidly and is metabolized within half an hour or so, which gives it a very short time to act. But if you ingest it rather than apply it, you can start to reap the benefits of resveratrol at any age—even if you begin taking it at middle age and/or add it to a Western high-fat diet. So long as you add resveratrol-rich foods to your life every day, you should reap significant anti-aging benefits.

2. Gorgeous Green Tea

Green tea is another powerful sirtuin activator with multiple bene-fits. Epigallocatechin-3-gallate (EGCG), a component of green tea, has been shown to lengthen telomeres—an essential part of human cells that affect how they age—in damaged heart cells. This is an extraordinary finding, since this process prevents cell death. EGCG also protects the skin from UVB- and UVA-induced sun damage and protects collagen from degradation by collagenase, an enzyme responsible for collagen breakdown. Levels of collagenase increase as we get older, leading to a loss of collagen, thinner skin, sagging, and wrinkles. What's more, EGCG promotes hair growth in hair follicle cultures, depletes fat accumulation, and stimulates lipolysis in human adipocytes. In plain English, this means that the marvelous compound gets rid of fat from your fat cells, effectively and safely. It will help to improve your heart, boost your brain function, and smooth your skin. EGCG has been shown to prevent bone loss, ward off tooth decay, and protect against all kinds of cancer, including leukemia and melanoma.

And for aging purposes, here's what's truly impressive: compounds from green tea have been shown to stimulate the mitochondria, or energy cells, in your brain, skin, all over. They can stimulate cellular function and can help make every one of your cells young, and in doing so should expand your lifespan. On a hormonal level, green tea compounds decrease dihydrotestosterone, or DHT, a form of testosterone known to increase with age in both men and women. DHT is responsible for many of the signs of old age women hate—thinning hair or baldness and unwanted facial hair.

3. Garlic the Great

Garlic, known unfairly as the stink bulb, is reputed for its ability to help fight infections, but this herb also activates SIRT1. This means it is a heart protector, energy giver, skin saver, and lifespan extender. One of its primary benefits is as an infection fighter. Steering free of infective illness is vital for a long lifespan. Your immune system declines with age unless you take steps to prevent this, and many people succumb to lung infections and flus that could have been prevented.

☀ Sirtuin-Stimulating Spotlight: Gotu Kola and Ginseng

Gotu kola—known in Latin as *Centella asiatica* or *Hydrocotyle asiatica*—also activates SIRT1, and with no negative side effects. Gotu kola has been shown to protect the brain, increase collagen production, and strengthen hair follicles. For centuries, gotu kola extract was used topically for hair follicle stimulation, wound healing, and increasing collagen. When taken internally, it activates the sirtuin pathways, exhibiting powerful anti-aging potential for the whole body. It has been shown to be highly neuroprotective, preventing glutamate-induced neurotoxicity, which kills brain cells.

Gotu kola contains ursane triterpenes, complex organic molecules with anti-cancer effects that are also powerful stimulators of collagen synthesis, with or without vitamin C. The ursane triterpenes and many other remarkable compounds make gotu kola one of the most potent wound healers around, and one of the most effective anti-aging wrinkle treatments. It works if you take the powder internally, and it works if you apply it as a tea or extracted in an oil base. So you truly can look great, with smooth, firm skin, even at an age when others will be showing theirs.

Ursane and related compounds are also found in rosemary oil, which accounts for many of the plant's extraordinary neuroprotective and anti-aging properties. You will meet rosemary in the next chapter, since it is the main ingredient of a powerful anti-aging potion called Queen of Hungary water. Here's the bottom line: nature simplifies it for you by mixing up many powerful compounds in one plant, and by giving natural substances many varied, beneficial actions. So as you read about these compounds, please enjoy the fact that all you have to do is take gotu kola powder or use an anti-aging essential oil like rosemary, mixed into a cream, for all the mitochondrial stimulation, collagen synthesis, and anti-aging power you need!

The other Chinese herb I love for SIRT1 activation is called Panax ginseng, or Asian ginseng, and known in Chinese as ren shen, man root. It is one of the royal herbs in Chinese herbalism. Once considered so valuable that wars were fought over the right to the areas it grew in, ginseng does deserve its reputation. Among its many anti-aging properties, ginseng is a highly effective activator of SIRT1 in every cell of your body. In fact, this extraordinary root stimulates cellular function, and at the same time increases all hormones, particularly the sex hormones, which are so vital to looking young.

BIO-YOUNG TREATMENTS

Please choose preparations based on ease of availability, cost, and personal preference. One is sufficient for treating this anti-aging mechanism, but two or more can speed improvements or improve a particularly neglected situation. Each one uses an ingredient discussed in this chapter. Enjoy!

Fruit sirtuin: Choose resveratrol-packed fruits from this chapter for daily use. Or you can use four to six teaspoons of a fruit powder added to smoothies and yogurts.

Gotu kola: Take four capsules a day.

Ginseng: Take two teaspoonfuls of the tincture or six capsules of the powdered herb daily.

Roxy Dillon

Garlic: Use liberally in cooking, raw, and in salad dressings.

Yeast: Dissolve baking yeast in warm water and apply directly to your skin as a mask, but not around your eyes, since the skin here is sensitive and the yeast preparation is drying. I like to use coconut or red palm oil to moisturize the face afterward.

CHAPTER 2

Fibroblasts, Antioxidants, and Free Radicals—Oh My!

ANTI-AGING MECHANISM: Stimulation of fibroblasts

USE: Increasing collagen and elastin

STARRING: Rosemary and dill seed essential oils, coconut and red palm oil, oats

The Queen of Hungary's vibrant health and long life are a great example of how much you can achieve if you put even a fraction of the *Bio-Young* philosophy to use. The alchemist who created the recipe for what is now known all over the world as Queen of Hungary water didn't have a clue about antioxidants, fibroblasts, or cellular and hormonal dysfunction. But he did use some of the principles of *Bio-Young* when he came to the queen's rescue, and she obtained spectacular results.

Elizabeth of Poland, Queen of Hungary, died in 1380 at seventy-five, which was a remarkable age for that time. Advancing years had taken their toll and when the queen called on her alchemist for help, she was riddled with gout, looked wrinkled and stooped over. An alchemist was primarily an herbalist who also dabbled in the use of poisons, and whose goal was to produce gold from base, or cheaper, metals. But it was the alchemist's herbal knowledge that led to the formulation of Queen of Hungary water, and the queen's astonishing transformation—from an old, withered woman to one who looked young and lovely at the age of seventy—is revered to this day. Such was her allure that the twenty-five-year-old Duke of Lithuania fell hopelessly in love with her and asked for her hand in marriage.

It may seem extraordinary that the alchemist knew so long ago what science is proving to be true today: that you can rejuvenate your whole body with antioxidants to an astonishing degree. The primary antioxidant ingredient in the Queen of Hungary water is rosemary. Scientific evaluation has shown that this Mediterranean herb is very high in antioxidants.

In this chapter, I will explore the role of antioxidants and fibroblasts in the aging process. Antioxidants form a large, biologically active family of compounds with astonishing anti-aging benefits. They have been used for this reason for centuries, long before the term *antioxidant* was coined. You'll soon learn that antioxidants stimulate aging fibroblasts to produce young, firm skin thanks to revived collagen, elastin, and other structural skin components. If your skin has become loose and slack, fibroblast stimulators can help make it firm and young again.

Meet Collagen, Procollagen, and Elastin

Collagen, elastin, and other structural components essential for firm skin decrease with age. Collagen and elastin are structural proteins, and procollagen is the precursor of collagen—that is, it is the protein that must be made first, before collagen can be synthesized. Raising levels of procollagen is a good way of increasing collagen levels. Collagen gives skin its integrity and firmness. Young skin, which contains a lot of collagen, is thick and firm. Collagen in youthful skin is also highly regular—it is arranged in a symmetrical "scaffold," also known as a matrix. Older skin loses this symmetry, which results in uneven thickening, grooves, and lines that form when thin skin moves repeatedly as we talk or smile. The rapid appearance of lines in the eye area from the age of thirty onward comes from collagen loss. Elastin is also a structural protein. As its name suggests, elastin provides elasticity. If you pinch the skin on the back of your hand, and then let it go, it should snap back to its original position within one second. If it moves only slowly back, this indicates lowered levels of elastin. Loss of elasticity, or pliability, caused by low levels of elastin results in deep wrinkles around the mouth, jowls, "turkey neck," and deep folds that form along the line that leads from nose to mouth.

The herb amla, also known as amalaki, or in Latin as *Emblica officinalis*, increases procollagen production in your skin and inhibits those damaging matrix metalloproteinases—enzymes that break down protein—leading to a noticeably thicker collagen layer almost overnight. This means that when a metalloproteinase is activated, more proteins, including collagen and elastin, both structural proteins, will be broken down and their levels will decrease. Amla's common name is Indian gooseberry, and it is one of the richest sources of vitamin C in the world. This little fruit has long held a privileged position as one of the most effective anti-aging herbs in Ayurveda. Amla has been shown to be a highly effective liver protector and an anti-inflammatory, and is very common in treatments for hair loss and for reversing and preventing natural color loss.

Through a complex interaction of many beneficial biochemical mechanisms, amla stimulates procollagen synthesis and prevents the destruction of your skin collagen by ultraviolet radiation, thus producing significant protection against photoaging. It has been shown to increase hyaluronic acid, which keeps your skin soft and smooth and springy, and it also increases mitochondrial activity.

In India, amla is traditionally prepared by cooking it in coconut oil, a method that enhances the effectiveness of both ingredients. This is yet another example of the kind of synergy at work between tomato products and olive oil, which will come up throughout this book. Amla, tomatoes, olive oil, and coconut oil all have fibroblast-stimulating properties, and the effects of amla and tomato are enhanced when combined with either of the two oils. Isn't it extraordinary that olive oil, so easy to obtain in your local grocery store, actually stimulates your fibroblasts to produce more collagen?

Why Are Antioxidants Important?

The level of antioxidants in your body and their activity from moment to moment, with every breath that you take, make you young or make you old. Remember when Neil Young sang, "It's better to burn out than it is to rust"? With the help of antioxidants, you don't have to do either!

The basis of antioxidants' effects on aging is oxygen. As you know, we need oxygen every second of our lives; it's a molecule so vital that we cannot survive more than three minutes in its absence. In fact, the human body is about two-thirds oxygen. Oxygen enters your body through your nose and lungs, is transported into your bloodstream, and gets delivered to every single cell in your body. This powers the energy in your cells that is used by mitochondria, the energy factories found in every cell. Releasing the energy is what keeps you alive. This energy can also keep you young for decades, if you know how to help it work at its optimal, cellular level.

While oxygen is essential for survival, after it's performed its role in providing us with energy, it is broken down into metabolites that are then excreted. These metabolites are the superoxide ion, hydrogen peroxide, and the hydroxyl radical, and they're collectively known as reactive oxygen species, or ROS. They are also popularly known as free radicals.

Oxygen is a highly reactive molecule, which is a good thing, because this reactivity enables it to take part in millions of biochemical reactions in your body, every second of your life. But this same quality also causes oxygen to form highly reactive compounds, which are free radicals. Free radicals are electrically charged molecules that are looking for electrons. They are highly active and remove these electrons wherever possible—from your collagen, from the lipids in your cell membranes, or from the protein in your heart muscle. Normally this scenario is kept under control by the antioxidants that inactivate these highly active free radicals. When you are young, your collagen, your cell membranes, your heart muscle, your whole body, in fact, functions as it should, and repairs what needs to be repaired. It synthesizes fresh, healthy tissue when necessary. Free radicals are very effectively kept under close guard by antioxidants, which perform essential life functions as gene regulators and cell activators and other roles at the cellular level. As we get older our natural antioxidant systems become less efficient, and if we don't supply natural antioxidants directly to the skin, and eat them in our diet, aging is the result.

As these free radicals overwhelm your body, your cells experience a condition called oxidative stress, which causes cell damage. Blood vessels can rupture, heart muscle can weaken, and neurons can die. Free radical damage has been shown to play a part in nearly every disease associated with aging—Alzheimer's and Parkinson's diseases, cardiovascular disease, diabetes, and macular degeneration among them. It is the cause of damage to the heart or the brain when normal circulation returns following a stroke or after surgery. Free radical damage causes diabetic blindness and neuropathy, and its oxidative stress is also the cause of sagging skin, wrinkles, and the thickened skin that forms permanent folds in older people. When collagen is damaged by free radicals, it forms a stiff, crisscrossed scaffold that we see as lined, coarse skin.

What we call wrinkles is actually collagen, elastin, and lipids damaged by free radicals. Gray hair is the result of many processes, but chief among them is the damage to hair melanocytes caused by hydrogen peroxide, a free radical. It is fascinating to note that estrogen, melatonin, testosterone, and many other hormones are, among their numerous attributes, also highly effective antioxidants. This is an important example of the interaction between hormones and cellular functioning and shows yet another way in which hormones are vital for looking young. Hormones synthesize vital proteins and oversee essential functions, but they also participate in these vital moment-to-moment protective biochemical reactions.

Free radical damage doesn't result only from purely biological processes. It also occurs when you are stressed—either emotionally, which results in cortisol and adrenaline hormone releases, or physically, which results in actual bodily injury. Physical injury also involves the release of stress hormones. Cortisol, in particular, is now known to produce catastrophic changes in the body, aging and killing cells wherever it is found. It causes a tenfold loss of vital skin proteins, particularly collagen. Physical trauma, as you would expect, is very damaging to your body. A lot of this damage occurs via the formation of free radicals and results in cell death. If you hit your head, free radicals are released in your brain, and if you suffer a cut, an infection, or a bruise, free radicals are formed. Sunlight, artificial light, and pollution all produce free radical damage in your body, most visibly on your skin. Free radical production is the necessary consequence of being alive, but the accumulated results of unchecked free radical action can manifest as signs we associate with aging.

The good news is, you can prevent and reverse any free radical damage, including uneven skin tone and wrinkles caused by the sun, slack skin due to improper collagen and elastin formation, and inflexible skin cells that have been damaged by peroxides, a very common species of free radicals. Every single layer of your skin is susceptible to free radical damage. But if you have a sufficient number and adequate range of antioxidants circulating in your body, you might be able to stop or even reverse the harm that's been done.

How Low Can You Go?
Antioxidants and the Skin

Although antioxidants help fight and reverse aging throughout the body, skin damage is the most visible repercussion and one that a lot of my clients bemoan. Skin becomes dry with age, and as I've said, this is one of the causes of visible lines, particularly crow's feet. Skin is your body's largest organ, so it's imperative to keep it young and healthy. Its strength isn't just a vanity issue, either—dynamic skin function plays a role in wound healing and skin integrity acts as a protective outer layer that's constantly barraged with inevitable foes like too much sun and pollution. Antioxidants like green tea and ginkgo, for instance, are well known. When applied directly to your skin, both have been shown to improve smoothness and moisture. The best way, then, to discuss skin here is to consider its structure and how that will influence the ways we protect it from, and reverse, free radical damage.

The outermost layer of your skin, also known as the stratum corneum or the epidermis, is composed of a protein called keratin, which is the same protein that forms the hair shaft. Keratin gives strength to both your skin and hair, which means that anything that enhances the formation of keratin also protects your skin from external damage from the sun and environmental pollution while also making your hair resilient to breakage. Using coconut oil is one of the most effective ways to strengthen keratin, as it diminishes lines and wrinkles in skin and adds shine and elasticity to hair. If you have had problems growing your hair long because it breaks off constantly at shoulder level, you will find that regularly using coconut oil will help give you the shiny, long, healthy hair of your dreams.

Below the epidermis is the dermis, a scaffold comprising collagen and elastin that provides support and structure for your skin. This layer is richly supplied with blood vessels and fibroblasts, which synthesize new skin cells. A topical substance that stimulates fibroblasts has great anti-aging potential for the deeper layers of skin. What's interesting is that cosmetic companies are banned from producing products that affect the dermis and hypodermis—any topical substance that impacts the skin below the very outermost layer is deemed to be a drug, and over-the-counter creams are not allowed to advertise such claims or to possess such activity. This is yet another pro in the column of using natural substances. They easily penetrate the top layer of your skin and into its deepest layers. They also do so safely and effectively, producing fresh, new skin.

The base of the dermis contains sugars, hyaluronic acid, chondroitin sulfate, and glycoproteins, which are mixtures of sugar molecules and protein. These molecules can keep your skin looking fresh, springy, and moist. The hypodermis forms the lowest layer of your skin. It contains adipocytes, or fat cells, which preserve body heat and give your body and face a plump, youthful look.

A Dynamic Duo: Antioxidants and Fibroblasts

Antioxidants have the power to penetrate into the dermis of your skin and stimulate cells called fibroblasts. Fibroblasts are found in the dermis, and their role is to synthesize collagen, elastin, keratin, glycoproteins, and the cellular matrix. They are crucial for wound healing. When they're stimulated, fibroblasts produce rapid and visible anti-aging. In other words, a substance that activates fibroblasts makes your skin young.

Fibroblasts become slower as we age, which causes lower levels of those all-important structural molecules that provide structure to the skin. So slower, or less numerous, fibroblasts will result in skin that is less firm, elastic, and pliable. Antioxidants are an important substance that can protect fibroblasts and make them more active. This means any compound that reaches the dermis, where these fibroblasts are situated and stimulates them, will have serious anti-aging properties. They can help protect your skin from the damaging effects of sunlight, pollution, and aging.

You have probably heard of, and maybe even used, face creams containing antioxidants. You may be surprised to find out just how far-reaching their benefits really are. We now know that antioxidants like vitamin C or natural vitamin E, when applied to the skin's surface, can reverse sun damage. This includes long-term damage that occurred years, even decades, before. This is revolutionary, since it's only been a few years since sun damage and wrinkles were considered irreversible, and certainly not accessible to something as simple as the topical application of vitamin E oil. Vitamin E has some estrogenic activity, too, which is yet another example of an interaction between cellular and hormonal effects. You can also eat and drink your skin-nourishing antioxidants, as they're found in blueberries, goji berries, pomegranate, spinach, strawberries, prunes, broccoli, turmeric, and green tea.

Scientists have conducted studies on the safety of synthetic antioxidants, but the natural ones continue to reign supreme. Does that mean synthetic antioxidants aren't safe? Over the past decade or so, several reports have claimed that when taken internally, some synthetic antioxidant supplements and vitamins increase the progression of lung cancer and other tumors. So far beta-carotene,

N-acetyl cysteine (NAC), and vitamin E have been implicated. These studies show that synthetic antioxidants have a detrimental effect in cases where tumors are already present, speeding growth and making them more malignant. A possible explanation may be that free radicals are toxic to tumors, but when they are removed or lowered by these synthetic antioxidants, tumors grow unchecked. This effect has been seen in other diseases, such as heart disease, and with other types of cancer, such as prostate, and with a variety of synthetic antioxidants, including synthetic beta-carotene and synthetic vitamin E. My advice is to avoid the synthetic supplements that have been shown to be more effective in their natural form, and opt instead for whole herbs and foods, and natural vitamins and supplements.

More of a Good Thing: Fibroblast Synthesis

Apart from collagen, fibroblasts synthesize many other anti-aging substances, including the remarkable elastin, a structural protein that is fast becoming the new buzzword in anti-aging skin care. Why? Because it can make your skin as elastic as it used to be. Levels of enzymes that synthesize elastin decrease as you get older. Increasing them is easy and effective, and rapidly produces elastic, youthful skin that looks and behaves exactly the same as younger skin. This means you can sleep on your side without getting pillow creases and lean on the edge of a table without getting a deep groove in your arm.

Dill seed essential oil is one of the most effective stimulators of elastin synthesis, because it activates dermal fibroblasts, and increases the production of tropoelastin, the precursor of elastin. Licorice also increases elastin production in the same way, but not to the same extent as dill seed essential oil. Every substance that activates dermal fibroblasts has a positive effect on both collagen and elastin levels in your skin, but dill targets elastin so powerfully, it's really worth making a big noise about it.

As we age, levels of both collagenase and elastinase increase, while the production of these youth-giving structural proteins decreases. Collagenase and elastinase are enzymes that break down collagen and elastin, respectively. Unfortunately, with age, the collagen and elastin synthesis slows, so the effect is compounded. This leaves your skin looking very old and saggy. So the goal is to increase collagen to make your skin thicker and stronger, and increase elastin to make it spongier, springier, and more elastic. In practice, you should see a wonderful effect around your eyes, particularly if you have under-eye bags. Dill seed essential oil, which should always be diluted in an oil base like coconut or red palm, can help make under-eye pouches vanish because it stops the sagging that causes them.

Other elastin-increasing ingredients to be aware of: helichrysum essential oil, creatine, and hibiscus. The essential oil of helichrysum, commonly known as everlasting, and which is a member of the sunflower family, is becoming very popular and is easily available online. Along with dill seed essential oil, helichrysum should anti-age your skin. Increasing elastin produces serious anti-aging results wherever you apply your elastin-stimulating product. It is now known that levels of elastin are low in varicose veins, and this deficiency causes the condition. Applying a treatment containing dill seed, or helichrysum, essential oil directly in the affected area should make a huge difference to this unsightly problem. Hibiscus is also an impressive stimulator of elastin synthesis, much more so than creatine and folic acid, which are often recommended. The only problem with hibiscus is its rich, dark crimson color. You can use it as a strong tea and apply as needed, but you do need to be careful to avoid splashes, since it stains fabrics.

Ultraviolet radiation is now believed to be the number one cause of premature facial skin aging, and the damage typically caused by such exposure can be reversed by ursolic acid and asiatic acid. Ursolic acid, one of the many beneficial compounds found in rosemary, and asiatic acid, isolated from gotu kola, are impressively effective at keeping your skin young. These and many other compounds found in herbs and plants have been shown to protect keratinocytes, the cells responsible for synthesizing keratin, which makes your skin resilient.

Because daily fibroblast stimulation produces youthful, robust skin, in this next section I'll focus on some of my favorite fibroblast stimulators that will play a role in the treatment you create at the end of this chapter—rosemary, vitamins E and C, lycopene, oats, coconut oil, and red palm oil.

✳ Fibroblast Spotlight: Rosemary

Rosemary is a very effective fibroblast stimulator. When you apply rosemary essential oil that's been diluted in a suitable base to the surface of your skin, its active ingredients penetrate the dermal layer and stimulate fibroblasts to produce collagen and elastin. Carnosic acid, one of the components found in rosemary, has been shown to have impressive anti-photoaging properties— in other words, damage associated with chronological skin aging, or aging caused by the passing of time, such as wrinkles, loose skin, and uneven pigmentation. This also means they offer significant protection against the damaging increase of matrix metalloproteinases. These are enzymes that break down skin collagen when it is exposed to UV radiation and is the process that underlies photoaging—the wrinkles, sags, uneven pigmentation, and coarse skin created by sun exposure. Carnosic acid also stimulates keratinocytes, or cells that produce keratin, the protein that is so vital for strong, resilient skin and hair. Ursolic acid is also found in rosemary, and studies find it to be highly effective at protecting skin fibroblasts against sun damage by increasing every vital protein for young skin—keratin, elastin, and collagen.

Rosemary is also effective because it contains rosmarinic acid, a powerful antioxidant that has a wide range of anti-aging properties. It may not surprise you that rosmarinic acid stimulates SIRT1, turning on a very important longevity pathway. You may remember from the last chapter that SIRT1 is a protein. It is also known as a longevity gene, and when it is stimulated, it's capable of extending your lifespan and producing marked and visible anti-aging effects. Rosmarinic acid is also an antioxidant that has the power to deactivate free radicals, which as we've seen are at the very basis of aging.

Other antioxidants and active compounds found in rosemary are carnosol, carnosic acid, ursolic acid, caffeic acid, betulinic acid, and rosmanol. Rosemary is so effective that it is commonly used as a food preservative. Rosmarinic acid also has anxiolytic properties that alleviate anxiety; it does this by increasing levels of the inhibitory neurotransmitter gamma-aminobutyric acid, or GABA.

Rosemary also aids memory. A 2013 study at the University of Northumbria showed that rosemary's smell alone improved memory in healthy adults. Even Shakespeare knew rosemary's value in this way. In the play *Hamlet*, Ophelia says, "There's rosemary, that's for remembrance," and she was right. This is obviously essential as you age, since memory is critical for everyday functioning. Rosemary can help us collect our thoughts, get organized, complete tasks at the required times, recall the reasons for doing something, and generally enhance our cognitive function.

✳ Fibroblast Spotlight: Vitamin E, Vitamin C, and Lycopene

Vitamin E, vitamin C, and lycopene also stimulate fibroblasts. Vitamin E is a highly effective, fat-soluble antioxidant that reaches the dermis very easily. It acts as a very effective inhibitor of matrix metalloproteinases by suppressing the damage that UV radiation would cause. Vitamin C is also highly effective. You may have come across lycopene in some skin preparations—beware. On its own, lycopene, one of many beneficial compounds found in tomatoes, does not prevent the rise in matrix metalloproteinases, and so will not prevent the damage caused by ultraviolet radiation in your skin. However, when vitamin E is added to the lycopene skin preparation, then significant protection against photoaging occurs, even more than with vitamin E alone. So there is synergy at work between the two. A similar beneficial interaction occurs between vitamin E and beta-carotene, the antioxidant found in carrots and spinach. On its own, beta-carotene, like lycopene, is ineffective at stopping sun damage, but again, once vitamin E is added, serious anti-aging is the result! It has been found that tomato paste is better absorbed, and is much more effective, when eaten with olive oil, the way it is traditionally used in Mediterranean cuisine. The same principle is at work when tomato paste is used externally, mixed with olive oil, or even alone as a quick, refreshing face mask, which you can rinse off after a few minutes. An ideal time for this treatment would be in the shower or in the bath.

✳ Fibroblast Spotlight: Oats

Oats also stimulate fibroblast activity. You may have come across oat-based products that are formulated for use on irritated skin.

Surprisingly, humble oat bran contains antioxidants that are highly effective at stimulating dermal fibroblasts. Oat bran was able to offer significant protection against damage by hydrogen peroxide, a free radical that's now implicated as the cause of gray hair. Oat bran extracts produced a dose-dependent effectiveness at inhibiting hydrogen-peroxide-induced injury, clearly demonstrating their well-deserved reputation for preventing and healing skin irritation. This also means that oat bran and its constituents are great candidates for age reversal.

Hydrogen peroxide is a free radical that creates real havoc in our skin, because it produces wrinkles and loose, saggy folds. Because it is similar in its effects to the destruction wrought by strong sunlight (sunlight produces hydrogen peroxide, among other free radicals, in our skin), anything that keeps hydrogen peroxide in check is a welcome ally in the war against looking your age.

✳ Fibroblast Spotlight: Coconut Oil, Red Palm Oil, and Rice Bran Oil

Coconut oil performs its magic through its antioxidant capacity, stimulating fibroblasts. Coconut oil has been shown to help with many diseases, including Alzheimer's, but it is also amazing when it's applied to wounds, because it greatly speeds up healing and increases beneficial collagen formation. This involves the right kind of cross-linking, creating a strong, resilient skin structure. This type of cross-linking differs from the process triggered by aging, sun damage, and high blood sugar levels. These harmful factors lead to the formation of faulty, stiff, damaged collagen. Healthy cross-linking of collagen results in strong, firm skin.

Red palm oil and rice bran oil are highly effective anti-aging skin and hair solutions. They are becoming more popular and more widely known, and with good reason. They possess the qualities of coconut oil and vitamin E oil respectively, but with far greater potency. They are also both cheap and easily available. What's more, both red palm oil and rice bran oil are particularly rich sources of tocotrienols, compounds that are related to vitamin E but show even higher activity in the human body. Vitamin E is spectacular at mopping up free radicals when applied to the skin, and tocotrienols outperform this amazing vitamin! When applied to skin damaged by hydrogen peroxide, red palm oil and rice bran oil protect the skin and produce an increase in collagen synthesis, offsetting the dramatic decrease in collagen production and collagen levels that normally occur with sun exposure.

BIO-YOUNG TREATMENTS

Please choose preparations based on ease of availability, cost, and personal preference. One is sufficient for treating this anti-aging mechanism, but two or more can speed improvements or improve a particularly neglected situation. Each one uses an ingredient discussed in this chapter. Enjoy!

Red palm oil with rosemary, eucalyptus, and dill essential oils: Mix 30 drops of each essential oil into 100 grams of red palm oil. You can substitute 100 grams of coconut oil for the red palm oil to avoid the orange color on your face and body. Coconut oil increases collagen and elastin.

Oats: Aveeno stands out as a very good commercial oat-based product. You can also mill 100–250 grams of oat flakes into a fine powder, keep it in a container on your bathtub, and use a little every time you have a bath, as a fibroblast-stimulating exfoliator. To avoid a blocked drain, pour oats or oat powder into a stocking, tie it up well, swish it in hot water, squeeze it, and use the liquid on your skin.

CHAPTER 3

Powerful Proteasomes
for Skin and Body

ANTI-AGING MECHANISM: Proteasome activation

USE: Breaking down old proteins and clarifying skin

STARRING: Broccoli, kale, onions, oak bark, vitamin C
with glycerin

M ost of us don't like being told to act our age, but to have skin that acts downright immature? That would be terrific, if you ask me! After all, skin that doesn't act its age has an extremely efficient repair system, so a scratch or a cut heals quickly and without scarring; a fast cell turnover that produces a radiant, childlike bloom; and a supple, moist quality that doesn't wrinkle or sag.

Proteasomes are the answer to making aging skin act immature again, and they're found in every cell of our bodies. They break down and clear away old proteins to make way for new ones, a process that results in fresh, clear, youthful skin. Because proteasomes become less active with age, the buildup of old cells leads to sallow, rough skin. But if you can activate your proteasomes, you'll improve your skin's tone and texture, and if your skin is already young, you'll be rewarded with clear, trouble-free skin that's resistant to wrinkles, pigmentation problems, dryness, and a coarse texture. And while I won't go into this too deeply in this chapter, activating proteasomes improves more than your looks. In a group of centenarians, those who were the most active *and* looked the youngest had the most active proteasomes. That's because proteasomes affect the lifespan of every cell in the body. Their activation removes cellular debris and keeps cells functioning at their optimal levels throughout your body—and as you might guess, it's most noticeable in the skin. In this chapter, you'll learn how to activate your body's proteasomes to break down old proteins and clarify your skin from within.

What's a Proteasome?

Proteasomes are involved in the breakdown of old, or faulty, proteins. One of the most obvious signs of aging skin, and aging in general, is "breakdown" itself. That is, the breaking down of elastin and collagen, muscle atrophy, and the breakdown of cell-to-cell communication. But breakdown—also called catabolism—is not all bad. It's true that too much breakdown produces old-looking, sagging skin, but not enough breakdown of proteins results in sallow, dull, rough, thickened skin. So if too much collagen or elastin is broken down and this is not replenished, then skin becomes weaker, thinner, and far less resilient. But if collagen, elastin, and other proteins are not broken down on a regular basis, a buildup occurs that leads to skin thickening and this, too, ultimately results in a loss of resilience— which creates deep lines, folds, and droopy skin most easily seen around the jawline and neck. In the previous chapter, we discussed how young, springy skin is the result of highly active fibroblasts that produce healthy levels of collagen, elastin, and other structural components. Proteasomes help clear away unwanted old cellular debris (old and damaged proteins, for example) that will otherwise clog cellular mechanisms and lead to the slowing down of the biochemical processes we recognize as aging. That means sallow skin, saggy skin, and wrinkles.

A healthy balance between synthesis and catabolism is under the control of a huge variety of enzymes and occurs in every cell of your body, at every moment of your life. The very act of breathing produces waste products in every one of your cells that must be regularly and efficiently disposed of. When you eat, your body utilizes amino acids, sugars, and fats to make new tissues, but just as important, it must clear away and dispose of, or recycle, amino acids, sugars, and fats leftover from previous biochemical processes. A body that is chronologically young carries out these two opposing tasks, anabolism (the building up of tissues) and catabolism (breaking down), with beautiful precision, efficiency, and balance. A chronologically older body needs a little help from proteasomes.

Proteasome activity is closely linked with aging at the cellular level, involving an interplay between the mitochondria, the cell's energy factories, and the proteasomes, which are responsible for clearing up faulty or old proteins. When proteasome activity decreases, as it does with age, for example, this leads to a decrease in mitochondrial function. Conversely, increasing proteasome activity will stimulate mitochondria, too. This is great news for anti-aging, providing yet another easy way to produce cellular youthfulness. All you have to do is eat foods and herbs that stimulate proteasomal activity every day!

Though proteasome activity is most noticeable on your skin, it has far-reaching effects on your entire body. Proteasomes are not directly involved in cellular energy production, but anything that slows down optimal cell function will ultimately result in an overall loss of efficiency and, therefore, a slowing down of energy production further down the line. This means less energy is produced by the cells, and this will be perceived as fatigue. What's more, proteasome activity is closely linked with aging at the cellular level, involving an interplay between the mitochondria and the proteasomes. When proteasome activity decreases, as it does with age, for example, this leads to a decrease in mitochondrial function. Conversely, increasing proteasome activity will stimulate mitochondria, too.

If you think about aging in its simplest form, it can be viewed as a slowing down, of sorts—a lack of cellular energy, and a lack of energy in hormone-producing glands such as ovaries. *Energy* is the single word that best describes what children have and old people don't—in their bodies, muscles, eyes, hair, minds, you name it. And when I ask elderly clients what they truly miss from their youth, *energy* is typically the word I hear most. They have experience, and they still have dreams. But without energy, it's all useless. And there's no point to looking young if all you want to do is sleep! The great news is that restoring cellular and hormonal function automatically produces a vibrant level of youthful, energetic functioning, a level that results in feeling happy, strong, positive, and optimistic—all the qualities we associate with youth. They return automatically when cellular and hormonal functioning is brought back to youthful levels in every aspect of your life by turning your cellular and hormonal pathways to "young."

Back to proteasomes. One of the proteins that exhibit less energy as we get older is poly [ADP-ribose] polymerase 1, or PARP-1—a protein found in the nucleus of your cells that is closely involved in maintaining youthful cell turnover. This protein performs its tasks more and more slowly as you get older. When PARP-1 is active, your skin makes fresh new cells every day. Your fibroblasts produce abundant collagen and elastin, and other vital structural skin components, keeping your skin young.

PARP-1 is just one of the proteins that activate proteasomes and enable them to act the way they did when you were young. When proteasomes are working at peak capacity, not only are all faulty and old proteins efficiently degraded and cleared away, but the proteins that are synthesized are also highly resistant to DNA mutation and free radical assault. All your cells reach their longest lifespan!

The Ultimate "Peel": Proteasome Activators

Proteasomes keep your skin and body young by performing the equivalent of an inside-out chemical peel. Stimulating them makes your skin, in particular, feel new and immature. Healthy, active proteasomes are of vital importance in the fight against all aspects of aging, including heart and brain diseases. And as for your skin, natural substances that activate proteasomes make your skin act, well, exactly as young skin acts—fresh and radiant. All you have to do is reveal this new skin, and activate the processes that make sure it remains gleaming and vibrant for decades to come.

I'm sure you've heard of chemical peels, and versions of this treatment have been around for as long as women have wanted to look younger—and with good reason. Removing the buildup of cellular debris that clogs the surface of aging skin is one of the fastest ways to look refreshed. Chemical peels are more invasive, and even though the process may only take minutes, it will result in serious skin damage that will take weeks to heal. A scab will form, and when the scab falls off, fresh, new skin is revealed. This skin is, and will remain, acutely sensitive to the effects of sunlight, which means covering up and staying indoors or at least in the shade for a long time. The new skin that debuts after a chemical skin peel is thinner than normal and more fragile.

Truly young skin, a child's skin, is not thin. It may be sensitive, but it is not fragile. It is healthy and robust. This is a significant cellular achievement and is done by specifically stimulating the activity of aging proteasomes and getting them to behave as they used to.

Several natural compounds have been found to achieve this amazing feat, among them resveratrol, which we met in chapter 1, and quercetin, a compound first isolated from oak bark (*Quercus* is the Latin name for oak). Oak bark is used in traditional herbal medicine as an astringent, an herb that tightens loose, flabby tissues, such as inflamed, spongy gums or twisted varicose veins.

Eat Your Way to Proteasome Activation

An easy way to activate your proteasomes every day is to choose foods from the following list, and be sure to consume at least one a day. All of these foods contain compounds that should stimulate those sirtuin longevity pathways. There are many effective natural substances that will stimulate your proteasomes, like sulforaphane, which is found in broccoli. You should feel the results and see them when you look in the mirror!

Foods	Proteasome-Activating Compounds
broccoli	sulfuraphane
brussels sprouts	sulfuraphane
olive oil	oleuropein
olives	oleuropein
olive leaf	oleuropein
cabbage	sulfuraphane
kale	sulfuraphane

Of these, I find olive leaf, olive oil, and olives to be particularly remarkable. They are very effective proteasome activators. This is one reason I like to suggest olive-oil-based creams for a fresher, younger complexion. Every time you use that olive oil preparation, your skin cells experience effective DNA repair, protected against oxidative stress. Oleuropein is what's at work here. It's a proteasome-activating compound isolated from olives, olive oil, and olive leaf. You may not have come across olive leaf before, though it can be highly effective against the flu and also helps to lower high blood pressure, and you can find olive leaf capsules at your local health store. If you would like to take it as a supplement, follow the instructions on the bottle. For the purposes of activating proteasomes in your skin, I suggest applying extra-virgin olive oil topically. You can also use it in your hair as a prewash conditioner. If you're dirty blond, it will help lighten your hair by a few shades and make it brighter, so that's an added bonus! It will not affect the color of dark hair to any substantial degree. Proteasome activation is very much a part of the Mediterranean diet, which is often tied to longevity. Research has shown that the more olive oil people consume, the healthier they are, and the longer they live.

Consider Proteasome-Based Consumer Products

Proteasome-activating skin treatments that you can buy online, at a health store, at the drugstore, or at the cosmetics counter are becoming increasingly popular. Broccoli extract is beginning to appear in face treatments, as is olive oil. The skin care company Korres has pioneered the use of quercetin for proteasome activation in the skin, showing increased collagen and elastin levels with the use of their products. Quercetin is also found in red onions, tea, blueberries, cranberries, broccoli, dill, and capers, and has been shown to increase proteasome activity in the skin when applied externally if you prefer to DIY. You may find it difficult to use them in their whole form directly on your skin, however, so for that purpose you may wish to find a cream that contains active extracts from these foods.

BIO-YOUNG TREATMENTS

Please choose preparations based on ease of availability, cost, and personal preference. One is sufficient for treating this anti-aging mechanism, but two or more can speed improvements or improve a particularly neglected situation. Each one uses an ingredient discussed in this chapter. Enjoy!

Proteasome-stimulating foods: Eat a four-ounce serving of broccoli, cabbage, or brussels sprouts every day.

Olive oil: Pour 500 ml of olive oil into a saucepan, add 100 grams of oak bark (either powdered or cut), bring to a boil on the back burner (be very careful!), and then simmer for thirty minutes. Let it cool in a safe place, strain, label, and bottle. This oil has the extraordinary ability to make under-eye bags and dark circles vanish with the first application. The rest of your face, and your neck, should reward you with an almost instant increase in firmness, improved skin tone, and youthful freshness. Or you can have four teaspoons of olive oil every day or a handful of olives, if you prefer.

Dill seed essential oil: In chapter 2 you saw that this oil stimulates fibroblasts to produce elastin, so the palm oil preparation from chapter 2 can be used to achieve everything that quercetin can do to stimulate proteasome activity. Red palm oil stabilizes proteasomes, so you can use the preparation exactly as it is given in chapter 2. If you are prone to developing under-eye puffiness, then coconut oil is the one for you. Out of a range of oils tested, it was the only one that stimulated liver proteasomes. You can safely use coconut oil around your eyes, even overnight, and you shouldn't suffer from under-eye bags or dark circles as a result. Coconut oil doesn't usually cause your skin to break out, even if you're acne prone, so that's another bonus. If you add dill essential oil (30–100 drops per 100 ml of coconut oil), then you should significantly improve the delicate skin around your eyes, on your face, and on your neck within a few days. Use this formula on your breasts and just might see them firm up! You will learn more about firming up your breasts, and the rest of you, in the following chapters.

Vitamin C serum: Dissolve four teaspoons of pure ascorbic acid powder in enough water so the crystals disappear (about a quarter of a glass), then add this solution to 100 ml of glycerin and shake well to mix. And that's it! Your proteasome-activating vitamin C serum is ready for use! Shake it before use, but you don't need to keep it in the fridge; it will stay active for a few weeks even in your bathroom if kept out of direct sunlight. You can adjust the vitamin C concentration to suit your needs, decreasing it if your skin is sensitive or increasing it if you need more robust clarifying and refining.

CHAPTER 4

Here Comes the Sun— Embrace It!

ANTI-AGING MECHANISM: Reversing and preventing skin aging caused by sun exposure

USE: Erasing wrinkles, uneven skin pigmentation, skin sagging

STARRING: Red palm oil, tomato paste, rice bran oil, gelatin, squalene, aloe vera, honey

It may come as a shock to you, but sunscreen does not provide complete protection from sun damage—no matter what form it's in, what its SPF is, or how often you apply it. For complete sun protection and to reverse its damage, you must protect yourself on a cellular level.

Sun damage, or photoaging, is caused by UVA and UVB radiation, but also, as recent research has shown, by visible light. This damage ages every part of you, from the collagen in your skin to the increased risk of skin and metastatic cancer. Natural cellular defense mechanisms, which protect our skin from sun damage, decline with age. This is one reason why, without additional protection, people tend to be more susceptible to skin cancer as they grow older. This chapter will show you how natural, safe substances protect your skin from sun damage, repair existing damage, and even prevent the dangerous cancerous changes that we now associate with sunbathing.

It's time to stop fearing the sun and see it as the life-giving essential energy it is meant to be.

The Facts on Photoaging

Sun damage, or what's also called photoaging, is caused by ultraviolet light, which is really electromagnetic radiation. Though light serves various and obvious purposes for us and the universe, the damage it can cause to your body can age every part of you, from zapping your skin's collagen to increasing your risk of skin and metastatic cancer.

UVA and UVB rays have different wavelengths that penetrate your skin to different depths. There are no sunscreens that completely filter out UVB rays, and those with UVA filters only provide partial protection, even though recent research shows that UVA rays penetrate the skin more deeply and are far more damaging than UVB. What's more, data show that sunscreen is associated with an *increased* incidence of melanomas, the dangerous skin cancers caused by ultraviolet damage. Whether this relationship is causative or due to some as yet unknown factor is not yet clear. But to me, there seem to be at least two plausible theories. First, when sunscreens filter out UVB rays, they actually block the formation of vitamin D in the skin, which may correspond to the increased numbers of people in recent years with vitamin D deficiency, which can lead to increased risk of various diseases. Second, some of the agents used to filter out UV light may be harmful themselves and possibly cancer-forming. For that reason, I suggest avoiding sunscreen with these ingredients: micronized titanium, zinc oxide nanoparticles, octocrylene, octylmethoxycinnamate, and benzophenone-3.

Natural cellular defense mechanisms, which protect your skin from sun damage, also decline with age. This is one reason why, without additional protection, people tend to become more susceptible to skin cancer as they age. Aging and sun exposure cause widespread disruption in the body and in the skin. Fortunately, natural substances can prevent all of these detrimental changes.

Four Mechanisms in Sun Damage

To understand the effects of sun damage—from drastically aged skin to dangerous reactions in the human body—you must first understand the four main types of damage that occur:

• *Pyrimidine dimers:* Sunlight leads to the formation of thymine and pyrimidine dimers, highly active and dangerous free radicals that attack DNA strands and lead to genetic damage and cancerous changes.

• *Free radicals:* Sunlight generates ROS, reactive oxygen species, aka highly dangerous free radicals. This leads to DNA damage, destroys collagen, and can cause cancer.

• *Metalloproteinases:* Sunlight activates matrix metalloproteinases, which break down collagen and elastin that manifest as loose, saggy skin and wrinkles. Metalloproteinases are also involved in metastatic cancer. Recent research has shown that rosemary prevents the rise of matrix metalloproteinase-1 (MMP-1) in skin exposed to sunlight. Carnosol, found in high concentrations in rosemary oil, also possesses estrogenic properties, which enhance its efficacy against skin aging.

• *Glycation*: Sunlight produces AGEs, or advanced glycation end-products. AGEs are formed when a sugar molecule attaches to a protein. This causes thick, darkened skin, much like the skin of a roasted turkey, due to inelastic molecules. When collagen is affected, this causes wrinkles, but the damage can occur anywhere in the body. The eye lens is particularly vulnerable to AGEs. The proteins in the lens, called crystallins, become cloudy when they're damaged by glycation—this is the cause of cataracts. Eating sugar can also increase glycation and cause your skin to burn more easily.

Sunny Delight: The Benefits of Sunshine and Vitamin D

Though sun exposure comes with dangers, it is not a good idea to avoid sunlight, because it is also essential for good health. According to a recent study, sunlight produces nitric oxide, an essential molecule that dilates blood vessels and improves blood flow that benefits blood pressure. Your circadian clock also depends on sunlight. A daily rhythm of light and dark, preferably from bright sunshine and nightfall, is essential for your pineal gland to produce melatonin. Melatonin affects sleep, of course, but it is also vital for ovulation and fertility and affects many other cellular and hormonal functions, influencing your moods and energy level. Perhaps most important, sunlight reacts with your skin to form vitamin D, a vitamin that has far-reaching health benefits including decreased risk for heart attacks, diabetes, and multiple sclerosis. Activated vitamin D is also one of the most potent cancer cell growth inhibitors, stimulates your pancreas to make insulin, improves dental health, aids muscle tone, clears migraine headaches, and regulates your immune system, among other benefits.

The vitamin D factor is central to the cellular and hormonal aging discussion, because vitamin D possesses a very definitive combination of cellular and hormonal effects. It plays a role in the formation of sex hormones and protects against cancer by preventing cancerous proliferating (cell division that's gotten out of control). This makes this vitamin a very powerful ally against all kinds of cancer, including melanoma. It enables the uptake of calcium into your bones and makes the ovaries sensitive to estrogen, so estrogen can perform its functions. Without adequate levels of vitamin D, a woman's ovaries will not respond to estrogen even if circulating levels of the hormone are normal. In that way, it makes estrogen more efficient in women. And since the naturally formed vitamin D in your body is superior to the store-bought kind, and rapidly eliminates a deficiency, it is very wise to be in the sun for a half hour a day, but it's important to make sure the skin is a little oily, either by topically applying a good-quality vegetable oil like red palm oil, taking it internally, or just making sure the skin hasn't been stripped of its natural oils. Unrefined natural oils possess potent antioxidant activity, which means that your skin should be protected from burning in the sun. Vitamin D is not made if there is no oil on the skin. I do recommend vitamin D supplements when the sun is scarce and low on the horizon during the fall and winter.

I particularly love vitamin D's role in sun protection and the effects it has on subsequent damage. For one, it helps prevent damage to DNA by pyrimidine dimers, the dangerous free radicals we discussed above. It can reduce sunburn and also stop metalloproteinases from breaking down collagen, thus causing wrinkles and loose skin. And it helps prevent sun-related cancers like melanoma. The only "drawback" is that vitamin D takes time to synthesize in your skin, but you can speed this up by consuming some olive oil, or applying a thin layer of a suitable oil, chosen from the ones recommended in this book, before going in the sun.

Block Sun Damage but Keep Its Benefits

That being said, ideal sun protection would block its damage but keep its benefits, right? Well, that's exactly what I'll help you do by preventing and reversing photoaging. A perfect sunscreen would prevent all sun damage, including every aspect of photoaging from uneven pigmentation, dark spots, loose wrinkled skin, and cancer. It would enable you to benefit from sunshine by reaping the anti-aging benefits, from simple relaxation to heart health, vitamin D synthesis, and hormonal health.

I'd like to now explore the natural substances that possess the potent, beneficial biological properties that can be eaten, taken as supplements, or applied externally to do exactly that. They can help prevent, stop, or reverse every detrimental effect of sunlight on your skin and in your body, even if you have sun damage already in the form of wrinkles, uneven skin coloration, and/or thinning skin.

✳ Sun Protection Spotlight: Squalene

Squalene is a compound that made it possible for life to flourish on earth during a time when our planet's surface was hot enough to boil water. Bacteria are one of the earliest life-forms, and they were protected by squalene, which allowed them to survive, and even thrive, in our planet's extreme and hostile heat. Bacteria gradually evolved to become green plants and, later, multicellular life-forms, including animals. Without squalene, emerging plant life would have burned to a crisp, and in a similar way, squalene can protect you from sun damage, too.

Squalene is an isoprenoid, a member of a large family of chemicals found in every living thing. Isoprenoids are lipids, or fats. They are present in cinnamon, rosemary, turmeric, and ginger, but the richest sources of squalene are amaranth oil, olive oil, rice bran oil, red palm oil, and shark liver oil. In fact, the word *squalene* comes from the Latin term for the great white shark, *Squalus carcharias*, for this very reason. In the last few years, isoprenoids have emerged as nutrient molecules with impressive bioactive properties, particularly effective in influencing cellular growth and proliferation. They influence signaling pathways, which means they can protect you against cell dysfunction, including cancer formation, at the earliest stages. Since squalene is one of the most effective and easy-to-use isoprenoids, its effects on cellular function make it incomparable to any other sunscreen in the world. Again, squalene doesn't act through an attempt to block ultraviolet, or any other, radiation. It simply makes radiation—whether UVA, UVB, or visible light—harmless to you, because it protects at a cellular level.

Squalene is also able to achieve amazing protective effects against free radical formation, particularly against lipid (fat) free radicals, which create visible and internal signs of aging. It is even better when combined with natural vitamin E. Squalene achieves its anti-aging and photoprotective effects not by blocking sun rays, but by preventing sun damage. We all have natural squalene in our skin, and this is actually the primary skin-protective lipid.

Squalene is best combined with vitamin E for high-powered sun protection. Olive squalene is available with added tocopherol, or you can simply obtain a good natural vitamin E oil and mix olive squalene and vitamin E in one bottle for results that offer maximum sun protection. Squalene and vitamin E are your first line of defense against the formation of lipid peroxides, which are formed when fats are oxidized by sunlight or pollution, including tobacco smoke. It is clear that sun damage and aging have much in common and affect the same cellular mechanism, causing dysfunction and decline. Correcting one, in this case sun damage, also corrects the other, chronological aging. The threat of cancer also dramatically decreases.

Women are more vulnerable to lipid peroxidation dangers than men, so squalene and vitamin E are particularly helpful to them. Not only do women require more fats and fatty acids in their diet than men to sustain peak hormonal function, but their bodies form free radicals from fat more readily. This increases the risk of cancer, including breast cancers. Estrogens (there are several different types) are intimately involved in this increased vulnerability. Estrogens without adequate antioxidant protection can lead to cancer. It is therefore vitally important for women to obtain antioxidant protection from their diet and from the topical applications of antioxidant skin products.

Squalene is particularly helpful as an antioxidant. When light hits the skin, it generates catastrophic levels of free radicals in a short amount of time—levels that natural antioxidants in the body cannot manage on their own. The body has natural antioxidant protection, but this is exceeded when intense sunlight causes a surge of free radical formation. Sun damage occurs only when this protective system becomes overwhelmed and the free radicals are not deactivated by antioxidants. The result is internal and external damage—some you can see, some you experience from disease. Yet consciously consumed antioxidants increase your collagen before, during, and after exposure to the sun.

By protecting your cells with squalene internally and topically, this natural antioxidant prevents and reverses damage. Again, it takes care of wrinkles, loose skin, and uneven pigmentation. It evens and brightens skin tone and also reduces any redness you have. Squalene reverses coarsened skin texture, crisscrossing lines, and deep wrinkles. As a natural antioxidant, it controls free radicals to prevent collagen thinning, molecular lesions, and DNA damage that causes sun-related cancers and disease. It also removes under-eye circles. Squalene earns bonus points by eliminating various toxic chemicals from the body that do nothing to support your body as it ages, including phenobarbital and strychnine. The oil also removes hexachlorobenzene, a popular fungicide banned in 1965 but still found in our food chain. Dietary intake of squalene, at a concentration of 8 percent of the diet, markedly increased the elimination of hexachlorobenzene from the body.

Squalene Protects the Eyes

Squalene can also help prevent sunlight-related damage to your eyes—a concern most people don't realize is happening until they're diagnosed with cataracts. Cataracts are faulty proteins formed in the lens of the eye as a result of light-generated free radicals from artificial and natural light. Sunglasses are not the simple answer here, since it's hard to know how much light is filtered out. Also, you don't want to live in shades because light beneficially enters the eyes and signals travel to the pineal gland in your brain, which helps produce necessary melatonin at night. Finally, very dark glasses that do not filter out substantial ultraviolet light may cause *more* damage than not wearing any sunglasses at all! This is because the pupil naturally opens very wide in the dark, and all the more so with dark lenses, which actually allow even more sunlight to enter your eye than would be the case otherwise. When your pupils are forced open in this way, they're kept from naturally constricting to protect your retinas.

When squalene is taken internally in the form of rice bran oil, red palm oil, or amaranth oil, it will help protect your eyes' lenses against free radical damage caused by sunlight or artificial light. I particularly love using rice bran oil and red palm oil as my internal sources of squalene. If it seems that squalene is a panacea of sorts, that's no coincidence! As you're no doubt realizing, foods and nutrients that reverse one aspect of aging often reverse others. There is a great deal of interaction between every aspect of aging, and natural substances affect several factors at once. This means you can use one product to reverse aging on many levels.

Eat Your Sunscreen

You can maximize sun protection by adding antioxidant foods to your diet to prevent burning, the formation of cancer-causing compound, loss of collagen, and glycation. Ultraviolet light causes damage from the surface of your skin deep into your internal organs, creating potentially lethal carcinogenic changes. This means your body needs to be protected all the way through. Fortunately, this is exactly what happens when you eat foods and herbs rich in natural antioxidants—they accumulate in your skin, and they bathe your eyes and internal organs in damage-limiting, protective compounds at a cellular and hormonal level. Here are some of my favorites.

Foods	Their Antioxidants
cocoa powder	resveratrol
olive oil	oleuropein, luteolin
broccoli	luteolin, sulforaphane
black tea	quercetin
green tea	epigallocatechin-3-gallate
apples	quercetin
onions	quercetin
carrots	carotenes, quercetin
red palm oil	carotenes
red grape juice	resveratrol
blueberries	resveratrol
tomato paste	lycopene

While all the foods listed above have incredible properties, tomato paste is really special. If you can increase your consumption of tomato paste during summer months, you'll significantly help protect your skin from sunburn (you can also apply it to your skin as a mask, but this can get messy and may leave some pigmentation behind). Tomato paste can also improve collagen production if you combine it with olive oil, as in a sauce or bruschetta. This is because the complex of compounds found in tomato paste, including lycopene, prevents the formation of free radicals called pyrimidine dimers, and AGEs, and inhibits metalloproteinases. In other words, eating tomato paste, particularly mixed with extra-virgin olive oil, helps protect you against cancer, wrinkles, and thin skin.

As I mentioned above, tomato paste contains a whole complex of sun-protective factors that do wonders for your skin. Lycopene is one of a number of carotenoids (carotene-like compounds) found in tomatoes. A new family of carotenoids found in tomatoes, the colorless carotenoids, or CLCs, has now been identified. Two of them, phytoene and phytofluene, are highly protective against ultraviolet radiation, which means they prevent the formation of wrinkles in chronological aging as well as in sun-damaged skin. They inhibit metalloproteinases, preventing the breakdown of collagen by these enzymes, and via the same mechanism, these two colorless carotenoids also inhibit metastatic cancer.

Progerin Protection

Recently, science has discovered that a protein called progerin ages us. It is implicated in progeria, or Hutchinson-Gilford progeria syndrome, which is an extremely rare genetic disorder characterized by dramatically accelerated aging. In fact, the term *progeria* comes from the Greek and means "premature old age." Sufferers die in their teens or early twenties of age-related diseases. This tragic disease is now helping us understand the very mechanisms involved in aging, including skin aging, photoaging, and cancer. For one, it is now known that progerin is not only formed in progeroid (caused by progerin) diseases. Progerin is a protein formed in normal bodies, too, and its formation dramatically increases during normal aging. Progerin formation is vastly accelerated by the action of UVA rays on the skin.

This is cutting-edge science and represents the first steps in our understanding of this novel mechanism, which is vitally important to the study of chronological aging and aging caused by sun damage. It is clear that any substance that has the ability to prevent the formation of progerin has huge anti-aging potential, reversing damage on a fundamental, cellular level and protecting the body from a whole range of life-threatening diseases, as well as preventing and reversing wrinkles and skin cancer.

And while we know that progerin leads to aging, natural substances stop progerin. These remedies include ferulic acid, resveratrol, rapamycin, and madecassoside. Let's take a closer look at ferulic acid and madecassoside, since these are readily available in many natural sources.

1. Fantastic Ferulic Acid

Ferulic acid acts as a UV absorber, stops the formation of pyrimidine dimers, stops the activation of matrix metalloproteinases by sunlight (preventing collagen destruction), controls the browning reaction (glycation), and prevents the formation of AGEs. It is also anti-inflammatory. Beyond sun damage, ferulic acid reverses age by dramatically decreasing cancer risk and cardiovascular disease, improving brain functioning, and, externally, neutralizing every harmful aspect of sun radiation. Ferulic acid is found in the bran of rice, wheat, oats, and barley, plus coffee, the herb dang gui, and strawberries.

Rice bran oil contains esters of ferulic acid, which are very effective at protecting human skin from the effects of sunlight and exhibit a wide range of absorption across the ultraviolet spectrum, extending into the visible light spectrum, and in this way offering highly significant anti-aging benefits. Rice bran oil has been shown to prevent every aspect of ultraviolet damage and to reverse aging at the genetic level. It also protects against UVB and UVA radiation. When you use rice bran oil, you get exactly the benefits you need to reverse skin aging, including the synthesis of vitamin D, essential for good health. This amazing oil is also rich in tocotrienols, compounds that clear arteries and are closely related to vitamin E. Vitamin E alone is not as effective at preventing burning and cancerous changes following UVB irradiation as a combination of vitamin E and tocotrienols—all the more enhanced by a compound called sesamin, which is capable of decreasing your skin's absorption of ultraviolet radiation by a whopping 30 percent.

Rice bran oil and one of its major constituents, oryzanol, also exhibit estrogenic qualities, and stop, or greatly diminish, hot flashes during menopause. Rice bran oil is famous in Japan for producing a beautiful, glowing, even-toned complexion, which is a direct result of its ferulic acid activity. Many of what we now call home remedies lean on the power of ferulic acid for anti-aging results. Our grandmothers used to use barley water to keep their skin wrinkle-free, and it seems they were on to something, since barley is a great source of ferulic acid. Coffee is, too, and contains caffeic acid, which protects the skin from sun damage. Dang gui, also known as *Angelica sinensis*, or Chinese angelica, and sometimes written as dong quai, is very easy to obtain in tincture or capsule form, and offers huge anti-aging benefits, but do not use the alcoholic tincture form on your skin, because it is drying. I suggest you evaporate the alcohol by boiling the tincture in water in a saucepan without the lid for fifteen minutes, as described at the end of this chapter, or taking it as a supplement.

Ferulic acid's ability to stop every damaging aspect of ultraviolet radiation has recently brought this natural compound to scientific attention, making it a model for a completely novel method of sun protection. Ferulic acid takes care of the damage that occurs on the surface of your skin as well as the potentially catastrophic changes that occur a little further down the line. This compound stops the formation of pyrimidine dimers. We saw earlier in this chapter that sunlight activates matrix metalloproteinases, enzymes that dissolve collagen and can lead to metastatic cancer. Ferulic acid very effectively blocks the activation of matrix metalloproteinases caused by sunlight. This means that the skin thinning that normally results from sun exposure, and which leads to catastrophic wrinkling, is prevented. This allows the preservation of your skin's thickness, resilience, and bounciness.

It is interesting to note that in one study, ferulic acid combined in a formula with vitamins C and E was shown to completely prevent sun-induced damage. Skin creams with exactly this combination of ingredients are now available at cosmetic counters. If you wish to make your own ferulic acid skin treatment, you can use instant-coffee granules dissolved in water as an instant facial refresher, but this lotion is most definitely *brown* and therefore not suitable as a sunscreen before you go out. You will find instructions for making a preparation using dang gui at the end of this chapter.

2. Marvelous Madecassoside

Madecassoside is a novel compound isolated from gotu kola, or *Centella asiatica*. Gotu kola is a potent SIRT1 activator. In one study, madecassoside was found to be the most effective progerin inhibitor out of a whole range of plant compounds studied. This herb is impressively anti-aging when it's added to skin treatments. The inhibition of progerin is clearly a powerful anti-aging mechanism.

The Secrets of Amla and Hyaluronan

I first mentioned amla, or *Phyllanthus emblica,* also known as *Emblica officinalis,* in the context of collagen and procollagen production in chapter 2. But it also contains a vast range of powerful polyphenols that can make it a valuable sun protector. When human skin fibroblasts are irradiated with UVB light, collagen synthesis decreases and matrix metalloproteinases increase, leading to collagen breakdown. But amla has been shown to prevent this and inhibit yet another damaging process that is caused by ultraviolet radiation: the stimulation of the enzyme hyaluronidase. Amla is impressively effective in preventing this sun-induced destruction of hyaluronan in your skin. Boots No7 Protect and Perfect anti-aging treatments, one of the biggest success stories of recent years, contain amla extract. You will find a recipe to make your own amla treatment at the end of this chapter. Of course, you can also take amla powder internally and boost its anti-aging effects in your skin and the rest of your body, enhancing your protection against sun damage and cancer.

So what exactly is hyaluronan? Hyaluronan, or hyaluronic acid, is responsible for the plump, moist look of young skin. It declines with age, and its levels fall even more rapidly with sun exposure. When the enzyme hyaluronidase is stimulated by the action of sunlight, hyaluronan is broken down in the skin. Dry, shriveled, thinning, saggy skin is the result of falling hyaluronan levels in your skin. The dramatic decrease of hyaluronan levels in the skin following sun exposure is yet another reason why skin loses its youthful plumpness and resilience. Lines around the mouth and a thinning of the lips, cheeks, and the area around the eyes are the highly visible consequences of this process.

Hyaluronan provides the extracellular matrix of the skin with a kind of bouncy filler, retaining moisture and plumping up older skin to a lovely youthfulness. The extracellular matrix is a collection of cells that secrete molecules that support and provide structure for the skin. Conventional moisturizers can help stop flaky skin, but unless your skin treatment also increases hyaluronan or its equivalent in your skin, you will be left with nonflaky, saggy skin. Of course, all of the measures we have seen so far can contribute to plumpness and collagen production. Increasing hyaluronan directly in your skin can significantly add to the freshness and prettiness of your face. Hyaluronan is also essential for wound healing. When applied to wounds, hyaluronan might result in faster healing and can prevent or significantly minimize the formation of scars. This healing process diminishes significantly with age. Because it is high in vitamin C, amla is very effective in increasing hyaluronan in the skin. Vitamin C has been proven to increase this amazing substance.

You can also increase hyaluronan production by eating fish with skin, chicken skin, goose fat, or amaranth. Chicken and fish are two animal proteins that lengthen telomeres rather than shorten them, and the fat can be highly beneficial for hyaluronic acid levels, but if you are prone to under-eye bags, keep your intake of animal fats low. Animal saturated fats, particularly from meat, especially beef, can produce under-eye bags even if you didn't have them before, so do watch out for that.

Hyaluronic acid serums are now available, and they offer very good results, but be careful around the eyes because they can produce puffiness. Soy makes a very good alternative to these serums. You can apply a mask of soy protein powder and water directly to your face and neck. This can lighten dark circles, tighten the skin around the eyes, and can provide a firm plumpness. Soy is perfectly fine to use externally, even if it doesn't suit you internally, unless you are genuinely allergic to it. Soy helps to increase hyaluronic acid content in the skin and even out skin tone. You can see the results from the very first application, and these can intensify over time.

Sodium lactate liquid or plain yogurt is a great alternative to hyaluronic acid and its derivatives. Sodium lactate is part of the skin's natural moisturizing factor, or NMF, but its water-holding capacity is a little lower than that of hyaluronic acid and related compounds, which means sodium lactate or yogurt can be used to increase moisture near the eyes if you dilute the lotion even further, without causing puffiness. Hyaluronan, by virtue of its potent moisture-locking ability, can cause swelling in the sensitive eye area, leading to puffy eyes. Sodium lactate and yogurt lighten and clarify the skin. Apply the lotion to your face, neck, arms, and décolletage if you wish, leave it on for five minutes, then rinse and apply a thin layer of emu oil, rosehip oil, squalene, or jojoba oil to moisturize.

Firm Your Face

Gelatin is an incomplete protein derived from the collagen of various animal by-products. It is commonly used as a gelling agent in food, pharmaceuticals, and candy (think: marshmallows, gummy candies, and Jell-O). It's also a popular ingredient in cosmetics, since it helps improve hair condition and nail strength, and can make your skin thick, young, and supple. For our purposes, new evidence shows that a daily intake of gelatin effectively antidotes the damaging effects of sun exposure on skin collagen, not only preventing the thinning that normally occurs, but actually making your collagen layer thicker. When people were exposed to ultraviolet radiation while taking gelatin supplements, their collagen increased by 16 percent!

This, as mentioned, led to thicker, firmer, younger skin. For a good gelatin that's sourced from pig, I like ClassiKool, which is available on Amazon. For a vegan alternative, you can also use a good vegan protein powder like pea or brown rice.

Anti-Inflammatory Benefits of Natural Solutions

Inflammation plays havoc with numerous cellular processes and has a significant role in the skin aging that results from long-term, unprotected skin exposure. Inflammation can lead to the production of toxic compounds within the skin and body that play foreboding roles in cancer and aging. Too much sun exposure can cause localized redness, which is, of course, inflammation; it may be mild or progress to a more serious burn, with or without blisters, but even a mild redness indicates inflammation that is clearly skin damage. The good news is, antioxidants and progerin inhibitors such as ferulic acid and gotu kola compounds protect the skin and body from inflammation and the biological stress it causes. Let's look at chamomile and helichrysum oils, rosehip and tamanu oils, licorice, honey, aloe vera, and black cumin oil as means to prevent, remedy, and reverse this.

1. Chamomile and Helichrysum Oils

The oils of German chamomile (blue chamomile) and helichrysum, also known as everlasting, are impressively potent anti-inflammatory substances, and you can use them topically to help anti-age your skin with wonderful results. You can use chamomile and helichrysum combined or singly, and you will be amazed by the results! They are both gentle enough to use undiluted, although I recommend you always test them first on the inside of your wrist and dilute them in a carrier or base oil such as almond or rice bran oil. Two of the best oils to use as carriers for chamomile or helichrysum are rose-hip and tamanu, which we'll discuss in a bit. Chamomile evens out and brightens skin tone so effectively you can see the difference even after the first application. Uneven patches of darker skin are a common effect of sun exposure, and chamomile corrects this almost overnight. As for helichrysum, it is a wonderfully regenerating oil. It diminishes varicose veins, fades scars, and makes lines and wrinkles disappear. Try it in one of the base oils mentioned above.

Chamomile contains many active compounds, among them terpene bisabolol, which possesses anti-irritant, anti-inflammatory, and antibacterial properties. You can use chamomile oil, diluted in a suitable base oil, on your face and even around your eyes. Chamomile stops conjunctivitis and sties within hours. If you don't have the oil, you can use a cooled chamomile tea bag instead. Chamomile oil diluted in rosehip, rice bran, coconut, red palm, or tamanu oil anti-ages your skin very rapidly, lending it the bloom and freshness of childhood. This wonderful oil also helps you fall asleep easily and wake up refreshed, and not at all groggy.

2. Rosehip and Tamanu Oils

These oils can be used alone or mixed together on their own or as a base to chamomile or helichrysum oils. All four of these oils, both essential and carrier, fade scars. This shows powerful regeneration properties, which would be put to good use in the prevention of sun damage. In one study, researchers found that when women who habitually spend months on the beach applied rosehip oil to their skin, signs of sun damage such as wrinkles and uneven pigmentation began to disappear within three weeks. And in just four months of daily rosehip oil application, the women's skin became soft, smooth, and evenly pigmented. That represents some serious sun damage repair!

Tamanu oil is another remarkable oil with anti-scarring activity. Sun damage is sometimes known as "solar scarring" in scientific literature. Each time skin is damaged by sun exposure, small solar scars remain. In time, this produces visible signs of photoaging such as wrinkling, skin coarsening, loss of firmness, and uneven pigmentation. A substance capable of preventing or reversing this damage is an extremely valuable addition to any skin anti-aging program, turning the clock back to an age when sun damage was repaired quickly and efficiently by the body's own systems. Tamanu oil is highly anti-inflammatory, which makes it very protective against sun damage.

3. Licorice

Licorice is an extraordinarily effective anti-aging herb, but because it raises blood pressure, use it externally only. Licorice is anti-inflammatory and prevents the free radical species from forming when skin is exposed to ultraviolet radiation. This creates significant increases in collagen and elastin levels. Combine it with red palm oil or avocado oil for a highly effective sun-protecting preparation.

4. Honey

After spending all day in the sun with Tigger, Winnie the Pooh may have been on to something. This sticky, delicious food also protects your skin against sun damage. It inhibits the formation of pyrimidine dimers and also very effectively inhibits COX-2 expression induced by ultraviolet light. COX-2 stands for cyclooxygenase-2. Put simply, COX-2 produces inflammation. The redness, swelling, and itching you experience as part of sunburn are largely caused by COX-2. Not only is this reaction uncomfortable, it causes cell damage. Nonsteroidal anti-inflammatory drugs (NSAIDs) inhibit COX-2, but COX-2 inhibitors also have negative side effects, due to the fact that they inhibit COX-2 everywhere in the body, including the gastrointestinal tract and kidneys. Some of these side effects can be very serious. They include indigestion, stomach ulcers, internal bleeding, shortness of breath, gastrointestinal perforations, heart failure, heart attack, and stroke. It's extraordinary, then, when you consider that honey also inhibits the negative, inflammatory effects of COX-2, yet does not produce a single one of the negative side effects! Because of its anti-inflammatory properties, hospital burn units have been known to use thick layers of honey to speed healing even on the most serious, extensive burns, and with fantastic results. In the case of burns and cuts, it's been known to heal them without residual scarring. As a sunscreen, honey inhibits metalloproteinase activation by sunlight, preventing collagen breakdown. Surprisingly, because honey is intensely sweet, it prevents glycation, which is the culprit behind AGEs. Though its topical use is limited because of its stickiness, I'll suggest ways to incorporate this into your daily sun protection regime at the end of this chapter.

5. Aloe Vera

Simply put, aloe vera is your skin's guardian angel. There is now a whole body of research that describes the remarkable properties of this plant. From it, we now know why aloe vera is such an extraordinary healer of burns, wrinkles, and saggy skin: it protects the skin from sun damage by preventing the activation of metalloproteinases and free radicals. Aloe vera increases collagen and elastin levels in your skin and reverses photoaging when it is taken internally in the form of a juice and when it is applied externally as a gel. Use both methods for truly visible anti-aging effects in a matter of days.

6. Black Cumin Oil

Black cumin oil is an extraordinary oil, highly effective at inhibiting elastase, the enzyme responsible for the marked decrease in elasticity in the skin following sun exposure and during chronological aging. You can also use carvacol as an alternative topical treatment, as it's one of the active anti-elastase compounds found in black cumin oil. In fact, the same compound occurs in dill seed and dill seed essential oil, too. If you find essential oils a little drying for your skin, which they can be, then black cumin oil is an ideal alternative. It is available as an essential oil, but I recommend the edible, milder version, used externally, which can be used even in sunlight without any fear of irritation. This oil also possesses estrogenic activity, so it is wonderful to use all over. Apply it at least once a day on your face to help skin look more elastic, pliable, and younger. You should see significant improvements in texture, smoothness, plumpness, and radiance. I also like to mix it with red palm oil.

Boost Your Cholesterol

Cholesterol is found in every cell of your body, including your skin cells. If your skin has sun damage, then cholesterol-containing fats can come to your rescue. Cholesterol possesses antioxidant properties, but it is its ability to restore barrier function in aging skin that makes it so important for dehydrated, wrinkled skin. As skin ages, it loses its capacity to restore its integrity, otherwise known as its barrier function. It becomes dry, lined, red, and irritated. It is no longer the strong, resilient protective barrier it used to be when you were thirty and didn't think about moisturizing your face as often as you do now. Applying cholesterol-containing fats directly to your skin's surface can help replenish this all-important lipid, and your skin will start to rehydrate rapidly. In my own clients, I've seen lines vanish and a youthful bloom replace flaky redness. Cholesterol-containing fats include emu oil, goose fat, duck fat, and lard. In addition to cholesterol, these fats contain hyaluronan, essential fatty acids, and other helpful compounds, but it is the cholesterol that is so vital in this instance.

Caution When Using Essential Oils in the Sun

Natural substances such as essential oils, edible oils, herbs, foods, and supplements are very safe and have profound benefits on the human body. However, please be cautious about using certain essential oils in the sun, because they can make your skin more sensitive and vulnerable to damage. If you're in a bright climate, do not use any citrus oils like lemon, lime, orange, or bergamot to avoid redness or sensitivity reactions. And if you like to use myrrh and frankincense oils diluted in a carrier base, please don't apply them before and during sunbathing, and wait a half hour after exposure to use them.

A Word About Sourcing Squalene and Red Palm Oil

When purchasing squalene and red palm oil, look for Certified Sustainable Palm Oil (CSPO), which is produced by plantations that comply with globally agreed environmental standards and are independently audited. Vegan versions of squalene, such as olive squalene, are also readily available online. Amaranth oil is not yet easily available, but it is the richest natural source of squalene.

BIO-YOUNG TREATMENTS

Please choose preparations based on ease of availability, cost, and personal preference. One is sufficient for treating this anti-aging mechanism, but two or more can speed improvements or improve a particularly neglected situation. Each one uses an ingredient discussed in this chapter. Enjoy!

Squalene: I like Life-Flo Pure Olive Squalene. Apply frequently during the day to sun-exposed areas.

Antioxidants: Choose one antioxidant-rich food from the list in this chapter to eat at every meal.

Rice bran oil: Mix 50 ml rice bran oil, 50 ml sesame oil, and two teaspoons or the contents of eight capsules of natural vitamin E oil in a small bottle. Use this mixture on exposed skin before going out in the sun, and take rice bran oil as a supplement (four teaspoons a day).

Dang gui: Take internally to supply yourself with ferulic acid. If you obtain the powder or capsule form, take one teaspoon of the powder or six to nine capsules per day. If you buy dang gui tincture, take four to six teaspoons a day, divided into two or three doses. You can also make a dang gui face lotion by adding eight tablespoons of dang gui tincture to 250 ml of boiling water. Keep the solution on boil for ten minutes with the lid off to allow the alcohol to evaporate, let it cool, bottle, and refrigerate. Use as needed. This lotion will keep in the fridge for about three days.

Ferulic acid serum: You can find ferulic acid preparations online quite easily. Make sure your chosen product contains at least 0.5 percent ferulic acid combined with vitamin C (15 percent) and vitamin E (1 percent).

Cocoa powder: I like dark chocolate for this, preferably unsweetened. Plain cocoa powder is fine. Mix eight teaspoons into warm milk, or make a smoothie with raspberries, red grape juice, blueberries, and cocoa powder.

Gotu kola: Take six to nine 500 mg capsules or one teaspoon of the powder every day. You may safely double this dose when you are on holiday in a sunny country. You can make your own gotu kola gel by simmering six teaspoons of gotu kola powder in 500 grams of aloe vera gel.

Amla: Pukka Herbs is one of my favorite suppliers of amla powder. Take two teaspoons of the powder mixed with water or juice as daily sun protection. Make an amla skin treatment by simmering six teaspoons of amla powder in 500 grams of coconut oil for fifteen minutes. Strain carefully and transfer to a jar. This cream will solidify, but it melts very easily with body heat.

Hyaluronic acid and related compounds, sodium lactate, yogurt: Hyaluronic acid is widely available in serum form, but my favorite is sodium lactate liquid (60 percent), from Amazon. Use all over your face, neck, arms, and décolletage. You may leave the lotion on or rinse off after five minutes. Unflavored low-fat yogurt makes an easily available substitute for sodium lactate. Apply it in a thin layer.

Gelatin: Four teaspoons of quality gelatin powder daily, stirred into yogurt and eaten, will help keep your skin collagen thick.

Chamomile, helichrysum, rosehip, and tamanu: Combine 50 ml each of rosehip and tamanu oil, add twenty drops each of German chamomile and helichrysum oils, and mix well. Tamanu oil can sting the eyes, so be careful with this and gently pat away excess with a soft tissue.

Red palm oil and licorice sun protection cream: Combine 500 grams of red palm oil (or avocado oil) with eight teaspoons of licorice powder. Simmer for fifteen minutes, stirring regularly to prevent burning the herb, then take off, let it cool a little, but strain through a muslin cloth or a clean tea towel while still warm so the oil is liquid. Press gently to extract the last of the oil, then discard the solids and store the cream in a jar. It will keep up to three months in the refrigerator.

Honey: Melt 500 grams of coconut oil over a low heat, add eight tea-spoons of honey, and stir well. Continue stirring while the mixture is cooling, then pour or spoon into a wide-mouthed jar.

Aloe vera: Use this internally in juice form and externally in gel form as a daily anti-aging treatment. You can smooth a little gel on your wet hair after washing it, as a leave-in conditioner. Take 10 ml of pure aloe vera juice once a day, and use a pure gel on your face before applying a light oil such as squalene.

Black cumin oil: This amazing oil is available from Amazon in one-liter bottles. Apply a thin layer from the bottle, or as a base for your choice of herbs and essential oils.

Cholesterol: Choose from emu oil, duck fat, goose fat, or lard. Add fifteen drops each of fennel and dill oil to every 100 ml of emu oil or 100 grams of solid fats to enhance estrogenic and anti-aging benefits.

CHAPTER 5

DIY Stem Cell Therapy

ANTI-AGING MECHANISM: Activation of stem cells

USE: Stimulating skin repair mechanisms

STARRING: Red palm oil, whey protein, avocado oil, comfrey, barley extract

Stem cell anti-aging is based on the fact that as we get older, our adult stem cells are less able to self-renew, and this causes a significant deterioration in our skin, hair, tissues, and organs. Proposed treatments to improve this have involved using embryonic stem cells, injections of adult stem cells into your body, or using plant stem cells in creams. But a lot of these options are accompanied by ethical concerns, safety issues, and efficacy questions.

My stem cell activation plan, however, is different. The aim is to activate your own skin stem cells with herbs, oils, supplements, and food, plus lengthen the lifespan of your stem cells, so more of them are active for a longer period of time. The result? Biologically younger skin and a healthier body. Surprising new research shows that we have more adult stem cells than was previously thought, just ready and waiting to be activated, which is great news for us all. These stem cells are present in significant numbers throughout the human body, even as it ages, and can be safely activated using natural substances.

Before we go on, I'd like to explain how this information relates to the bigger picture of anti-aging, and what you've read so far. By necessity, scientists examine one mechanism at a time. This is because a mechanism needs to be isolated as much as possible in order to evaluate its role in the body. However, as you've learned from this book, mechanisms do not function in isolation. There are millions of interactions that occur every millisecond in your body. Improving one aspect will improve a whole range of other mechanisms when we use natural, safe substances. Similarly, harming one mechanism, or system, will harm others. The scientific approach, which attempts to isolate individual components of any mechanism, leads to the erroneous impression that such mechanisms are unrelated. Mechanisms are, of course, closely related, and your body acts as a harmonious whole when all is well. So as an example, rosemary oil's various mechanisms—antioxidants and other compounds—interact with each other and can have a beneficial effect on hair follicle stem cells, protect telomeres, increase a cell's ability to allow water to flow through it, stimulate fibroblasts into producing collagen, and much more. And it's the body's ability to use amazing interactions like these that makes stem cell treatments with natural solutions not only possible but very cutting-edge science.

How Does Stem Cell Science Work?

Stem cell science is a revolutionary anti-aging concept with enormous potential for helping us look younger and live longer. But there are problems, both ethical and empirical, with how science often approaches this solution, and this limits the use of this information in an anti-aging program. Embryonic stem cells are at the forefront of most stem cell research, but they are also culled from nonviable human embryos, which is not an option for an anti-aging beauty program. Injections of adult stem cells directly into the skin or muscle are another approach, but they have produced dangerous, even life-threatening, anaphylaxis, and very disappointing results otherwise. For instance, when a group of bodybuilders directly injected their muscles with stem cells, they suffered anaphylaxis, and when clients at a beauty clinic in eastern Europe had stem cells injected directly into their facial skin, they experienced adverse reactions including anaphylaxis and facial swelling. Then we have plant stem cells delivered in creams and serums, and while they were initially hailed as a breakthrough, it now seems unlikely that they're capable of directly activating human stem cells when applied topically.

The main job of stem cells in your body is to produce young, fresh cells in all of your tissues—including those found in your skin, muscles, brain, bones, and elsewhere throughout the human form. In this way new, fresh cells replace old or injured ones. As you age, however, your stem cells die and fewer remain. The goal of using stem cells in anti-aging is to stimulate the growth of new stem cells in your own body, including your skin.

There are two broad categories of stem cells: embryonic and adult. Embryonic stem cells are undifferentiated, which means they have not yet matured into fully functioning cells. Embryonic stem cells are also pluripotent, which means they have the potential to become any type of cell, so they pose unique and extreme dangers, specifically the growth of extremely active tumors. The original thought behind using embryonic stem cell injections was that these unformed cells would simply make new, fresh cells of whatever type was needed—epidermal cells, neurons, or muscle fibers. Unfortunately, it proved extremely difficult to coax the embryonic stem cells to form exactly the type of neuron, or other cell, that a damaged area needed. And because stem cells are undifferentiated, they have huge potential to keep differentiating and multiplying. This is why they readily form tumors. The second issue here, as I'm sure you've heard and as I've noted above, is that embryonic stem cells are harvested from nonviable human embryos. This is controversial, since embryos are destroyed during this process.

On the other hand, adult stem cells, also known as somatic stem cells, are found throughout your body. Like embryonic stem cells, they are also undifferentiated. They have not matured into the cells that they will eventually become. However, adult stem cells are only multipotent, meaning that their fate is already decided and they can only become what they are meant to be. Their development is more controlled than that of embryonic stem cells. And the big news is this: adult stem cells are capable of forming various cells and tissue types. While it was once thought that adult stem cells were found in extremely low numbers in the adult human body, and so were not useful for regeneration, we now know this is not so. Adult stem cells are found throughout your body, in numbers high enough to accomplish very real regeneration! This means the stimulation and maintenance of a large population of adult stem cells in your body will make you look and feel decades younger for a very long time.

Adult stem cells are classified further, according to the body tissue in which they're found. For example, mammary stem cells help grow breasts during puberty, and neural stem cells enable the brain to grow neurons. A special category of stem cells that's of interest to rejuvenating skin is that of the mesenchymal stem cells, which play a vital role in wound healing, which we'll explore later.

We now know that we have more adult stem cells throughout adulthood than was previously thought, and that these stem cells can be safely and naturally activated. The latest stem cell research demonstrates that very important interactions occur between stem cells, estrogen, and molecules called telomeres, which protect your genetic material and extend the lifespan of your cells, including your stem cells—so an efficient anti-aging plan revolves around making the most of these factors.

Fibroblasts also play an important role in stem cell activation. When your cells reach their capacity limit for replication, they die, and as you age, this happens to all cells, including all-important fibroblasts that keep your skin taut and thick. As old fibroblasts increase and become sluggish, this results in lowered levels of collagen. This process accelerates with every decade after thirty years old, speeding up as you age. Stimulating fibroblasts, as we have already seen in this book, is a brilliant way to keep those fibroblasts active and to produce youthful levels of collagen, elastin, and the extracellular matrix, skin components that make your skin firm, resilient, supple, and well hydrated.

No Cancer Concerns Here

While some of the stem cell treatments mentioned above seem to promote cancer, there are ways to definitely avoid this using certain natural substances. Ashwagandha (*Withania somnifera*), for instance, both stimulates stem cell activity and inhibits cancer growth. It also restores melanin to graying hair, can help stop metastatic cancers (including melanoma), and protects the brain. As a result, it's been revered in Ayurvedic medicine for millennia, and I was one of the first practitioners to use this wonderful herb in the United Kingdom, almost thirty years ago. Skin creams featuring ashwagandha are not yet on the market, but you can make your own preparations using the information at the end of this chapter.

Ashwagandha is known as a JAK inhibitor. The Janus kinases (JAKs) are a family of compounds found within your cells that are implicated in inflammation, a mechanism that's detrimental to your health, longevity, and youthfulness. JAK inhibitors have powerful anti-cancer properties that can prevent and even stop metastases.

The compound found in ashwagandha is amazingly effective against all kinds of cancer, including liver, breast, and lung metastases.

One thing to keep in mind: ashwagandha has the ability to remove opiate tolerance. This means anyone taking opiate-type medication must not take ashwagandha, as there is a very real risk of overdose. Do not take ashwagandha in any form if you are taking, or have recently taken, any of the following: codeine or codeine-containing medication such as co-codamol (these are metabolized into morphine), morphine, Percocet, Vicodin, heroin, oxycodone (as in OxyContin), or in any other form. If you are not sure whether your medication may be opiate-based, avoid ashwagandha just in case and consult with your doctor.

Wound Healing and Stem Cell Activation

Wound healing is a great model for stem cell activation. In chapter 4, you saw how sun damage accelerates skin aging. Fascinatingly, many substances that prevent photoaging do so because they activate stem cells. Burns, cuts, and wounds are forms of stress as far as your skin and deeper tissues are concerned, and to an extent, face peels and mechanical exfoliation cause controlled stress in the skin and thereby mobilize stem cells and growth factors that lead to increased collagen, elastin, and extracellular matrix components. So when wounds heal, a similar process happens, because stem cells and vital growth factors are stimulated to heal and remodel skin.

A skin wound activates many growth factors, including mesenchymal stem cells. These are undifferentiated cells found in the bone marrow, fat cells, and blood. The role of mesenchymal stem cells (MSCs) is to repair and replace damaged tissue. When you have skin and deeper tissue injury, MSCs differentiate into fibroblasts, keratinocytes, and other skin cells. This means there is a hugely beneficial increase in exactly the types of skin cells we wish to utilize to anti-age the skin, leading to higher collagen and elastin production. This also increases the production of extracellular matrix components and structural and hydrating factors such as hyaluronan. And while mesenchymal stem cells are activated by inflammatory molecules, such as cytokines, they can also be activated by vitamin C, sirtuin, estrogen, and wound-healing substances like aloe vera. Aloe is famous for healing burns very rapidly, as it stimulates stem cell production in your skin. Mesenchymal stem cells in the bone marrow decrease in number as we age, which may be one of the reasons older people heal less well, and more slowly, than younger people—not to mention a reason their skin is thinner, less firm, and duller than that of those who are younger and have larger numbers of MSCs at their disposal.

Two natural wound healers with potent anti-aging activity that I love are avocado oil and almond oil. When a study measured wound healing, examining several parameters involved in this process that are also vital to keeping the skin young, avocado oil was superb at activating the skin-healing mechanisms. Petroleum jelly, on the other hand, was much less effective. Avocado oil works both internally and externally to increase cell proliferation and cell differentiation of skin cells. During wound healing, this leads to a vital increase in the numbers of fibroblasts during the first twenty-one days.

In aging skin, an increase in fibroblast activity leads to smooth, unwrinkled skin. This declines dramatically with aging, and it is the aim of stem cell facial treatments to increase this. Avocado oil is extremely effective at activating fibroblasts directly in your skin, keeping their numbers and activity at youthful levels. The effect of avocado oil involves the activation of several growth factors in the skin, and does not lead to the overgrowth of collagen, which happens when epidermal growth factor (EGF) is used singly in a facial serum. As for almond oil or sweet almond oil, as it's also known, this wonderful oil helps speed up wound healing and prevent skin degradation caused by ultraviolet light. It is also excellent for removing dark under-eye circles.

Every natural substance capable of rapid wound healing will stimulate the production of MSCs, epidermal growth factor, and other factors responsible for healing, which can also anti-age your skin. In the same way as when wounds heal, you can stimulate your skin to produce new fibroblasts and keratinocytes by using natural agents that cause mesenchymal stem cells to differentiate into cells that produce fresh, young skin. Let's examine how vitamin C, sirtuins like resveratrol, comfrey, barley, and gotu kola activate stem cells on a cellular level.

※ Stem Cell Spotlight: Vitamin C

Human skin cells can be transformed into stem cells during healing, when stressed, or when certain natural substances are applied directly to those cells. Vitamin C increases the numbers of skin cells that turn into stem cells and increases the lifespan of those cells. To put it very simply, vitamin C stops cells from dying—particularly fibroblasts. Vitamin C also kills cancer cells at the same time. Fibroblasts synthesize collagens, elastin, and other components of the extracellular matrix, all of which are essential for firm, youthful skin and rapid, effective wound healing. Albert Szent-Györgyi, who was awarded the Nobel Prize in 1937 for his work on vitamin C, found that the more purified his vitamin C preparation was, the less effective its biological activity. He found "dirty" lemon juice to be far more potent than pure ascorbic acid powder. In essence, he discovered the synergistic interaction between ascorbic acid and bioflavonoids (an important category of antioxidants), long before they had a name.

You may, of course, use a vitamin C serum on your skin, and

this should produce good results, but some of the best results are obtained when we take into account Szent-Györgyi's findings and include bioflavonoids in a broader skin preparation. Pure lemon juice contains both vitamin C and bioflavonoids, but it can be ir-ritating. My favorite vitamin-C-enhanced preparation is the amla and coconut oil preparation at the end of this chapter.

✳ Stem Cell Spotlight: Resveratrol

Resveratrol activates a vitally important longevity gene, SIRT1, which is great, since new research shows resveratrol prevents progerin-induced cell death of SIRT1 stem cells. One of the ways progerin causes accelerated aging is via the inactivation of sirtuins, including SIRT1. Aged and worn-out sirtuins, just like all other cells, need to regenerate and repair in order to survive. The rapid decline in sirtu-ins is one of the serious damaging effects of the aging protein proger-in. Resveratrol prevents the death of the adult stem cells responsible for the production of sirtuins. In turn, sirtuins stimulate stem cells in your skin. This is an extraordinary anti-aging circle. Resveratrol is in this way able to prevent one of the most serious cellular dysfunc-tions in progerin-related diseases and to anti-age healthy adults, too. Grape seed extract, red grape juice, red wine polyphenols, and pine bark extract are all great resveratrol sources. Chapter 1 includes a list of delicious natural resveratrol sources.

✳ Stem Cell Spotlight: Comfrey

Comfrey, or *symphytum,* is a plant most gardeners consider to be an annoying weed, but it's also been shown to stimulate and regenerate epidermal stem cells when applied externally. This means the cells responsible for keeping your skin lovely, thick, and hydrated by producing collagen, elastin, hyaluronic acid, and many other structural components—these cells are activated. These cells actually die off, and decrease in number as we age. By applying comfrey directly to your skin, you keep these cells from dying and even increase their numbers. The topical use of a comfrey cream, whether from root or leaf, has been shown to stimulate the skin to produce fresh, new skin and is perfectly safe to apply anywhere on your body.

A few years ago comfrey got a bad reputation, because when rabbits were fed a diet that contained a very high percentage of comfrey leaves, they developed liver cancer. Comfrey contains pyrrolizidine alkaloids (PAs), compounds that have definitely been linked to liver cancer. Many people claim to have used comfrey internally, both in leaf and root form, without harm, obtaining great health benefits, and many farmers feed it to their livestock, improving the animals' health. Just to be safe, I don't suggest ingesting it, but I do like it as an external treatment.

Comfrey's Jekyll and Hyde identity brings up a very important point about stem cells. Comfrey is, without a doubt, a powerful cell proliferator, which means it really does activate your skin, and even your bone, to make fresh, new cells. But that kind of stimulation, if it isn't controlled, can lead to out-of-control cell proliferation, otherwise known as cancer. Obviously this is not something that the approach given here ignores. But rest assured, the natural substances recommended in this book actually control stem cell activity, activating aged stem cells but not allowing cell growth to become cancerous. One of the dangers associated with stem cell injections and the introduction of ready-made embryonic or adult stem cells from human sources is tumor growth. Despite the potential for problems when pyrrolizidine alkaloids are ingested, the external use of comfrey does not pose this risk.

Comfrey extract is also great for wound healing. When you cut a fruit or plant, the liquid that oozes out is very rich in stem cells. The same thing happens if you cut yourself! A wound stimulates the release of MSCs and a whole host of epidermal growth factors (EGFs) that work together to repair the injury as quickly as possible. It's not a coincidence that comfrey, one of the best wound healers around, stimulates stem cell production and related growth factors in your own skin.

✳ Stem Cell Spotlight: Barley

Barley contains compounds that have been shown to produce very effective stem cell stimulation in human skin. This is a rich source of epidermal growth factor and was once used as a very popular antiwrinkle remedy. Unlike the above stem cell activators, barley possesses estrogenic activity, and this may explain some of its anti-aging effect on the skin.

✳ Stem Cell Spotlight: Gotu Kola

Gotu kola (*Centella asiatica,* also known as *Hydrocotyle asiatica*) is a potent anti-ager that affects stem cell stimulation. In chapter 1, we saw that this herb activates the longevity genes, sirtuins, particularly SIRT1. Gotu kola also inhibits the aging protein progerin. Gotu kola is one of the most effective wound healers known and can be used both internally and externally to switch on repair and skin anti-aging.

Keep Them Long and Strong:
Stem Cells and Telomeres

The human body consists of systems that react with one another. These systems are made of organs, such as the lungs, liver, kidneys, and skin. The skin is the largest organ of the human body. All organs, including bones, blood, and the brain, are made of tissues. These tissues are made of cells. Each cell contains a nucleus. Each nucleus contains twenty-three pairs of chromosomes. And every chromosome has a telomere on each end. Telomeres protect the genetic code of your cells from damage during replication—the process of making new cells, such as skin, muscle, or bone. Chromosomes are codes that enable your body to make proteins, the building blocks of everything from collagen to hormones. Replication is the process by which your body heals injury and replaces worn-out cells.

The telomeres at either end of the chromosomes prevent loss of essential genetic material during replication. Imagine the genetic code as the fabric part of a shoelace. The telomere is the plastic covering at each end, preventing that genetic code from "fraying." However, with every replication, the telomeres themselves become damaged. Little pieces are lost and the telomeres become shorter and shorter. When this damage reaches a critical point and the telomere at the end of a particular code becomes too short, the cell dies. This is truly the most basic mechanism of aging, occurring at the cellular level. Telomeres protect your chromosomes, and so prevent cellular aging. But telomeres are themselves damaged in the process. Preventing this damage, then, makes every one of your cells, from collagen to your bones, significantly younger.

Adult stem cells die when their telomeres become too short, but the adult stem cells in your body are capable of highly effective renewal. The number of times that a cell can replicate is determined by the length of its telomeres. But it is not necessary to inject adult stem cells into your body to activate their anti-aging potential. Adult stem cells in the skin can continue replacing fibroblasts, for example, and they can be activated by natural plant extracts.

Keeping your telomeres long means that the lifespan of all of your cells is extended. This applies to your stem cells, too. It was once thought that there were very few adult stem cells in the human body and, therefore, that regeneration was severely limited. We now know that adult stem cells are widely distributed throughout the body. Your skin is rich in these stem cells, providing you with an extraordinary anti-aging opportunity at this vital, basic, cellular level. The link between telomere length and youthfulness is very strong. It is as simple as this: the longer your telomeres, the longer your life span. The longer your telomeres, the younger you look.

When we speak of stem cells and telomeres, then, we are talking about truly reversing the aging process at the most fundamental, cellular level, because we are now in the domain of genetic information. The one vital constant in being young is the activation and protection of cells that produce anti-aging compounds. In the skin, these cells are the fibroblasts. They can be activated, as you've seen in prior chapters, by essential oils, sirtuin activators, and progerin inhibitors. And because of the latest stem cell research, we've learned that aging fibroblasts can be revived and declining fibroblast numbers can be restored. Natural agents can activate your own adult stem cells and their production, and then keep them youthful and extend their lifespan by activating telomerase and keeping their telomeres long. And if you look after your telomeres, you will encourage your stem cells to function at their most youthful optimum, including your skin's capacity to regenerate and renew itself at its peak, youthful levels.

Natural Substances That Lengthen Telomeres

There are natural substances that, when applied directly to the skin, activate stem cells in the treated area. In addition, many natural substances also protect your telomeres on a deeper level. Some substances even lengthen already-shortened telomeres, reversing aging in a powerful way. But because one treatment can affect multiple systems, telomere-lengthening substances can protect your stem cells in the skin, hair, muscle, bone, and every cell of your body at once. In fact, anything that makes you healthier, including a reduction in stress, will have a highly positive effect on your stem cells, anti-aging you to an astonishing degree.

Although there has been some concern about the possibility of telomere-lengthening agents increasing cancer risk, there are many safe, natural substances that protect and lengthen telomeres and actually *prevent* cancer. As you'll see in the list below, there is a very close relationship between stem cells, telomeres, antioxidants, and estrogen that keep your body healthy. Antioxidants provide powerful protection for telomeres, preventing their shortening and even lengthening them. Estrogen is one of the most potent telomere stimulators and lengtheners so far discovered, especially for women.

Natural substances that support telomeres:

red palm oil, taken internally

vitamin D, taken in the D3 form, at least 800 IU (international units) a day

whey protein (ricotta cheese is made from whey protein)

fish oil

rosemary

cocoa

bilberries

folic acid

sulfur-rich proteins such as eggs, chicken, and cottage cheese

green tea

berries

red grapes

olive oil

unrefined avocado oil

estrogenic herbs and essential oils

There are also foods that shorten and damage your telomeres. These include:

processed meats like bacon

sugar, with the exception of ribose and honey

easily oxidized saturated fats like bacon, cheese, butter

There are also herbs that do wonders for your telomeres. *Astragalus membranaceus,* or huang qi in Chinese, is particularly effective, and has been shown to increase telomere length and lifespan. This herb has a long history in Chinese medicine as one of the revered royal herbs, a category known in Ayurveda as *rasayana* and in the West as adaptogens. These herbs possess a wide array of hormonal and cellular properties that create significant anti-aging. Astragalus has been used in Chinese medicine for two thousand years, and I've personally used it for over thirty. In fact, I have used it in all of my anti-cancer programs with great success. I have also used it to raise the white cell count in patients undergoing chemotherapy, which typically reduces white blood cells, since the thymus gland that produces them is damaged by anti-cancer cytotoxic drugs that kill all rapidly dividing cells. Remarkably, astragalus restores thymus gland function. Since a gradual deterioration that leads to eventual atrophy of the thymus gland occurs during aging, astragalus is able to reverse the immune function loss that occurs as people grow older. The thymus gland is the immune system's master gland. Astragalus also helps protect against cancer and lengthens telomeres. Used internally, and applied externally, astragalus is capable of fast, visible anti-aging in your whole body, including the skin, where the results—a lovely clarity, freshness, and glow—are highly visible, very quickly.

Estrogen: Stem Cell Stimulator, Wound Healer, Telomere Lengthener

Estrogen stimulates cell growth because stem cells possess estrogen receptors. It stimulates the growth of breast cells, the endometrium, uterine cells, and brain cells. But the most important effects, in terms of cancer risk, are the cell-proliferating effects on these hormone-sensitive tissues. When this cell growth is not controlled, cancer can occur. Antioxidants keep that cell growth in check, and in this way, antioxidants keep this estrogen-induced cell growth in check, too, protecting against cancer. In fact, it is the uncontrolled activation of mammary stem cells by estrogen that can lead to breast cancer. The aim in this book is to produce anti-aging stimulation without increasing the risk of cancer. This represents cellular stimulation with cellular control that is easily and safely achieved by natural substances.

The relationship between estrogen and wound healing is also significant. One study found that topical estrogen significantly improved wound healing in both elderly women and men, speeding up the rate of healing and greatly improving the integrity of the wound eighty days post-injury.

Estrogenic oils activate stem cells and growth factors when you apply them, increasing collagen, elastin, hyaluronan, and every structural cellular matrix component that collectively makes your skin firm, dewy, and young. Estrogenic oils, applied directly to your face and neck, will help plump up your cheeks, the area around your eyes, your forehead, and your lips, and they can make your neck rounder so you no longer have ropes of muscle just under the jaw.

Estrogen also lengthens telomeres, which ultimately helps protect your skin from ultraviolet damage and your brain from Alzheimer's, as well as increasing the lifespan of your stem cells. Youthful hormone levels should be achieved by using natural substances, not synthetic or even bio-identical hormones.

The most effective natural estrogenic preparations for the skin are licorice and fenugreek herbs, and dill seed and fennel essential oils. Honey is also powerfully estrogenic, aiding against bone loss and uterine and vaginal atrophy in postmenopausal women, and protecting against cancer, particularly hormone-sensitive ones. Honey very effectively increases growth factors in the skin, stimulating mesenchymal stem cells and fibroblasts as well.

BIO-YOUNG TREATMENTS

Please choose preparations based on ease of availability, cost, and personal preference. One is sufficient for treating this anti-aging mechanism, but two or more can speed improvements or improve a particularly neglected situation. Each one uses an ingredient discussed in this chapter. Enjoy!

Comfrey: Use comfrey root powder externally only. You can make a very simple stem-cell-stimulating lotion by simmering six teaspoons of comfrey root powder in 500 ml of water. Let it cool, strain the liquid, bottle, and store in the fridge. Alternatively, you could gently simmer the same quantity of comfrey root powder in 500 grams of aloe vera gel, then strain and store in the fridge. Apply to your face, neck, arms, and body at least once a day. In practice you can use external treatments more often on your face, which is where they are most needed. For the face, I like to use my chosen treatment at least twice a day, more frequently if I really feel I need help! Leave the treatment on for five to ten minutes, then rinse off. This treatment, like all non-oil-based treatments, can be a little drying on facial skin, so choose from the range of oils in this book and apply your chosen treatment after you rinse off the comfrey.

Barley: Boil 15–200 grams of pearl barley until it is soft, allowing it to cool, and straining the liquid. Store this in a bottle in the fridge. Apply to the face, neck, and arms, leave on for five to ten minutes, then rinse off and follow with an oil-based treatment, as above.

Astragalus: Take six capsules of this herb per day.

Amla (contains vitamin C and antioxidants): Melt 500 grams of virgin coconut oil in a saucepan over a gentle heat and stir in six teaspoons of amla (*Emblica officinalis*) powder. Simmer the mixture for fifteen minutes, making sure it doesn't catch, then take it off the heat, let it cool, and strain while still pourable. Store it in a wide-mouthed container, as it will set solid, though it melts on contact with the warmth of your skin. Store in fridge. Use this treatment on clean skin, devoid of makeup. Use it on your face, neck, and arms. This treatment can be left on, but gently wipe off excess if your face is a little too oily.

Resveratrol: Eat a resveratrol food every day, or use a lotion high in resveratrol directly on your skin. I recommend unsweetened cocoa powder dissolved in warm water, applied to your face, and rinsed off after five to ten minutes. After, use squalene, coconut oil, or avocado oil to compensate for the drying.

Red palm oil: Take four teaspoons daily and apply a little to your skin, particularly your face. This oil is orange, so be careful with light-colored fabrics, and also wash off or wipe off the oil before you venture out!

Estrogenic oils and plants: Licorice tea, to be used externally, is easy to make—just brew a strong tea using three tea bags and two cups of boiling water, let cool, and apply as a lotion to your face, neck, and arms. There is no need to rinse off the licorice tea. Fennel and dill essential oils can be added to avocado oil, at a ratio of 30 drops of essential oil (or 15 each of fennel and dill) to 100 ml of avocado oil. Apply at least twice a day to your face, neck, and arms.

Telomere-lengthening foods: Incorporate at least two kinds of these into your daily diet. See the list of telomere-lengthening foods earlier in this chapter.

Honey: Make a pure honey mask for the bathtub or shower, or a honey lotion by dissolving two teaspoons of honey in 500 ml of water. This preparation is a little sticky, and it will ferment over the course of a week, but it is very effective and makes your skin smooth and young if used daily.

CHAPTER 6

Good to the Bone

ANTI-AGING MECHANISM: Reversing and preventing
bone loss

USE: Reducing bone loss, restoring facial features,
strengthening spine and hips

STARRING: Prunes, onions, fenugreek, fennel, maca,
boron, fennel essential oil

Looking young is no longer about softening fine lines or filling out wrinkles. Even cosmetic surgeons know that stretching
the skin during a face-lift cannot conceal the drastic effects of
bone loss and bone remodeling that occur with age. This produces
visible aging that no makeup, cream, cosmetic procedure, or filler
can restore or realistically simulate to resemble its natural contours.

Bone loss can be prevented, and halted. Bone can even be re-
grown! Bone is alive—every day, bone is both lost and built. You can
see it and you can feel it. Age-related bone loss doesn't just lead to
a stooping back or broken limbs. Its effects are visible in your face,
which dramatically changes its shape as the years pass by. You can
see the loss of bone mass in the cheek and eye areas. This type of
bone loss produces under-eye bags. Bone loss in the jaw area alters
your profile. Bone mass lost anywhere in your skeleton, the very
structure of your body, leads to catastrophic loss of support for

muscle, fat, and skin, producing sagging and wrinkling. Some surgeons advocate cheek implants, and new procedures involving the breaking and resetting of jawbones are being perfected to correct the loss of facial bone mass, but the underlying bone structure is not improved by these surgical techniques. Facial bone will remain as thin as it was before these surgical interventions. Unless steps are taken to stop bone loss, and to build up existing bone, aging will lead to further erosion of facial structure as bone continues to thin and degrade.

Bone loss also feels bad. Just as wrinkles are a sign that you need to anti-age your skin, and hot flashes signal the need to increase your estrogenic activity, sore, loose teeth and lower back pain indicate that your bones are in trouble. The great news is that raising hormones to optimum levels using natural foods, herbs, and supplements thickens bone. Doing all you can to maintain and restore bone mass is necessary to your looks and quality of life.

You can return your vulnerable bones to their youthful strength and flexibility by following the instructions given in this chapter, so that you look and move like your younger self.

The Other Big O: Osteoporosis

Severe bone loss can lead to osteoporosis. As we have seen, bone is live, active tissue that is broken down and repaired daily. When you are young, bone growth is greater than bone loss. But as you age, bone loss accelerates, and bone growth slows down or even stops altogether. This process eventually produces a condition characterized by holes or spaces between the solid parts of the bone, making the bone porous. *Osteoporosis* is the medical term for the thinning of bone that results when the process of breaking bone down outweighs the rate at which it is repaired and rebuilt.

Osteoporosis is one of the most common and well-known consequences of aging. In the five to seven years following menopause, women can lose up to 20 percent of their bone density, and approximately nine million people in the United States have osteoporosis, which occurs in all ethnic groups. People with osteoporosis break bones—commonly, the wrist, spine, hip, leg, or arm. This typically happens with minimum impact, so a person with osteoporosis can break a bone simply by sneezing, hugging or being hugged, bumping into furniture, or stepping off a curb. Fortunately, osteoporosis can be prevented and reversed, even if you are already a sufferer.

Cellular and hormonal factors play a role in osteoporosis. Since much of osteoporosis is due to hormonal decline, restoring hormonal function will prevent bone loss and replace bone that has already been lost due to low hormone levels. Estrogen is the main hormone involved, but other hormones like progesterone are also involved. Cellular factors involving minerals and biochemical mechanisms that act in concert with hormones also play a significant part in protecting and restoring lost bone mass. Elemi, a little-known essential oil, has been helpful in speeding up the healing of bone injuries in my practice, where I deal with many martial artists, and the aftermath of their competitions and training. I suggest that you mix elemi into a facial preparation to firm up skin and benefit your facial bone structure, but remember to also use it on your hip bones, shinbones, and forearms.

Are You at Risk for Bone Loss?

Bone maintenance and building are complex processes involving several hormones and many nutrients, which is great news, because naturals are complex, affect several hormones at once, and contain a vast range of bone-beneficial nutrients. Although we usually think of bone density as a marker of bone health, because medical tests only measure bone density, there is one other hugely important measure of bone health: bone flexibility. Flexibility is essential in the prevention of fractures, for example. So using natural agents to support various aspects of bone health is integral to having strong bones throughout your life.

Estrogenic activity maintains and rebuilds bone mass, so if you're perimenopausal or going through menopause and experiencing hot flashes, you are also losing bone. Increasing your intake of estrogenically active herbs like fennel, hops, fenugreek, and evening primrose oil then becomes vital to preserving bone mass, and restoring any that has been lost. Fenugreek and fennel, for instance, have estrogenic activity, and they also contain a compound called diosgenin, which builds new bone. These herbs increase beneficial hormonal activity while decreasing cancer risk. And while synthetic estrogen has been shown to maintain bone, it does not build new bone or restore bone mass. It was once thought that synthetic estrogen in the form of estradiol was the only answer, but natural compounds such as diosgenin increase osteogenesis, too, and actually make new bone.

Let's pause a moment on the term *diosgenin*, since this will come up again in later chapters. Diosgenin is a compound found in plants that possesses hormonal activity, acting primarily, but not exclusively, as an estrogen, in a wide range of mechanisms. The best way to obtain diosgenin is by taking diosgenin-rich herbs, such as fenugreek, fennel, sarsaparilla, boron, and maca. Diosgenin and diosgenin-containing herbs can achieve what synthetic estrogen cannot—they stop bone loss, and they stimulate the formation of new bone. They increase blood supply to the bone, which is a necessary condition for repair and growth; increase bone matrix protein synthesis; and increase the formation of calcium deposits that leads to increased bone formation. Diosgenin increases blood supply as it enhances bone growth, and it does this via estrogenic stimulation. Based on studies that used synthetic estrogen, researchers thought that estrogen only maintained bone density following menopause, but experiments with diosgenin indicate that this compound produces bone growth at least partially via its estrogenic activity. In fact, diosgenin acts as a precursor to estrogen, progesterone, and testosterone.

Herbs such as fenugreek and fennel contain diosgenin, which inhibits metalloproteinases and increases collagen in the skin. Wild yam is the most well-known diosgenin-containing herb, but it does not suit all women. Some women find it makes them feel blue and weepy. It can also reduce your breast size. Sarsaparilla, on the other hand, also contains diosgenin, but it makes you feel energized, and enhances breast growth. These herbs contain other compounds that add to their beneficial effects, but it is their diosgenin content that impacts bone building. Diosgenin builds bone everywhere in your body, including the jaw, which is essential to bone mass and structure. Diosgenin also helps keep your teeth strong, white, and healthy. Tooth loss in later years is very much a consequence of lost jawbone density, though gum disease also plays a part. Interestingly, gum shrinkage is the result of declining hormone levels, particularly estrogen. All vitamins and minerals mentioned in this chapter, which help with bone strength, also strengthen teeth.

Hormones are the primary factors involved in bone growth and bone loss, but lifestyle and diet can affect bone health, too. These include alcoholism, smoking, being very thin and tall, exercising too much, anorexia, a sedentary lifestyle, and a diet high in sucrose. Medication such as anticonvulsant medications, benzodiazepines, steroid medications such as asthma inhalers, and too-high doses of medications for hyperthyroidism or hypothyroidism can also produce bone loss.

Natural Solutions for Bone Health

Our knowledge about bone health has greatly advanced in the past two decades. We now know that minerals, fatty acids, antioxidants, and vitamins play a role in preventing bone loss and maintaining bone mass as we age. Here are, in no particular order, some of the major participants in bone health: calcium, magnesium, boron, vitamin D, vitamin K, vitamin C, silicon, omega-3 fatty acids, omega-6 fatty acids, manganese, copper, zinc, sulfur, and iodine. A pill that contained every nutrient necessary for healthy bones would be impossible to swallow! Fortunately you can combine foods, herbs, and supplements to obtain powerful bone-building benefits. And the sooner you begin to care for your bones with these substances, the better. It is never too early or too late to start. However, while a forty-five-year-old woman whose bone loss is still in its very early stages will be able to improve her bone mass quite rapidly, an eighty-year-old woman who has lost a great deal of her bone mass will find that improvement takes longer.

Magnesium, vitamin K, and hops are a few agents worth highlighting here. Magnesium is involved in more than three hundred biochemical reactions in your body and plays a vital role in energy production and bone building. Vitamin K, from green vegetables, is also vital for strong bones. Beer builds strong bones, too, as it's a good source of silica, yet another mineral vital for healthy bones. Most beers also contain hops, an estrogenic herb. This estrogenic activity very effectively offsets the fall in the sex hormone estradiol that occurs in the years before, during, and after menopause, so that you can retain more bone structure. Green tea, black tea, barley, chicory, and cocoa also possess valuable bone-building properties, so include them in your daily diet.

✳ Bone Health Spotlight: Maca

The human body is very complex, and the interactions between hormones are highly dynamic. The ideal situation is one where bone building and bone repair outweigh bone breakdown. This is exactly what happens during childhood and early adulthood, and continues until we reach thirty years old. After this age, bone breakdown begins to outweigh bone repair and bone building, a process that speeds up with aging. As we have just seen, this is by no means inevitable, even though such an imbalance is so common as to be considered normal. It is not normal; rather, it is the result of less than ideal food and lifestyle choices that cause bone to be broken down in order to restore acidic blood to neutral.

Women's low levels of estrogen and progesterone after menopause depletes bone mass in their bodies, including the jaw, which changes facial structure. Estrogenic activity maintains bone, and if this activity is coupled with the actions of polyphenols, a type of antioxidant, lost bone is restored.

Maca, or *Lepidium meyenii*, is a root vegetable with astonishing anti-aging powers. Maca contains many compounds with antioxidant properties coupled with complex, highly beneficial hormone activity. This makes it a bone-building dynamo! It increases fertility in both sexes, but its action on the sex hormones can seem confusing. In some experiments, it possesses definite estrogenic activity and increases uterine weight, yet in others it seems to be progestogenic, or progesterone-increasing, which in this case is good news for us because progesterone is a very effective bone builder. It is considered to be the major bone-trophic (bone-growing) hormone.

It is possible that the wide-ranging effects of maca are also due to a novel mechanism that has not yet been fully elucidated. It seems highly probable that maca may act via the brain, in a way that is similar to the action of Panax ginseng—by stimulating the pituitary gland, for example, which then activates hormonal systems in the body, particularly the ovaries in women and the testes in men, to produce the relevant sex hormones. This would explain why the effects of maca supplementation often do not become fully obvious until the herb has been taken for at least four months.

Maca increases collagen IV and integrin synthesis, which makes your skin firm. It stimulates hair growth and forms the protective coating around the hair shaft, making your hair visibly thicker. Maca protects you against the detrimental effects of stress, increases your energy and memory, and acts as an antidepressant and antioxidant, even if you've gone through menopause. Maca is very effective at stimulating ovulation, greatly increasing the numbers of maturing egg follicles. What's more, maca is very effective at protecting your skin from sun damage, whether from the inside out or applied directly to the skin as a topical treatment. Maca protects the liver and prevents breast cancer. All of these effects are very valuable and highly anti-aging. But maca also strengthens bones via an estrogenic mechanism even after menopause.

✳️ Bone Health Spotlight: Boron

Boron is a mineral responsible for normal growth and plays a pivotal role in preventing and reversing osteoporosis. Excitingly, boron raises 17-beta-estradiol levels in postmenopausal women, an effect that makes this mineral a vitally important supplement in any anti-aging program. Boron is so effective at increasing the concentration of estradiol in postmenopausal women that it can be used as a very effective alternative to synthetic hormone replacement therapy. On top of raising estradiol, boron stimulates parathyroid hormone. In fact, boron appears to have the same relationship to this hormone that iodine has to the thyroid. The four parathyroid glands are situated in the neck near the thyroid gland. The parathyroids secrete the parathyroid hormone, which is responsible for keeping calcium within an optimal narrow range. In cases of boron deficiency, the parathyroids overreact and increase their parathyroid hormone output, which stimulates osteoclasts to break down bone to release calcium. This causes bones and teeth to lose calcium.

Inadequate boron intake impairs bone repair and formation, which leads to decreased bone volume. Sufficient boron intake increases bone growth, or osteogenesis. Boron increases osteoblast activity; osteoblasts are cells that make new bone. We are not simply talking of preventing bone loss, because boron actually thickens bone—even bone damaged and thinned by osteoporosis!

Boron makes old bones young again, which is a truly wonderful feat. It also protects your teeth from decay, keeping your jaw strong and your teeth firmly embedded and healthy. Crumbling, decayed, and loose teeth play a huge role in malnutrition in elderly people. And that strong jaw and youthful cheekbones and forehead mean your facial features and profile will remain their best. Facial bone thinning typically flattens facial features and alters the look of a face beyond recognition.

✳ Bone Health Spotlight: Prunes

Prunes are a rich source of boron and a polyphenol. In a study comparing two groups of women, one group supplemented their diet with ten prunes a day, while the other ate dried apple. The results? The prune eaters had significantly higher bone density! A compound found in apple, phloridzin, has huge benefits for bone health, but it may be that it is not present in large concentrations in dried apples. In the study, eating prunes caused increased bone density while dried apples did not, or did not do so to the same extent. True anti-aging power comes from knowing which fruits, vegetables, herbs, or other natural substances are best for which particular aging mechanism. Because while prunes did better than dried apples here, researchers would have seen great performance from apple juice, apple cider vinegar, and apple polyphenols. So when comparing dried fruit, prunes are better than apples, but if you want overall bone health, other apple products can do wonders, so do include them in your diet. Apple polyphenols are also effective at stimulating aquaporins, the pores found in cell membranes that regulate water and fat content inside your cells. Aquaporins become less numerous and active with age, resulting in dry skin and weight gain, and apple polyphenols both stimulate that process and revive aquaporins.

The amazing benefits of prunes on bones are enhanced even further when they are eaten with fructooligosaccharides, also known as oligofructans or oligofructose. These are sugars found in bananas, agave, chicory, and onions. Fructooligosaccharides (FOS) can be used as a sweetener. They stimulate the growth of beneficial bacteria in the gut, producing increased well-being, health, and protection against infectious diseases. Healthy gut bacteria also contribute to a positive mental outlook, decreased depression, and less fatigue. When FOS and prunes are taken together, the result is one of the most powerful bone builders around! It is almost impossible to avoid some gastrointestinal discomfort in the form of a very bloated, painful stomach when fructooligosaccharides are taken in concentrated powder or liquid form, so it is much better to eat them as bananas or chicory coffee, a beverage that also contains melanoidins, yet another amazingly effective compound.

✳ Bone Health Spotlight: Onions

Onions contain polyphenols and fructooligosaccharides and are a rich source of sulfur—all necessary for bone health. Onions are good for the heart and the brain, they make bruises vanish if they're applied directly to them, and in the right preparation they get rid of wrinkles and stiff joints and even regrow hair. These humble little bulbs also regrow bone, making you look as great as you did when you were young! You can eat onions fresh, or you can take onion powder daily to build bone. Onion powder is remarkably effective at stimulating osteoblast activity even when estrogen is low, which occurs after menopause, and even when bone is exposed to cigarette smoke.

Finally, onions, particularly red onions, are also a very good source of quercetin, which prevents the formation of pyrimidine dimers after sun exposure and prevents metastatic cancer.

✳ Bone Health Spotlight: Quercetin

Quercetin binds to estrogen receptors and prevents bone break-down, particularly after menopause. Osteoclasts are bone cells that break down bone as it is needed to release calcium. Osteoclasts are normally balanced by osteoblasts, which build new bone. After menopause, osteoclasts are very active, but the osteoblasts decline in number, and the ones that remain become progressively less and less active. The result is thin, brittle bone very prone to fracturing. This deterioration happens very rapidly after menopause. As you saw at the beginning of this chapter, in five years or so following menopause a woman can lose up to 20 percent of her bone mass. The following contain quercetin:

onions, particularly red onions

onion powder (without salt)

black tea

apples, apple juice, and apple cider vinegar

red wine

berries such as blueberries and strawberries

cocoa powder and high cocoa chocolate

chili peppers

capers

❋ Bone Health Spotlight: Kudzu

Kudzu possesses potent estrogenic activity. It compares impressively with the female sex hormone estradiol, exhibiting 80 to 90 percent of this estrogen's activity while being cancer protective. Kudzu enhances breast and uterus growth. Breasts, the vagina, and the uterus atrophy after menopause, as do skin, muscle, hair, and bone. Kudzu is remarkably effective at preventing and reversing these aging effects of low hormone levels. Kudzu, together with *Pueraria mirifica*, a closely related herb, contains puerarin. This compound is responsible for kudzu's estrogenic activity. Research shows that puerarin has astonishing effects on osteoblasts, increasing and maturing their cell numbers and in this way promoting new bone growth. And while kudzu has powerful beneficial estrogenic activity, it also protects against estrogen-sensitive cancers. It can also help with endometriosis, a condition linked to errant estrogenic activity.

Kudzu is a good source of genistein and daidzein, two plant hormones with estrogenic activity that are also found in soy.

Genistein and daidzein have powerful bone-building effects. Kudzu is a great alternative to soy for people who avoid soy products. Soy builds bone, makes your skin young, and grows hair due to its genistein and daidzein content, and kudzu achieves all this, too.

Is Sugar Bad for Bones?

Some sugars, depending on various factors, can be either bad or good for bone health. Let's tackle the sour news first, since the prevalence of a high-sugar, or high-sucrose, diet is such a pressing concern in America. *Sucrose* is the correct term for what we know as sugar. Sucrose is a disaccharide, which means that each molecule of sucrose is made up of two sugars, glucose and fructose (they are monosaccharides). Sucrose's color doesn't change its chemical composition, so it can be white, brown, or the colors of muscovado and molasses sugar. Refined sugar, specifically, causes skin and bones to age alarmingly fast and sugar substitutes like aspartame stimulate neurons, frequently overstimulating and killing them. One of the reasons sugar leads to bone thinning is that it doesn't contain minerals. Minerals have an alkalizing effect on the blood, whereas protein and sugar make the blood acidic. In order to make the blood neutral, rather than acidic, something alkaline is needed. Minerals are alkaline, the major one of these being calcium. If there is no calcium in the foods you eat, for example when you eat a sugary cake, your bones are broken down to release calcium, which then neutralizes the acidity. Magnesium is also a very important alkalizing mineral, which is one of the reasons it protects you against bone loss. Boron, which is found only in trace amounts in the body, can reverse bone loss and form new bone. What's more, the bone cells responsible for new bone formation, called osteoblasts, possess insulin receptors, and glucose actually stimulates osteoblasts to form new bone—but only if the glucose levels do not rise too high. High blood sugar levels, as in diabetes or a high dietary intake of sugar, can actually lead to bone breakdown. Cinnamon, fenugreek, and oats are all very effective at keeping blood sugar levels within safe limits.

Surprisingly, not all sugar is harmful to bones. Glucosamine sulfate, a supplement that can help repair damaged cartilage in knee joints, is synthesized in the body from glucose, the amino acid glutamine, and sulfur. Hyaluronic acid is one of the most important glucosaminoglycans, compounds that contain glucose. As we saw earlier in this book, hyaluronic acid is a highly effective hydrating molecule. Trehalose is another sugar that has been found to have extraordinary health benefits, including bone building. Trehalose is found in mushrooms and honey. Both of these foods firm and tone the complexion. Molasses is a mineral-rich sweetener that benefits bone health. Both honey and molasses possess estrogenic activity and contain minerals, including boron, and a range of B vitamins, all of which possess hormonal activity and facilitate the growth of new bone.

Exercise and Face Tapping

Exercise plays a huge part in building fresh bone. Inactivity leads to loss of bone mass, and this process is shockingly rapid. Astronauts have measurable bone loss after a few weeks in space. The pull of gravity on your bones is essential exercise, and the resultant stress on bones keeps them strong. When this stress is absent, bones become thinner very quickly. Walking, running, and weight training all stress and strengthen the bones in your body. They will help your facial bones to a certain extent, but to rebuild your cheekbones and jawbones, you might like to add gentle knuckle tapping every day. The process only takes a few minutes, but it will go a long way toward keeping your face looking young. Simply make loose fists with your hands and gently tap along your cheekbones and jaw and over your forehead with the knuckles of your folded fingers. Gentle, repetitive tapping is all that is needed. You can also gently tap along your upper brow bone and the fleshy area of your cheeks.

BIO-YOUNG TREATMENTS

Please choose preparations based on ease of availability, cost, and personal preference. One is sufficient for treating this anti-aging mechanism, but two or more can speed improvements or improve a particularly neglected situation. Each one uses an ingredient discussed in this chapter. Enjoy!

Fenugreek and fennel: Take four teaspoons each of fenugreek and fennel powder per day. Divide this into two or three doses, if you wish. Stir the powder into apple juice or water and drink.

Boron: Take 3–9 mg of boron per day. Solgar makes a useful boron supplement.

Maca: Take four teaspoons of powdered maca a day. You don't need to use the gelatinized version. You can add yogurt or juice to the powder, stir well, and drink or eat immediately before it thickens.

Prunes, bananas, and onions: Ten prunes a day, one banana, and an onion will build great bones for you. The onion can be fried in olive or safflower oil. You can also use pure onion powder, stirred into water. You may want to have a little yogurt after, in case the onion gives you indigestion. Onion powder gently fried in olive oil makes an excellent base for chilis, curries, and tomato-based sauces.

Kudzu and Clearspring-brand kudzu starch: Add two teaspoons of the powder to a mug with apple juice, stir well, and drink before it thickens. You can cook with kudzu, too, if you'd like. Tempura batter is traditionally made with kudzu, but make sure you consume the equivalent of two teaspoons of kudzu, which can be a bit tricky if you don't know how much is in the batter.

Apple juice: Get your dose of phloridzin from eight ounces of apple juice a day.

Beer: I am not advocating irresponsible drinking, but one bottle of good beer a day can produce stronger bones. The darker beers tend to have more silica, barley, and malt, so you'll be getting melanoidins in addition to the estrogenic properties of barley and hops.

Vitamin D, calcium, and magnesium: Take 400–1,000 IU of vitamin D3 a day. Plain goat's milk or low-fat or whole-milk yogurt is a great source of calcium. Magnesium supplements should be in the range of 200–400 mg of elemental magnesium, whether citrate, chelated, or another form.

Face tapping: Tap gently along the bones of your face once a day.

Elemi: Add thirty drops of this essential oil or the oil of your choice to an oil base. If you can't find this amazing but rare essential oil, you can substitute myrrh or frankincense essential oils for a comparable result.

CHAPTER 7

Turn Fat to Muscle

ANTI-AGING MECHANISM: Switching back to a youthful
fat-to-muscle ratio

USE: Reducing and eliminating fat and cellulite

STARRING: Ginkgo, apple cider vinegar, whey protein,
rosemary, blueberries, coffee, dill essential oil

Aging visibly increases the proportion of fat to muscle in our bodies. Many people complain about gaining weight as they get older, even though they aren't eating more than they did when they were younger. But the proportion of fat to muscle changes dramatically as we get older, resulting both in general weight gain and in a flabbier silhouette even if weight remains the same. The amount of muscle you have shrinks and your fat cells expand. While fat provides a reservoir of energy and essential padding and protection, for example, protecting vital organs in the abdominal cavity, too much fat is both unsightly and detrimental to good health. The fat-to-muscle ratio as we age negatively affects not only the way we look, but our strength, and even our susceptibility to heart disease and diabetes. Amazingly, natural foods, herbs, and supplements have been shown to be extraordinarily successful at correcting these negative changes. They will help you achieve what has always seemed impossible before: eating whatever (healthy) foods you want and not gaining weight. If you have never been that person, the natural substances in this chapter can help you get there now, no matter what age you are!

Both fat and muscle are necessary for health and an attractive appearance—the fat layer gives a woman her curves and shapes her face with a lovely femininity. But too much fat, and all that beauty vanishes. A five-pound lump of fat is much bigger than a five-pound piece of muscle. Muscle, of course, gives the body firmness, strength, and the kind of definition that was once thought only to be had in youth. Fortunately this is not the case. You do not have to lose your youthful curves, or muscle definition, at any age.

Do You Have Sarcopenia?

Recently, I was walking behind two women. Even from behind I could tell they were pretty and that they were mother and daughter. There was a great physical resemblance in their hair and body type, and in the way they moved. But it was easy to see that the woman on the left was much older than the teenager on the right. They were both slender, athletic, and dressed in a youthful, casual way. The older woman was thin with an unmistakable lack of tone in her limbs, which had nothing to do with whether or not she exercised. She clearly did exercise. But her body composition had altered. The teenager was slender and softer, while the older woman was more angular and thin.

This is sarcopenia in action, an age-related condition where you lose skeletal muscle mass and gain an altered fat-to-muscle ratio. Muscle fibers are lost and fat begins to predominate, where there once was natural muscle. This leads to a gradual loss of movement and strength and an increased risk of fall-related injury. Sarcopenia was once thought to be an inevitable aging consequence, but using the right natural substances can most certainly return your muscle-to-fat ratio to a youthful place.

The term *sarcopenia* was coined by I. H. Rosenberg in 1988. It originates from the Greek words *sarx,* meaning "flesh," and *penia,* meaning "loss." This adequately describes the loss of muscle quantity and quality. Fortunately, the loss of muscle fiber numbers and their size can be reversed, producing youthful muscle tone and the body composition of a thirty-year-old. You can restore energy and balance, vigor, and endurance through safe, natural means. Since achieving these goals means reversing the decline of cellular and hormonal mechanisms, the result is true anti-aging!

Sarcopenia is the result of cellular and hormonal decline. As mitochondria, the energy factories in your cells, slow down and new muscle cells are not made as efficiently, muscle fibers are lost and their numbers fall significantly. The muscle fibers' size decreases and their composition changes, too. At the same time, fat mass increases. All these factors lead to losing strength and balance and increased fatigue. Alarmingly, in the elderly this age-related reduced muscle mass is associated with decreased survival following illness.

Sarcopenia begins after age thirty and accelerates rapidly. In the decade between thirty and forty, we lose at least 5 percent of our total muscle mass to this wasting process. Once we hit forty, muscle loss accelerates until we have lost our strength, balance, and much of our muscle mass by the time we reach seventy years old. Lean muscle mass constitutes 50 percent of total body weight in young adults. This falls to just 25 percent in the 75–80 age group, but the deterioration, as we have just seen, begins long before. This muscle loss occurs in sedentary as well as in active seniors. In contrast, no muscle loss of this type (involving lost muscle fibers and muscle size) occurs in healthy young adults. Up to 65 percent of older men and women say they can't lift ten pounds using their arms.

Muscle loss is an important health concern, because having

muscle isn't just about looking sleek, fit, strong, and attractive. While the altered fat-to-muscle ratio and the loss and atrophy of muscle fibers give older people a withered look, a lack of muscle also doesn't move your body as effectively. This dramatically reduces quality of life for many elderly people. Muscle loss is also associated with kidney disease, heart disease, vascular disease, blindness, and liver disease. Muscle is an important metabolic organ, vital for proper blood glucose control. Muscle loss means a higher likelihood of type 2 diabetes. It is also associated with increased mortality and an increased incidence of lung cancer. Cyclic AMP (cAMP), an energy molecule, plays a vital role in preserving muscle mass, but its levels decline with age. One of your goals here will be to significantly increase cAMP activity in your cells.

Should you ever give advice to a senior in the grips of sarcopenia, please don't tell him or her to get active, run, or lift weights. An elderly person with sarcopenia is physiologically unable to get active. Their muscles have atrophied, and they feel and are weak. Instead, hand them a copy of this book, and after they've used the treatments at the end of the chapter, then you can ask them to meet you on the tennis court. Just look out—they might even beat you! I have seen elderly men respond within days when placed on a program using the natural substances recommended here.

The Role of Growth Hormone

Growth hormone plays a part in sarcopenia, but synthetic growth hormone produces severe side effects. Naturally stimulating this hormone is highly beneficial and effectively reverses age-related muscle loss. This is what makes you grow in height during childhood and adolescence, and is often supplemented when growth is severely slow during these times. Once we have stopped growing, it is still essential. Instead of powering a growth spurt, and adding seven inches to a teen almost overnight, growth hormone maintains muscle mass, bone mass, and skin thickness as we get older.

Growth hormone, known as somatotropin or somatropin, stimulates cell regeneration. This hormone has a wide range of benefits in anti-aging, including, as we just saw, increased bone mass and firmer skin. Its effects on muscle growth occur because growth hormone stimulates sarcomere hypertrophy. Sarcomeres are the basic units of muscle, and hypertrophy is growth. So an increase in sarcomeres means more numerous, and bigger, muscle fibers, obviously a good thing for looking good and feeling strong as we get older. This is anti-aging at the cellular level producing some highly attractive results!

Growth hormone also stimulates lipolysis, cutting excess fat and so reestablishing that youthful fat-to-muscle ratio, which is so visible when it is disturbed. Growth hormone plays a role in many vital bodily functions, including the prevention of low blood sugar, which can be a problem under certain conditions. Many athletes use growth hormone off-label to improve their performance.

Growth hormone is licensed for use as a drug, but this is associated with many side effects, including carpal tunnel syndrome, the formation of dangerous blood clots, and Hodgkin's lymphoma. The risks associated with pharmaceutical forms of growth hormone have led to a search for safer ways to obtain the benefits of increased levels. It is therefore very fortunate that natural substances are highly effective at increasing growth hormone levels even in old age, offering great anti-aging benefits that include improved muscle fullness, decreased fat, and firmer skin, but without the threat of side effects.

Certain amino acids increase growth hormone levels when taken as supplements, producing the effects we normally associate with vibrant youth and reversing a whole range of factors associated with aging, back to the peak function of a thirty-year-old. Glutamine, for example, has been intensively studied and found to be very effective at raising growth hormone levels in human subjects. However, glutamine is also an ideal fuel for cancer cells, which makes its use controversial. There are also some problems with arginine, which significantly raises growth hormone levels and even helps prevent heart disease by increasing the levels of nitric oxide and dilating blood vessels, because arginine feeds the herpes virus, which can be problematic for many people.

Fortunately, there are other safe, highly effective ways of releasing growth hormone without side effects. For instance, ginkgo and whey protein very effectively raise growth hormone levels in the body. Externally, wild yam and apple polyphenols (which can be used both internally and externally, in the form of apple cider vinegar) stimulate a recently discovered, hugely exciting mechanism that drains fat from your cells. Hydroxycitric acid, extracted from tamarind, and tamarind itself stop your body from making fat and protect you from diabetes. Horse chestnut breaks down the fat that forms the unsightly condition known as cellulite.

✳ Fat-to-Muscle Spotlight: Ginkgo

Ginkgo biloba, or maidenhair tree, is a living fossil. The ginkgo trees we see in Japanese gardens today are botanically almost identical to specimens from a hundred million years ago. There are trees growing today in China that are more than three thousand years old! It seems a bit of a stretch to assume that such longevity could be transferred from the plant to a human being, yet ginkgo does possess impressive properties that restore youth, extend lifespan, and greatly improve quality of life.

Components found in ginkgo have an impressive ability to inhibit cAMP-phosphodiesterase. Why should that have you jumping up and down for joy? The formation of cAMP (cyclic adenosine monophosphate) releases energy in your cells. This process breaks down fat and shrinks fat cells. But cAMP-phosphodiesterase, an enzyme, lowers the levels of cAMP available in your cells for this energy and fat breakdown. Because ginkgo stops cAMP-phosphodiesterase, decreasing your cAMP levels, it produces optimal levels of this amazing energy-producing, anti-aging molecule in your cells. This does not contradict the principles of chapter 4, because the goal in both cases is healthy, firm, youthful support.

This idea, that healthy fat and healthy muscle are both needed for anti-aging and looking good, is supported by further studies, which show that ginkgo makes your fat cells, or adipocytes, healthy, not shriveled up, and not enlarged. Shriveled fat cells lead to the loss of fullness in cheeks and limbs. Enlarged fat cells occur in the overweight and aged, and they lead to health problems, plus lost firmness. What we are aiming for is a healthy relationship between the fat and muscle cells of your body—you know, the kind of relationship enjoyed by healthy young people. Ginkgo can play a pivotal part in getting you there.

Ginkgo seems to exert a positive effect on every mechanism studied. It helps in asthma and controls histamine release by an overactive immune system and prevents allergies. It alleviates ear-related conditions like Ménière's disease and tinnitus, and improves memory and cognition.

Ginkgo keeps body composition healthy and attractive, limits fat to a healthy, youthful range, and supports the growth of muscle mass in various ways. Ginkgo stimulates the release of growth hormone and raises sensitivity to gonadotropin. Since growth hormone is key to all kinds of repair and growth mechanisms, the results of its decline are immediately apparent when you meet an older person and see their lack of muscle tone. Flat, atrophied muscles in the limbs, coupled with a paunch, are the visible results of this decline. Without adequate levels of growth hormone (as well as other hormones, including testosterone), it is impossible to maintain muscle mass in old age, despite a good diet and exercise program. In a study that examined ginkgo's effects on muscle composition and the activity of genes involved in muscle synthesis, ginkgo remarkably reversed the decline in elderly muscles, bringing them back to youthful levels. Ginkgo produced impressive muscle gains in atrophied muscles and stimulated lethargic metabolism into producing more muscle, restoring the kind of activity that occurs in youth.

✳ Fat-to-Muscle Spotlight: Whey Protein

Taken as a supplement, whey increases muscle volume in young people and can enhance muscle growth even in the elderly. Whey is a very effective stimulator of growth hormone release, raising those all-important levels even in old age, when levels have declined precipitously. You may remember that whey also elongates telomeres, thereby protecting DNA.

✳ Fat-to-Muscle Spotlight: Ursolic Acid

Ursolic acid is found in apple peels, bilberries, prunes, lavender, oregano, sage, thyme, and rosemary. When scientists examined which genes were switched on or off in sarcopenia, they found that ursolic acid from apple peels produced a pattern that was the opposite of the pattern associated with muscle atrophy. Out of more than 1,300 compounds studied, ursolic acid was found to be the most effective muscle atrophy inhibitor. Not only does ursolic acid prevent muscle wasting, or sarcopenia, but it also enhances muscle growth when it is added to the diet. Ursolic acid accomplishes these astounding results even when a high-fat diet is deliberately given in order to increase weight.

The high ursolic acid content in rosemary, blueberries, and bilberries is responsible for much of the substance's anti-aging dynamics. There are numerous active plant compounds that affect multiple biochemical anti-aging mechanisms. Other compounds such as chlorogenic acid, found in green coffee beans, prunes, and raspberry ketones, are very effective at cutting body fat. Isolated chlorogenic acid appears to raise homocysteine levels, an effect that does not occur with prunes. Generally speaking, fruits are very effective at helping you turn fat to muscle by cutting fat and promoting muscle synthesis. Tamarind (*Garcinia cambogia*), a common ingredient in Indian cooking that is available as a paste or in dried form, contains hydroxycitric acid, or HCA, a compound that turns on fat-burning mechanisms in your body and disperses fat globules. Hydroxycitric acid stops the formation of fat, even when foods that would normally lead to fat formation in the body are eaten.

✳ Fat-to-Muscle Spotlight: DMAE and ALCAR

I first began researching the effects of DMAE (dimethylaminoethanol) in 1982, and ALCAR (acetyl-L-carnitine) about a decade later, but these two supernutrients go together very well. You can take them as supplements. Both DMAE and ALCAR increase cholinergic activity—the activity of the neurotransmitter acetylcholine—and they do this both in the brain and in the body. ALCAR improves cognitive function and hippocampal activity in Alzheimer's disease and in aging. The hippocampus is the area of the brain most involved with memory, and it is severely damaged in Alzheimer's disease. Acetylcholine is the major neurotransmitter in the hippocampus. This neurotransmitter is vital for cognition. It is also essential in muscle function. The link between brain decline and muscle weakness, as well as pain, is obvious in senility. DMAE and ALCAR are impressively effective in chronic fatigue syndrome, declining mental function, and muscle atrophy. Taking these two nutrients together is like an internal workout. Muscle becomes taut and lean, strength improves dramatically, pain vanishes, and bone-crushing fatigue disappears.

Zap Your Cellulite

Cellulite is the result of enlarged fat cells caused by overfull fat globules that pull on the surrounding tissue and form dimples. There is also a loss of collagen, the formation of tough, fibrous tissue, and localized fluid leakage. Anything that shrinks fat cells will restore firmness to the affected areas.

Cellulite can strike any woman after the age of sixteen years. Even thin women can have the dimpled "orange peel" tissue that characterizes this condition. It also gets worse with age, and the same approaches that tone up muscle and make the fat layer healthy so that it provides cushioning and not flab will also eliminate cellulite. In addition, there are certain techniques and topical treatments that you can use to speed up the process and improve any troublesome spots. Estrogen is seen as the primary culprit in cellulite because most of the people who have this are women, and so estrogenic herbs such as fenugreek, fennel, dill, and licorice can be very effective at treating this condition.

The simplest thing you can do to eliminate cellulite is to use an exfoliating massage glove before every bath or shower. What you're looking for here is a glove with scratchy bits—this will stimulate your cellulite in a beneficial way. Use this glove, dry, over your whole body and concentrate on your thighs, hips, buttocks, stomach, breasts, and arms. You can even gently use this glove on your face to help firm it up. The idea is to stimulate but not actually hurt your skin. You should see fresh, glowing skin and firmer flesh. The idea is to stimulate collagen synthesis in the skin and make scars and wrinkles disappear. You can enhance the effects of this with a preparation from the end of the chapter. You can also apply an oil to your face and body before using the glove. If your aim is to reduce cellulite and fat deposits, coconut and dill oils are your best choice (combine, if you wish).

Years ago, I used to make an anti-cellulite lotion from a horse chestnut tincture mixed half-and-half with distilled witch hazel. It looked rather brown, but women loved it. I knew it was a great formula, but imagine my delight when I came across scientific evidence of the molecular mechanism involved in this herb's amazing anti-cellulite activity! This exciting evidence shows that horse chestnut significantly reduces fat accumulation. Horse chestnut also strengthens cell walls, including those in the capillaries and larger blood vessels, to effectively stop fluid leakage. It increases collagen formation and raises the levels of elastin and hyaluronic acid necessary to restore suppleness and elasticity to the tough, fibrous tissue that gives rise to stubborn cellulite. The topical application of horse chestnut lotions or creams directly to an affected area will shrink and tighten the skin. You should notice a visible change within days of the treatment, and combining several treatments brings faster results. Additional massage will further help to break down tough, fibrous tissue. I also like juniper, caffeine, apple cider vinegar, dill, and gotu kola in cellulite remedies.

※ Cellulite-Busting Spotlight: Juniper and Seaweed

Juniper essential oil is wonderful for stubborn fat deposits and for cellulite. Combine it with dill, or use it on its own, mixed with coconut oil. It drains excess water from tissues and firms the stomach and thighs very effectively, and surprisingly fast. As for seaweed, it can be used topically to break down fat deposits. A seaweed body lotion made from bladder wrack, wakame, arame, or Irish moss is a very effective addition to the fat-to-muscle program.

✳ Cellulite-Busting Spotlight: Caffeine

You can apply cooled instant coffee directly to any area you wish to firm up and slim down. Caffeine works by stimulating cAMP (cyclic adenosine monophosphate), also known as a second messenger. The cAMP enhances the release of growth hormone in the body. Epinephrine (adrenaline) cannot function without cAMP. Caffeine's effects are catabolic. This means that caffeine breaks down fat. But because of its beneficial effects on growth hormone release, caffeine does not break down muscle, but stimulates its growth. Essentially, by stimulating cAMP, caffeine increases cellular energy.

Caffeine belongs to a family of compounds called the methyl xanthines, all of which possess these cAMP stimulating properties. Methyl xanthines are also found in green and black tea (the methyl xanthine contained in tea is called theophylline) and in cocoa (this contains theobromine). You can use any of these externally, but green tea is probably the easiest, as it doesn't leave a stain. If you choose coffee, be aware that it is very potent. Take 150 mg of magnesium citrate daily if you are consuming coffee on a regular basis. Caffeine can disrupt heart rhythms and magnesium offsets this problem. One well-known problem with caffeine is that it can lead to insomnia. If you find that you can't sleep after coffee, switch to green tea. Green tea is very effective at improving muscle synthesis and cutting the fat in your body and it also contains theanine in addition to theophylline (theophylline is similar to caffeine in its activity). Theanine is a nonnutritional amino acid that inhibits the negative effects of caffeine and theophylline, which makes green tea an excellent choice for anyone wishing to cut fat from their body but not lose sleep in the process. Using coffee externally, by the way, does not produce any unpleasant sleep or heart disturbances.

✳ Cellulite-Busting Spotlight: Dill Seed Essential Oil and Gotu Kola

Dill seed essential oil and gotu kola herb are two of my favorite go-to remedies for cellulite. In spite of the fact that estrogen is often blamed for causing cellulite, dill seed, which possesses estrogenic activity, is highly effective against this condition. A daily massage with dill seed essential oil, diluted in a coconut oil base, will help to lead to toned and youthful limbs, a smaller waist, and an athletic firmness in your body. Dill is a very potent activator of elastin production, which means it will help make varicose veins shrink and diminish under-eye bags, too. Elastin enables the fat cells affected by cellulite to regain their firmness. As a result, you should lose all of those unwanted fatty deposits. Gotu kola, also known as *Centella asiatica* or *Hydrocotyle asiatica*, stimulates SIRT1, increases type 1 collagen synthesis, protects the skin from sun damage, and speeds up wound healing. Type 1 collagen is the type of collagen that decreases markedly during aging. You have already seen that madecassoside, a compound isolated from gotu kola, possesses the extraordinary property of stopping the formation of progerin, the mutant protein responsible for aging. Gotu kola is also extremely effective against cellulite, draining excess water and shrinking fat cells. Since cellulite is a condition that involves the dysfunction of several systems, connective tissue abnormalities, blood vessel constriction, and the distending of fat cells, an agent capable of normalizing all of these parameters is exactly what you need. Applied topically, or taken internally as a supplement, this wonderful herb reverses every aspect of cellulite.

Amazing Aquaporins

The 2003 Nobel Prize for Chemistry was awarded to Peter Agre for the discovery of aquaporins, protein molecules that serve as pores or channels in cellular membranes. As so often happens in science, the discovery was an accident. At first, aquaporins were thought to only be involved with the regulation of intracellular (inside the cell) water, but now a family of aquaporins involved in removing excess fat from cells has been discovered, too. We now know that aquaporins are channels in the membranes of your cells that control cellular water *and* lipids (fat). They become far less active with age. Aquaporins 1, 2, 4, 5, and 8 are concerned with water transport, whereas aquaporins 3, 7, and 9, also termed aquaglyceroporins, or aquaporin adipose, also regulate the levels of fatty acids inside fat cells. Your cells, in fact, have "taps" (aquaporins) to let out water and fat, which is stored in the tissues as fat droplets. Stimulating aquaporin adipose pores causes fatty acids to leave fat cells. This is great news for those of us who wish to get rid of cellulite and stubborn fat deposits! According to the most recent research, aquaporins also transport urea and glycerol, a property that affects both dry skin and the growth of unwanted hair, as you will see later in this book.

The medical importance of aquaporins extends well beyond the shrinking of fat cells stretched by excess fat. Activating these pores has tremendous clinical potential in the treatment of fluid retention/hydration and, because the brain contains aquaporins, too, aquaporin activators could be lifesaving in cases of brain edema.

Aquaglyceroporins, or aquaporin adipose (AQPap), have been shown to be underactive in insulin sensitivity (type 2 diabetes) and in obesity. Both of these conditions are very closely associated with aging as well as unhealthy lifestyles, so agents capable of influencing them are extremely important for looking young and being healthy.

Wild yam and apple cider vinegar are great examples of aquaporin stimulators that open the tap on your fat cells and drain all the excess fat out, leaving a smooth, firm, and youthful body behind. Wild yam was one of the first modulators of aquaporins discovered. Apple polyphenols have also been shown to activate aquaporins involved with fat reduction and hydrated skin. Fat depositing goes haywire as we age, leading to a paunch, soft triceps, a sagging jawline, love handles, under-eye bags—stop me anytime. Less efficient aquaporins, particularly aquaglyceroporins that allow both water and fat to exit the cell, are very much involved. Apple polyphenols are supremely effective at activating aquaglyceroporins. Apple cider vinegar has a very long history as a folk remedy that leads to fat loss, and new data back that up. Recent research shows that apple polyphenols prevent the weight gain that would normally occur as the result of a sugar-rich diet.

Apple polyphenols are astonishingly effective at shrinking fat cells and increasing muscle synthesis. They're extremely effective at cutting fat, enhancing muscle tone and muscle growth, and increasing strength. The easiest way to make sure you obtain plenty of apple polyphenols is to add apple cider vinegar to your daily regime. Joan Crawford apparently kept her weight down by drinking a glass of apple cider vinegar before meals. Apple cider vinegar is superb at reducing fat and cellulite, both internally and when applied topically. You can leave the apple cider vinegar on your skin without rinsing it, but dilute it before you use it on your face and be careful around the eyes because it can be irritating. The result is soft, smooth, supple, unlined, and beautifully hydrated skin.

"Sculpt" Your Body With Natural Treatments

It has been said that when you're over a certain age, you have to "choose between your face and your behind." In other words, you either get to build a plump, pretty, youthful face and a behind that is similarly plump, or you can work on having a slender body but suffer a sunken, old-looking face. This is not true. You can have both! It is possible to reduce fat deposits and enhance fat store *exactly where you wish to do so* by using the principles given in this chapter. Eating a diet rich in beneficial fats like olive oil and avocados, and using the herbs you'll read about in chapter 9, will help restore an atrophied fat layer and give your tissues that youthful bounce. Olive oil contains hydroxytyrosol, which revs up the mitochondria in your fat cells, making them far more active and energetic, ensuring that calories are utilized rather than stored. You can also apply sarsaparilla oil to your cheeks and breasts to help enhance beneficial fat formation in these places. Taking apple polyphenols, in the form of apple cider vinegar, as described in this chapter, and massaging areas that need to be firmed up with a lotion or a cream containing one or more of the herbs described in the cellulite section, should keep fat deposits within a healthy, gorgeous, youthful range.

BIO-YOUNG TREATMENTS

Please choose preparations based on ease of availability, cost, and personal preference. One is sufficient for treating this anti-aging mechanism, but two or more can speed improvements or improve a particularly neglected situation. Each one uses an ingredient discussed in this chapter. Enjoy!

Ginkgo: Choose from a tincture, capsules, or powder. Take two teaspoons of the tincture three times a day, or six capsules twice a day. If you have a powder, then one teaspoon a day would be sufficient to produce the fat-cutting, muscle-enhancing effects of this amazing herb.

Whey: Purchase a good-quality pure whey protein powder and take according to instructions.

Apple polyphenols: It's possible to buy apple polyphenol supplements, but apple cider vinegar is very effective, is much cheaper, and contains a whole range of beneficial compounds including ursolic acid. Simply take two teaspoons of apple cider vinegar, diluted in water, two or three times a day. The ideal time would be just before a meal, or with the meal, but anytime is fine.

Ursolic acid: Use apple cider vinegar or apple juice. Both of these are good sources of ursolic acid. Take two teaspoons of the vinegar with meals. It should prevent your blood sugar levels from rising after the meal, which protects you from diabetes and enhances loss of fat and muscle building. In addition, you can use apple cider vinegar topically in those hard-to-shift places such as thighs or stomach. Dilute the vinegar in water for both internal and external use. Prunes are another easy-to-find source of ursolic acid, and since they are very protective against cancer, and neuroprotective, too, they are worth adding to your daily diet, perhaps chopped up in your morning muesli or yogurt. Rosemary and rosemary essential oil are easy to incorporate into your daily routine as well.

DMAE and ALCAR: Buy these supernutrients separately, but you can take them together. The optimum daily dose of DMAE is 100–300 mg. The best daily dose of ALCAR is 500 mg.

Massage glove: An exfoliating glove is ideal, as you can gently massage your body and the glove's roughness yields additional stimulation that breaks down fat deposits and tones up your body.

Horse chestnut: Purchase a tincture online, then mix 50:50 with water, store, and use as needed on any cellulite area or on any area you wish to firm up.

Juniper: Use 30 drops of this essential oil to 100 ml of coconut oil base for fast results, helping to decrease fat deposits and cellulite on hips, thighs, and stomach.

Caffeine: Make a strong cup of instant coffee. Let it cool, and use daily as an anti-cellulite treatment. This same preparation can be used to regrow hair on your scalp. If you find the coffee lotion too staining, use it just before you shower or bathe. Or make a strong cup of green or black (not herb) tea and use it when cool as a highly slimming body lotion. You can increase the body-firming effects by drinking green tea, black tea, or coffee daily. Do not add sugar!

Wild yam: Purchase a wild yam tincture, then mix 50:50 with water, store, and use as needed. You can also mix this with the horse chestnut tincture in a base of apple cider vinegar, using equal proportions of the tinctures and vinegar.

Dill seed essential oil: Obtain a good-quality dill essential oil and add 30 drops to 100 ml of coconut oil. It will stir in better if you gently heat the coconut oil before adding the dill. Let it cool, store in a wide-mouthed container, and use at least once a day.

Seaweed lotion: Purchase the seaweed you wish to use online. Choose from bladder wrack, Irish moss, wakame, nori, or any other seaweed. Most seaweeds can be in powder form, or as dried pieces. Simmer one large cupful of seaweed in one liter of water or in one liter of apple cider vinegar for fifteen minutes, let it cool, strain, and bottle. You can add the whole preparation to your bathwater, or use it as a body lotion after your bath.

Gotu kola: Take four teaspoons of gotu kola tincture or gotu kola powder, or twenty gotu kola capsules per day. This is not a large dose if each of those capsules contains 500 mg of the herb, which is usually the case. You may take twenty capsules if each one contains 1 gram of the herb, too. It's a lot of capsules to swallow, and you may like to empty them into a cup, add water, and drink them. You can divide the large daily dose into three smaller daily doses if you wish. If you find the capsules difficult, then do search for the loose powder or the tincture. Also use gotu kola directly on any troublesome areas. Add 20 teaspoons of gotu kola powder to 500 ml of apple cider vinegar. Simmer the mixture for fifteen minutes, let it cool, and then strain, bottle, and label. Apply this externally, and leave to dry. This can be used on the face and neck, but dilute the lotion with water first and avoid the eye area.

CHAPTER 8

Hair to Remember

ANTI-AGING MECHANISM: Restoring youthful hair

USE: Reversing hair loss and thinning hair, encouraging faster hair growth, reversing gray hair

STARRING: Rosemary and eucalyptus globulus essential oils, lard, onion, calcium pantothenate

We all know men lose hair as they age, but it happens to women, too. Female hair loss has a different pattern, though, which thins all over the scalp and not just in certain areas that leave bald spots. Hair is at its best when you're under thirty years old, though many women notice a decline in their twenties. If this is you, you know the signs—a wider parting, thinner ponytail, hair that won't grow past your shoulders. Like men, some women experience small patchy spots. Women also lose hair color, which happens because of a decreasing number of hair melanocytes, the cells responsible for hair color.

Hair follicles slow down, and shut down, because of declining cellular and hormonal function. But you can revive the cells and the hormonal functioning by using the right natural substances. Fortunately, it's possible to regrow your hair and revitalize its natural color. Reviving the melanocytes in your scalp can even reverse gray hair! In this chapter, we'll explore ways to make your hair grow faster, improve its condition, and regain its natural color, body, and beauty.

What Makes Your Hair Thin and Fall Out?

Hormonal and cellular decline produce distressing scalp hair thinning, loss, and unwanted hair growth. Thankfully, there are many natural cellular and hormonal stimulators that can reverse hair loss on the scalp and stop the growth of unwanted hair.

Declining estrogen in aging women is a huge factor in hair loss and thinning. As estrogen levels fall, the male hormone dihydrotestosterone (DHT), the same hormone that plays havoc with men's hairlines, becomes dominant, and this results in female hair loss and unwanted hair growth on the face and body. Even worse, just as in men, DHT levels rise with age in women, and hair follicles become more sensitive to DHT effects. Scalp hair follicles shrivel and become inactive. The hair follicles in facial and body skin respond to this extra DHT by growing coarser, thicker hair. Fortunately, the same strategies that rebalance estrogen in a woman's body and regrow hair on her scalp stop the growth of unwanted hair on her face and body.

However, any substance that stimulates hair follicles on the scalp may do the same on your face, too. This is a great example of the difference between restoring cellular versus hormonal function. Cellular stimulation will stimulate hair follicles all over the body. Hormonal balancing, with an emphasis on estrogenic increase in women, will produce the correct effects, depending on the area being treated. This means that a purely cellular stimulator, such as caffeine (or coffee), can increase the growth of hair on the scalp but also on the chin if it is applied to the chin. But fennel, or aniseed, or any other estrogenically active oil or herb can stimulate scalp hair follicles, yet might decrease the growth of unwanted facial hair in women.

There is more! A recently discovered mechanism further explains why unwanted hair growth in women, hair loss, and dry skin increase with age. This mechanism involves aquaporins, which, you may remember from chapter 7, are pores found in the cellular membrane. These pores regulate water and fat transport. Their numbers and efficiency decline as you age, which causes dry skin and weight gain. These pores, as we now know, also control the movement of urea and glycerol, and as they become less efficient with age and their numbers decline, urea and glycerol concentrations decrease in the skin. This makes the skin very dry and prone to wrinkling. It also feeds the growth of unwanted facial hair, because both glycerol and urea are involved in controlling hair bulb metabolism. This means you can use glycerin and urea creams to eliminate unwanted hair growth on your body (urea is also a great moisturizer). Both glycerin and urea, by the way, have been used as hair-growth stimulators on the scalp, which demonstrates that this effect is due to a normalizing of the deranged cellular metabolism that occurs with aging. In this way, urea and glycerin act via cellular function, not by producing a hormonal effect, Always test a small amount of any cream on your skin before you use it on a larger area to make sure you are not sensitive to it.

Although caffeine (or coffee) mostly possesses unidirectional cell-stimulating activity, it does have some anti-DHT activity, too. In fact, it shot to mainstream fame as one of the first cellular stimulators known to regrow hair and decrease levels of DHT.

Caffeine increases cAMP levels, which is how it stimulates cellular metabolism. It is this increase in cellular energy that also counteracts, albeit weakly, the effect of DHT. Caffeine awakens dormant hair follicles on the scalp back to youthful vigor. In a study that investigated the effects of caffeine on hair follicles, testosterone was found to produce a very effective inhibition of hair growth easily antidoted by caffeine. Moreover, caffeine stimulated hair growth even in normal hair follicles that had not been suppressed by testosterone. Translated to the real world? Caffeine works whether you are twenty or seventy years old. If the culprit is DHT, then caffeine can remove the negative effect of this hormone. If you wish to stimulate hair growth and you are not suffering from DHT effects, caffeine can help you, too. To benefit, you must apply caffeine directly to your scalp (instant coffee is fine), leave it on for at least two minutes, then wash or rinse off. It may interact with hair dyes, so please test a strand of your hair to check for reactions before you use coffee as a hair treatment. I'm sorry to report that drinking coffee will not keep you from hair loss.

Essential Oils for Hair Growth

There are several essential oils that very effectively stimulate the growth of scalp hair. One of the best is ylang-ylang, which can also brighten your hair and was once the basis of Macassar oil, a remedy for baldness in Victorian England. Macassar oil used palm oil or coconut oil as a base, and little white doilies that became known as "antimacassar" were placed over the backs of armchairs to prevent the inevitable grease stain when a gentleman came calling. Lavender oil has long been used to stimulate hair growth and has been shown to be highly effective. Oils of thyme and cedarwood can be combined with lavender. Head massages manually stimulate your hair follicles, which can speed up the rate at which your hair grows with or without oils. Hair loss can be distressing, but there are things you can do to try and reverse it, and you can enjoy beautiful, shiny, bouncy hair at any age.

Rosemary and eucalyptus are impressively effective, individually or as a duo. If you apply rosemary essential oil to an area in which you'd like to see hair grow, you may see results in as little as three weeks. It's best to apply the oil every day for the first six months or so; after that, you can skip a day or two, but don't leave more than three days between treatments. For even better results, combine rosemary oil with eucalyptus oil. *Eucalyptus globulus* increases ceramides in your hair to boost moisture and shine (and in the skin, when applied topically). If you use eucalyptus oil daily on your scalp and down the length of your hair, over a period of three months it can transform your hair from lank and thin to bouncy and shiny. Both rosemary and eucalyptus essential oils also have a great effect on hair color, helping to brighten and revive color that has faded with the passing years. Apart from increasing shine-producing ceramides, eucalyptus stimulates human hair melanocytes, the cells responsible for producing hair pigment.

Rosemary may act via a novel hair-reviving mechanism. Recent research has shown that the stimulation of potassium channels in the hair follicles increases hair growth. Rosemary is a very effective calcium channel blocker. Calcium channels act in opposition to potassium channels, so when a substance inhibits calcium channels, potassium channels open. Using rosemary, eucalyptus, and lard, I've managed to grow my own hair well past my shoulders, and my color has returned to its youthful blond.

Foods and Supplements That Revive Hair

The internal and external use of onion, polyphenols, cysteine, vitamin E, and vitamin C, and the external use of lard, can bring back your youthful hair texture and also hair color. Of these, onions and polyphenols are particularly interesting. Onion and onion powder can stimulate hair follicles to regrow hair. This is a very rich source of sulfur, which is essential for the formation of keratin, the hair protein. Sulfur is a veritable box of magic tricks for the hair—it improves texture, shine, and bounce the very first time you use it, whether as a pure sulfur powder added to your shampoo and conditioner or as an onion preparation on your hair. This will help your hair become visibly stronger and more resilient. Quercetin, one of the compounds in onion, has been shown to have potent estrogenic activity, which explains the effect of onion on bones, skin, and hair. As for polyphenols, I turn again to apple cider vinegar. This is a great source of apple polyphenols, which are powerful stimulators of hair growth on the scalp. Using apple cider vinegar topically on your scalp will help strengthen and thicken your hair very fast.

Onions and apple cider vinegar also affect hair color. The quercetin in onions stimulates melanin production, which influences hair and skin color in the hair follicle itself. So rubbing onion juice or applying onion powder to your scalp helps reverse aging effects on your pigment-producing melanocytes and restores your natural hair color. The onion may also color your hair from inside out when you eat it, because it increases the production of melanin in the hair follicle "enormously," according to the scientists who measured it. Furthermore, onion can lighten hair (and skin) when it is applied as a topical treatment. And it does this because this pungent bulb contains a whole array of beneficial compounds, including sulfur, quercetin, vitamin C, potassium, and folic acid. Some people even report a return of their original hair color. As for apple cider vinegar, this lightens and brightens hair, whatever its color, but if your hair is dyed, do a strand test first.

Calcium pantothenate tablets do double duty, too. They help stimulate pigment production and growth rate, enhancing both natural color and hair growth rate. Adding this supplement to a bottle of your favorite shampoo can maximize its hair-beautifying potential. You should see the results after the first wash, and they get better with time. I use 10 x 500 mg of Lambert's calcium pantothenate tablets, added directly to 250 ml of shampoo. You can also dissolve them first in a half cup of water, then add them to your shampoo. Your hair should be brighter, softer, and truer to your original hair color when it dries.

Why Aging Changes Your Hair Color

Decreased tyrosinase activity causes your hair to lose its pigmentation. Tyrosinase is an enzyme involved in melanin synthesis. Melanin is responsible for every hair color—from blond, to red, to jet black. Different types of melanin are involved, which gives rise to a variety of hair hues, but melanin is an essential component of each. Melanin is also involved in skin color, and it's the increase in melanin production in your skin in response to sunlight, as a protective mechanism, that gives you a tan. Tyrosinase activity in the hair follicles decreases with age, and with it the pigmentation in our hair becomes less intense, until there is no pigment synthesized at all and your hair is white. Tyrosinase also decreases in the skin, which is why older skin can look rather pale.

Two types of melanin are produced in mammals: the black-to-brown eumelanins and the yellow-to-red pheomelanins. Your hair's natural color is caused by the complex interplay between eumelanin and pheomelanin, and it is this complexity that gives rise to the many wonderful hues of natural hair color around us. Blond hair is the result of very little of either pigment, but particularly eumelanin. Gray hair has very little melanin of any kind, and white hair has no melanin at all.

Quercetin and cysteine increase melanin in skin and hair, shifting the balance from eumelanin to pheomelanin. In this way, they lighten skin tone and hair color. Cysteine, or N-acetyl cysteine (NAC), is even more effective at lightening skin and hair when combined with vitamin C and vitamin E supplements. The mechanism occurs both when these compounds are ingested and when they are applied directly to the area you wish to treat. Excitingly, we now understand a major determining mechanism for this effect called glutathione, which also explains why naturally blond hair darkens with age. Glutathione is like natural hair bleach. High levels of glutathione actually raise the levels of pheomelanin in your hair follicles. A depletion of glutathione, exactly as would occur with aging, increases eumelanin, the pigment that produces darker hair.

Hormonal changes can also affect hair pigments. For instance, many women find that their skin and hair darken during and after pregnancy. The measures suggested in this section will reverse this darkening. Declining hormones during menopause lead to a decrease in melanin that can cause gray and then white hair; it also affects skin, and eyes begin to seem pale. Lips lose their mauve and pink undertones, irises lose their intense coloring, and the complexion looks flat and beige. A facial treatment featuring ginkgo, or ginkgo and hops, helps restore this pigmentation by increasing melanin in the skin. Faded lips can help regain tone, skin bloom, brighten your eyes, and help your eyebrows and eyelashes will become coal-black.

Saturated fatty acids can help return hair to its natural color, and studies show these are more potent tyrosinase activators than unsaturated fatty acids like those found in vegetable oils. For centuries, India has favored sesame and coconut oils for restoring gray hair, and science says these oils work because saturated fats are the most potent tyrosinase activators of all. This is why lard is so effective at brightening your natural color. Lard also stimulates hair growth, which makes it one of the cheapest, most amazing hair treatments you can find. If you prefer a vegetarian alternative, then red palm oil is a very good substitute, because it is saturated and contains carotenoids that enhance natural hair color. Sesame, coconut, avocado, and castor oil are also very good at stimulating hair growth and color, though not as effectively as lard or red palm oil. If your hair is very fragile, avoid vegetable oils that can tangle it; the last thing you want is to end up losing clumps of hair due to breakage. Lard doesn't seem to tangle the hair, and makes it supersmooth with sheen and softness. Use it to remove eye makeup; you'll see that lard helps make your eyelashes long, thick, and gorgeous!

Want to Go Blonder? Or Darker? *Bio-Young* Hair Color!

Fascinatingly, onion, quercetin, and cysteine lighten hair if it started out blond, but they darken hair that is meant to be dark, such as eyebrow hair. Cysteine is actually a part of pheomelanin. A deprivation of cysteine, just like a deprivation of glutathione, leads to an increase of eumelanin and a decrease of pheomelanin. There is some debate over whether cysteine and NAC in supplemental form may cause some negative health effects. However, it is clear that onions and garlic, which owe their pungent smell to cysteine compounds, can be highly beneficial to your hair. Years ago an older client told me that she switched to commercial shampoos when she was in her twenties, but her sister always used an egg shampoo, and her sister's hair was still blond, even in her forties. Egg yolks are a very rich source of cysteine, and they raise glutathione, too, so this could explain her observation.

And there's more! Using tomato paste before you shampoo your hair will help brighten its blond color. Green juices such as spinach or kale (remember to strain out the pulp!) and green oils such as olive or avocado have been shown to effectively lighten blond hair, whether blond is your natural shade or created by a hairdresser. If you are a natural blonde whose hair has faded and darkened with time, used externally, senna conditions hair, helps make your hair grow very fast, makes it supersoft, and colors it a sunny blond. It helps cover gray hair well. Senna has estrogenic activity, so it is very beneficial for overall hair beauty and growth.

Lemon, chamomile, ylang-ylang, licorice, honey, and lanolin—all or any of these used singly or in any combination you wish—can lighten hair. Lanolin is wool fat, and quite heavy, so use that before shampooing. You can use a tiny bit of Lansinoh lanolin cream spread over the palms of your hands and apply it while your hair is still wet after you have washed it. You just might see something quite magical, blond highlights where you thought you didn't have any. Similarly, chamomile, which is best used as an essential oil smoothed over wet or dry hair in very small amounts, will help bring out an ethereal blond shine. Ylang-ylang essential oil can also lighten hair. Honey contains a very mild bleach, helping to transform flat, dull hair, and lemon is well-known for adding natural highlights. Licorice effectively nudges melanin production toward blond for lighter skin and hair.

But blondes aren't the only ones who can have fun with this. If you have dark hair, hops and ginkgo can enhance its color, intensifying it to its younger hues. Beer is an age-old folk hair remedy, with good reason. Hops contain 8-prenylnaringenin, which acts very much like 17-beta-estradiol, producing all of the beneficial activity associated with that feminizing hormone. Hops may also increase melanin levels in your body, which restores your natural hair color, enlivens your skin tone, and makes your eye color gorgeous—intense and very attractive. If you have henna on your hair, coffee can darken that, though when it's applied to the scalp and down the length of natural blond, not bleached, hair, it typically produces lightening effects. Brunettes can also benefit from walnut shells, which are available in powder form, and can add a chestnut sheen to dark hair that is losing its richness. Natural redheads may intensify their beautiful color by eating a diet rich in onions and cysteine. If you have red highlights in dark hair, you can deepen them with henna. Henna on its own will also intensify naturally red hair. Natural colors are harmless, are good for your hair, and look fabulous.

A boon for all hair hues? Wheat germ oil, a rich source of natural vitamin E. Take this as a supplement and use it regularly on your hair before you wash it. You should see soft, gradual restoring of your youthful hair color, especially if you also use onion. Hops and ginkgo, internally and externally, can help intensify everyone's coloring, so include them in your regimen if your hair, skin, and eye color are fading. Be sure to always test a hair strand first when working with pigment enhancers, and be especially careful if your hair is bleached, chemically colored, or in any way treated with chemicals.

BIO-YOUNG TREATMENTS

Please choose preparations based on ease of availability, cost, and personal preference. One is sufficient for treating this anti-aging mechanism, but two or more can help speed improvements or improve a particularly neglected situation. Each one uses an ingredient discussed in this chapter. Enjoy!

Caffeine: Make a cup of strong instant coffee, let it cool, and then apply all over your scalp. Leave on for at least two minutes, longer if possible. Do this every day. The easiest method would be to do this while you are in the shower or in the bath, then shampoo your hair and condition.

Rosemary and eucalyptus: Purchase rosemary and eucalyptus essential oils, and rub them into your scalp every night. I use them both neat, but strictly speaking, it is better to dilute them in a base oil such as lard, red palm oil, olive oil, or any other oil of your choice. Use 50 drops each of rosemary and eucalyptus to 100 ml of the base oil. This is a good dose, but you may wish to start with just 30 drops each of the essential oils, or even 15 each, if your scalp is sensitive. Do this before you shampoo, leaving the oils on your scalp to act for as long as possible but at least half an hour.

Lard: Use a half to two teaspoons of lard, depending on your hair's length and thickness. Leave on for at least half an hour, then shampoo. Lard washes out easily and leaves your hair soft, but do condition after shampooing to make sure you have no tangles that could damage hair.

Apple cider vinegar: Add apple cider vinegar to your shampoo, half-and-half. You can apply the vinegar to your scalp about half an hour before washing, too. I don't recommend leaving it on your hair overnight, because it's a little sticky and if your hair gets pulled, it might break.

Onion: Chop and blend an onion, then strain and bottle the juice. Keep refrigerated. Use this liquid daily, leave on for half an hour, then shampoo. Alternatively, you can buy pure onion powder, mix eight teaspoons of the powder with warm water, make it into a paste, and apply to your hair before you wash it. Do this every day until you see results, then every three days or so to maintain progress.

Honey, lanolin, and licorice: Spread six teaspoons of honey on your scalp and hair. Leave on for a half hour before shampooing. Another treatment I like is to spread a film of lanolin over the palms of my hands, then apply it very gently when my hair is wet. Both of these methods will bring out lovely blond highlights. Licorice can be made into a tea using two bags; brew for five minutes, allow it to cool, and then use it as a final rinse after you've washed and conditioned your hair.

Wheat germ oil: If your blond hair has faded, apply three teaspoons of wheat germ oil as a pre-shampoo. This will help your color return.

Walnut shells and henna: Do not use henna on light-colored hair! These two natural colors are for dark or red hair. If your hair has a lot of gray in it but is basically brown, then dye a strand with walnut shell powder before you dye all your hair. The great thing about natural hair dyes is they look completely natural. And there are no roots to worry about, because these colors fade gently with time. Leave on for no more than thirty minutes the first time and make sure your product has no additives.

Urea: Look for a cream that contains 40 percent urea and apply to the area you wish to treat for unwanted hair.

Part II

YOUNGER HORMONES, YOUNGER YOU

CHAPTER 9

A Natural Approach to Facial Contouring

ANTI-AGING MECHANISM: Restoring the deep fat layer and support for a more rounded look

USE: Filling out sunken cheeks, thin neck, loss of volume in breast, and creating roundness in limbs

STARRING: Honey, bee pollen, lanolin, sarsaparilla, olive oil

Though we've talked about the face in previous chapters—how to improve skin, bone density and regeneration, fat-to-muscle ratio—I want to specifically focus on boosting optimal levels of estrogen in the face to help you regain the youthful contours you may have once taken for granted. I feel this warrants its own chapter because injected fillers and collagen stimulators, silicone implants, and even fat transfers taken from your belly or thighs and injected into your face are increasingly in demand—more so than full face-lifts, even!

Age-related hormonal dips affect every corner of your gorgeous face. I'm talking about changes to your upper cheeks, cheek hollows, jowls/lip/eye/chin contours, and wrinkles around the mouth area. Another feature that vanishes is a pleasant resting face, caused by the shrinking of your face's supporting fat and muscle layers, which makes your mouth drop because its underlying layers are not engaged. All this happens because your skin's deepest layer contains a cushioning of fat, which is evident in the roundness your face has when you're young. Aging depletes this layer, which causes a shrunken, gaunt face. Restore this fat layer and return your face to its youthful loveliness.

At this point in the book, we will do something else—we will transition to treatments that are primarily hormone-based. Here we will discuss the face, but soon you will see how hormones play out in your brain, waistline, curves, energy, mood, and sex appeal. Hormonal levels become particularly important if they are unbalanced or diminished, and I am not overstating it when I say that poor hormone levels can wreck your looks, relationships, happiness, and other areas of your life. Of course, cellular activity will always be involved in returning your face and body to their optimal peak, but the balance of intervention will now focus on boosting hormones through natural means.

Facial Fat Is Good Fat

During the early days of cosmetic surgery, doctors thought that stretching the skin taut would be all that was necessary for a youthful look. But a decade or so of oddly stretched, tight faces has proved there is far more to looking young than cutting bits off and pulling the rest. Not only was the result an unnatural approach, but a fundamental part of looking young was missing: the facial roundness of youth.

Young faces have fat. Not flabby, unattractive fat. Youthful fat. This is healthy fat, fat that lends structural support and fullness to a face without any sagging. Cosmetic surgeons have attempted to replicate this look by injecting fillers, and later actual fat, beneath cheek skin and under the eyes to fill out hollows that form there when this supportive fat disappears with age. Unfortunately, these procedures' results tend to produce uneven bumps and puffy-looking features that are a far cry from true youthful beauty. The startling effects have been dubbed "pillow face," because the results of this intervention produce unnatural, pillowlike swelling in the cheek and eye area, quite unlike the youthful appearance that was the original aim.

It is the natural fat layer that lies just beneath the skin that lends a lovely roundness to a young woman's face, and it disappears as estrogen dwindles. When this happens, it is impossible to disguise. No amount of makeup, no face exercise, not even surgical intervention, as we have seen, can help. Fortunately, there are natural substances that can restore the contours to your face and make you look decades younger in a matter of weeks!

Why Does an Older Woman Look More Like a Man?

Studies have shown that when we look at people, we don't judge their age by how lined their faces are. Our estimates are based on the contours of their faces. A woman's face shape tells us her age, even before we have focused on her features. And that shape is under hormonal control.

As you read in chapter 8, women's hormones decline with age and male hormones such as testosterone and its derivative, dihydrotestosterone, or DHT, predominate. Their effects are fast and apparent. Unwanted facial hair appears on the chin, a woman's face begins to look harder, more angular—more masculine. Her cheeks become sunken, exaggerating the angular look.

As we saw above, the very physiology of male and female skin differs dramatically: while men have a thicker dorsal (uppermost) skin layer at all ages, women have a thicker hypodermal layer. This hypodermal layer contains fat cells. This layer lies beneath the skin and provides the cushioning and softness we perceive as youthful and attractive in a girl's face. It's a quality that cannot be faked or replicated by using ordinary anti-aging creams and serums, even ones that contain antioxidants such as vitamin C, and as we saw, cosmetic procedures are ineffective, at best. But you can regain that lovely, youthful roundness in your face at any age, starting today, by using the techniques in this book, and in particular in this chapter.

By applying hormonally beneficial essential oils to your face and body, or by taking hormonally active natural substances, you can help restore your face's lost hypodermal thickness. This approach can also improve the atrophied muscle and adipose tissue in your arms, stomach, breasts, and forehead by reversing aging effects, particularly the visual ones, at the cellular and hormonal level, because estrogen has such a wide-ranging impact.

Estrogen to the Rescue!

Look at any picture of a model in a magazine and you'll see the effects of estrogen on skin. That adorable little pout of the top lip, with the thickened, cushioned upper ridge? Estrogen. That pretty, rounded neck, with not even a hint of ropiness? Estrogen. That firm, sexy jaw angle? Estrogen. Delicate, unveined hands, rounded arms, firm breasts? Luxurious hair? Estrogen, estrogen, estrogen. All of that disappears with age. Your lips vanish into a crisscross of wrinkles and your neck droops in folds. You end up with jowls, and ropy veins appear on the backs of your hands and on your forearms.

There are three main types of estrogen: estradiol, estrone, and estriol. They work together to help you look gorgeous and feminine, but when you're at your peak and fertility is high, estradiol is the main hormone in your body. It is produced by the ovaries. As your ovaries slow down, your levels of estradiol fall. To make up some of the deficit, estrone levels rise, but the effects of this hormone do not entirely replicate those of estradiol. Estriol is the hormone that dominates during pregnancy.

So to look young, you need to raise estradiol activity in your body. The ideal way to do this would be to activate your own ovaries, but even without that option in menopause, you can still achieve estradiol activity in your skin by using natural substances that possess the same properties as estradiol itself. In this chapter the focus is on producing those estradiol effects directly in your skin, particularly your face. The purpose of restoring estrogenic activity to an aging body is to replenish the shriveled fat layers, while not allowing fat deposits to get out of control and become flab.

What's the Buzz? Honey and Bee Pollen Boost Estrogen Levels

Honey is truly a huge help for safely and effectively raising estrogen levels in the skin and reversing the effects of aging. It seems almost ridiculous that a food you can buy at your corner store can rewind the clock so your face regains its youthful prettiness! Once you try it, you should see that honey, when eaten or when used externally, will dramatically anti-age your face and neck. Under-eye bags and droopy eyelids can vanish, your neck might regain a pleasant roundness, the veins on the backs of your hands and forearms should be no more. You should notice a smoothing of lines, more moisture, and a lovely bloom, together with a definite plumping effect even after the first day of use. And all because honey contains natural hormones that plump up your skin and restore the deeper layers. Honey has been shown to be powerfully anti-cancer, anti-inflammation, and even antibiotic, so you can use it with joyful abandon! As a bonus, it also anti-ages your breasts, arms, and hair in many ways. It is sticky, though, so use it in the bath, either directly or in the form of the preparations I recommend.

The estrogenic properties in this wonder food work their magic when you apply it to your face. To show just how estrogenic it is, let's first take a look at how honey hormonally affects other parts of the body. In a series of experiments using an animal model of menopause, honey was shown to be highly effective at overcoming the effects of low estrogen levels. Showing highly effective estrogenic activity, it prevented the type of weight gain caused by declining estrogen levels, increased bone density, and even prevented vaginal and uterine atrophy. Honey also achieves this while being protective against cancer and heart disease, two significant risk factors that can occur with other types of estrogenic agents. Dr. Basel al-Ramadi and his team in the United Arab Emirates showed that manuka honey, at very low concentrations, is capable of stopping the growth of breast, skin, and colon cancer cells. This experiment used an intravenous delivery of manuka honey, but ingesting the honey, at the kind of doses you would normally eat, would also supply the body with this amazing food.

It may seem as if the examples above have nothing to do with your face, but they are in fact closely related. Whether used internally or externally, honey does what estrogen would do: it restores youthful contours and eliminates the unwanted effects of androgens that occur when estrogen levels fall. The benefits of estrogen on the skin include increased collagen for skin thickness, increased mucopolysaccharides and hyaluronic acid for moisture retention, improved stratum corneum function to stop flakiness, improved wound healing and skin repair to prevent wrinkles, increased elastin for skin elasticity, and that all-important plumper fat layer for the right kind of pillow face.

Every part of you contains estrogen receptors, and decreasing levels of this hormone age you on every level—visibly so on the skin and hair. Estrogen receptors are found in every layer of the skin, even in the blood vessels that feed the skin. When estrogen levels decline, every part of you suffers. You can see it as a general withering. The loss of collagen is dramatic—a woman loses 30 percent of her entire collagen layer in the first five years of menopause, and the loss, which continues at a slightly diminished rate from then on, is highly visible. Imagine a duvet with 30 percent of the stuffing taken out. But some of this can be replenished by improved cellular functioning.

Yet when it comes to the loss of fat layer and its change in distribution, only estrogen can truly help. The laying down of fat and its feminine distribution in the body are largely under this hormone's control, and even great cellular function can't replace its cushioning benefits.

I mentioned earlier that mucopolysaccharides are vital for keeping your skin moisturized. Their declining levels are responsible for the dryness and flakiness many women experience as they get older. These changes further aggravate wrinkle formation. Mucopolysaccharides are chains of sugar molecules. White, refined sugar, or sucrose, deserves its bad reputation as a health destroyer and accelerator of aging. However, certain sugars are in fact essential for cellular function. This includes skin cells. Various sugars, for example trehalose and ribose (the ending -ose denotes a sugar), have been shown to be of great benefit to skin when applied topically as wrinkle preventers and as moisturizers. Sugars are essential for cell-to-cell communication as well as cellular energy, and their anti-aging effects are proving impressive. This is a new field of anti-aging, called glycobiology, which deals with how certain sugars benefit the skin, body, and aging. Trehalose, for example, is able to untangle damaged proteins in Alzheimer's disease, and ribose energizes the heart. Honey contains both trehalose and ribose, among other sugars, and is very effective at anti-aging the skin.

And while honey is terrific as a topical treatment and delicious when stirred into tea or oatmeal, another bee product, pollen, is even more effective at restoring age-depleted female hormones when used internally. Bee pollen possesses the same range of estrogen effects as honey but in higher concentrations. In addition, bee pollen contains a good helping of protein. It can be eaten daily as a very potent food with wonderful anti-aging benefits. I like to mix it into yogurt or warm milk for a superfood that's hard to beat!

The estrogenic effects of honey and bee pollen are also highly desirable because they make the troubling effects of androgens such as testosterone disappear. They achieve this not by lowering the levels of testosterone, but by enhancing estrogenic effects in a woman's body. A woman's levels of male sex hormones don't necessarily increase as she gets older, but as levels of her female hormones fall, the effects of male hormones are no longer balanced by the female hormones, and the results of their physiological actions become more visible.

Cholesterol, Fats, and Fat-Soluble Vitamins

Maintaining healthy cholesterol levels is key to good hormonal function. Cholesterol is essential to your health, and your body manufactures it every day. Without cholesterol, your memory would suffer, and your synthesis of sex hormones, including estrogen, would grind to a halt.

Vegetable oils raise HDL (high-density lipoprotein) cholesterol, which is considered to be the "good" form of cholesterol. This is generally true, but LDL (low-density lipoprotein) also performs important functions as an antioxidant. It protects the brain, builds muscle, and even offers anti-cancer protection. So it is vital for your hormonal and overall health to include vegetable oils in your diet, and make sure that they are of the very best quality—unrefined and unbleached.

Animal saturated fats can pose problems, however. Particularly the ones found in meat are associated with shortened telomeres and with accelerated aging. Many people don't process animal fats well and this can result in milia and in under-eye bags. Fish oil is associated with lengthened telomeres, as is red palm oil. But fish oil doesn't produce the rounded appearance of a young woman's face. In fact, omega-3 fatty acids, which predominate in fish oil, tend to "cut" fat rather than repair the shriveled hypodermis, and so this type of fat may exacerbate an already gaunt face. A better option is evening primrose, rice bran, and avocado oils, which are very good at anti-aging the fat layers beneath your skin, and these oils do not lead to the kind of weight gain that results from fatty meat. Full-fat dairy tends to be less problematic for younger people, but as we get older all of us need to be aware that low-fat meat and dairy options are less aging and lead to younger-looking skin. There are benefits to using cholesterol-containing fats such as lard externally, however. If your skin barrier has been compromised and damaged, and your skin is feeling very tight and dry, cholesterol-containing fats can restore it in moments, and repair it in days. Similarly, there are huge benefits from using lard on your hair, as discussed in detail in chapter 8.

Squalene, cocoa butter, and lanolin are all fats that produce wondrous effects on your skin's fatty layer, when applied externally. Internally, squalene does possess hormonal activity, too, but can be difficult to find as a supplement. Squalene is the building block of steroid hormones and one of the most common lipids, or fats, already found in human skin. The conversion of squalene to steroid hormones occurs in the body and directly in the skin, with remarkable consequences for anti-aging. When a woman applies a layer of this thin, colorless oil to her face, estrogen levels rise in the treated area. This means that the beneficial synthesis of procollagen increases and offsets the loss that may have already occurred with decreased hormonal levels. This response to topical application is important because wrinkles can be treated with high concentrations of squalene, and the results are fast and reliable.

Internal squalene supplementation has also been shown to make wrinkles disappear and increase procollagen levels, but it did produce loose stools, so be aware of that. Cocoa butter is a powerful fat that plumps your skin when applied externally and combined with a liquid oil such as avocado or jojoba oil (technically a wax, even in its liquid state), and heated very gently until the cocoa butter melts. You can also add fennel, dill seed, or aniseed essential oils to the preparation for more impact. Lanolin, or lanolin oil, is a wool fat that is highly effective at plumping the skin.

Fat-soluble vitamins also support the fat layer and can be used to add pretty plumpness to your face. Vitamin E, in particular, has a long and distinguished history in nutritional science. Decades before vitamin supplementation became common, and as long ago as 1948, vitamin E was studied as a possible candidate for estrogen replacement therapy. It was found to be effective in most studies, with its natural form, directly derived from wheat germ oil, producing the best results. Vitamin E is a mixture of eight fat-soluble, closely related antioxidants: four tocopherols and four tocotrienols. Of the tocopherols, alpha-tocopherol is considered to be the most valuable biologically. The tocotrienols, also found in red palm oil and rice bran oil, have a most amazing range of benefits, including clearing the arteries. It is also possible to become deficient in tocopherol. One of the symptoms of this is the loss of feeling in hands and feet, known as neuropathy.

Both the dermis, which is the lower skin layer, and the epidermis, or the uppermost layer, contain vitamin E, which is the most abundant fat-soluble antioxidant in your body. If you take it as a supplement, it does reach your skin. But it takes seven days for ingested vitamin E to do so. The use of topical vitamin E oil supplies your skin layers with this wonderful substance directly, the moment you apply it. Vitamin E is highly fat-loving, or lipophilic, which means that when you apply it to the surface of your skin, it sinks right through all the layers and penetrates deeply. By simply applying pure vitamin E oil to your face, you can restore the all-important youth-giving estrogenic activity to every layer of your skin! Since sun exposure and ozone deplete your vitamin E levels, which also decrease with age, it makes sense to make sure you have enough of this vitamin in your body for good health. Vitamin E also possesses antioxidant and anti-inflammatory activity and protects against cancer, too.

You may be confused by the recent negative press about vitamin E. The reason some studies have seen negative effects when using vitamin E lies in the shape of the vitamin itself. Only the natural form of this vitamin will produce the desirable effects we associate with vitamin E. Unfortunately, the form of vitamin E used in studies is a cheap, synthetic form that has the wrong shape. Often more than one incorrectly shaped form of vitamin E is present. This not only fails to produce vitamin E's beneficial effects, but can produce negative effects, by blocking the true vitamin E activity in the body. So always use natural vitamin E.

As I've said, for younger-looking skin, apply a pure vitamin E oil directly to your face—truly, an anti-aging dynamo. Vitamin E helps restore a fullness to your face in moments, and the results should become longer-lasting, the longer you use it. Regular application of this amazing vitamin helps repair every kind of skin damage, whether it's due to the sun, pollution, age, genetics, or a combination of all these factors. There is no facial sagging for those who use vitamin E! If taken internally, fat-soluble vitamins like vitamin E need to be taken with a source of good fat like olive oil.

✳ Beautiful Face Spotlight: Aniseed and Sarsaparilla

You can help enhance your face, neck, and even cleavage with sarsaparilla or aniseed. Aniseed is an essential oil that is wonderful for adding a youthful fullness and firmness to a face grown a little gaunt with time. Aniseed resembles sweet fennel, but aniseed is even more estrogenic. Test it on a small area of your skin first, and always use it diluted in an oil or cocoa butter base. As with all estrogenic skin treatments, you can use this oil all over your body. It will not make you gain weight, but it will help firm up your body and lend a pretty roundness to your limbs. If you compare young limbs with older ones, you can see the change in the ratio of muscle to fat, as you saw in a previous chapter. But, paradoxically, even though with age there is a loss of muscle, and a comparative gain in fat, the fat layer in the hypodermis, beneath the skin, shrinks, resulting in a loss of fullness and roundness wherever this occurs. The conundrum disappears when you consider what happens to young overweight people: their skin is smooth, but lacks firmness and definition. Age actually damages the very architecture of your skin, from the uppermost to its innermost layers. This causes dramatic wrinkling on the skin's surface and less support overall. The natural substances in this chapter helps restore the correct, youthful amount of fat in the hypodermis, your skin's deep layer.

Sarsaparilla is an herb that may also restore the youthful, underlying layer of fat to your face (as well as your breasts, your neck, the backs of your hands, or anywhere else you need it). Sarsaparilla has always been a remedy for skin-related concerns, even if its anti-aging properties haven't always been recognized. For instance, it used to be very popular in the Wild West because cowboys used it as a cure for syphilis, and it may have had some merit in that sphere. More recently, sarsaparilla was found to adequately treat psoriasis and decrease desquamation, or skin shedding, in just a week by boiling the herb in water and drinking the consequent tea on a daily basis. Excitingly, the newest findings show that sarsaparilla stimulates pre-adipocyte differentiation and adipocyte proliferation.

In ordinary language, this means that putting a treatment containing this herb on your face can dramatically increase your face's subcutaneous fat layer without "making you fat." And if you want to improve other areas of your body, sarsaparilla can work its magic there, too. This herb is great for the backs of your hands, forearms, neck, around the lips and mouth, and on your breasts. In one study, women who used a gel containing sarsaparilla extract on their breasts every day for a month saw an increase in their cup size. I like to incorporate sarsaparilla prepared in avocado or olive oil (the recipe is at the end of this chapter) into my daily skin care routine.

BIO-YOUNG TREATMENTS

Please choose preparations based on ease of availability, cost, and personal preference. One is sufficient for treating this anti-aging mechanism, but two or more can speed improvements or improve a particularly neglected situation. Each one uses an ingredient discussed in this chapter. Enjoy!

Honey and bee pollen: Eat ten teaspoons of bee pollen a day; you can take more, if you like, but any less will not yield the full benefits of this food. Apply honey to your face, leave for fifteen minutes, rinse.

Squalene: I recommend olive oil squalene. Spread a thin layer on your face in the morning and evening, when your face is free of makeup.

Vitamin E oil: If it's not available in a bottle, buy vitamin E capsules intended for internal use. Use 400 IU. Pierce the capsule and apply the oil.

Sarsaparilla: Volufiline is a commercial product that contains sarsaparilla and is marketed for increasing breast size. You can also use it on your face, neck, hands, and forearms. You can make your own preparation by adding four teaspoons of sarsaparilla powder to 500 ml of olive oil, heating this up carefully, and simmering for thirty minutes. Let it cool, strain the liquid, bottle and label it.

Aniseed: Make a cream using cocoa butter and avocado oil in a 50:50 ratio. Melt the cocoa butter and avocado oil together over gentle heat, remove when liquid, leave to cool, and while it is still liquid, add 30 drops of aniseed essential oil per 100 ml of the oil base. Stir well and pour into a wide-mouthed container.

Fat: Include healthy fats in your daily diet, including avocado, wheat germ, and evening primrose oils.

CHAPTER 10

The Secret to Reversing Menopause

ANTI-AGING MECHANISM: Restoring estrogenic activity

USE: Reducing hot flashes, wrinkles, breast atrophy,
vaginal atrophy

STARRING: Royal jelly, vitamin E, ashwagandha, Panax
ginseng, boron, lanolin

I f you thought menopause was simply about no longer menstruating, think again. Menopause changes you on both the hormonal and the cellular level. Hormones are extremely powerful compounds with far-reaching effects. Their declining levels therefore affect every cell of your body. You have already seen that skin, fat distribution, muscles, bone, and hair all suffer as hormonal levels decline with age. Hormone levels, particularly levels of estrogen, fall dramatically with age, but these levels also decline after a hysterectomy, or with the use of certain medications that affect or shut down proper ovarian function. The result is always the same: wrinkles, saggy skin, poor muscle tone, weight gain, thinning hair, loss of bone mass. Old age.

So far in this book you have seen the damage caused by falling levels of estrogen. In this chapter I will show you how you can significantly increase those levels to the peak levels of a thirty-year-old. This can result in firmer, smoother skin, fuller breasts, a more defined waist, shinier hair, and more supple joints. In fact, these are the markers by which you should judge your hormonal status and improvements as you age, because improvements in these factors signal an aging reversal and a return to younger biological functioning. You will learn how you can anti-age your entire female system, restoring that all-important youthful hormonal activity, and even restoring your ovaries and uterus to a biologically younger state. The herbs and nutrients in this chapter also help protect against cancer and heart disease, which makes this program a highly effective, and safe, alternative to conventional hormone replacement therapy.

Welcome to Menopause

A list of the most common menopausal symptoms can read like a list of reasons to lock yourself in the house or ball up in a corner and cry. They include hot flashes, night sweats, anxiety, insomnia, low libido, fatigue, wrinkled skin, thinning scalp hair, unwanted facial hair, osteoporosis, vaginal atrophy, fertility loss, and the absence of menstrual cycles. As if that weren't bad enough, there is also the Breast Slap, which refers to what happens when breast tissue atrophies so badly as a result of low estrogen levels that the breasts thin to the point that the glandular middle part, the filling, so to speak, almost disappears. So when a woman makes a sudden move without wearing a bra—like turning over in bed at night—her breasts literally slap against her body. I know from my email inbox that this is an important subject and a cause of great distress to many women, some of whom are still in their thirties. But there's no need to despair! The natural remedies in this chapter actually rebuild breast tissue, increasing fat, volume, and heaviness.

For decades, the accepted scientific explanation for menopause was simply the depletion of eggs with aging. The theory stated that every woman is born with a certain number of eggs, which are gradually used up each time she menstruates. When they are gone, menopause occurs. But new data show this is not true. In fact, Harvard researchers have found new evidence that female mammals can produce egg cells throughout their life. It is not that a woman runs out of egg cells; the reason for the menopause lies in the brain, in the pituitary and the pineal glands, which control and oversee hormonal levels. When these brain areas are stimulated, menstruation returns, even in women who have been fully menopausal for years! The reason these brain areas stop doing their job is the slowing down of cellular processes, and damage accumulated over time.

So far we have looked at anti-aging largely through either cellular or hormonal function. When studying the reversal of menopause, we see the intimate interplay between these two systems. Cellular function slows down and affects the brain, which in turn slows down and affects the ovaries, uterus, breasts, skin, muscle, and bone. Cellular-level changes can be reversed in real, biological terms that lead to real, biological anti-aging. But making changes on a cellular level isn't always enough. Cellular changes do have visible benefits, but they cannot transform *all* of your traits into those of a vital thirty-year-old, visually and biochemically. For that, you need to raise your hormones, too.

Modern medicine has recently taken up a new, revolutionary position with respect to menopause. Instead of seeing it as an inevitable decline, medical scientists are studying possible avenues of reversing menopause, with a view to extending fertility and reversing aging. The approach taken involves ovarian transplants and drugs that kick-start the return of healthy, youthful ovarian function. Kick-starting ovarian function is possible with natural substances, and this approach is preferable, as it is free from side effects.

Menopause begins when ovarian function declines. The cells responsible for estrogen production slow down with age. As we just saw, the whole process begins with the brain, in the pituitary and the pineal glands, which control the levels of estrogen and other hormones in the body, and even determine the sensitivity of ovaries to any estrogen circulating in the blood. But whatever the starting point, the drop in estrogen levels is detected by another part of the brain, the hypothalamus. The hypothalamus reacts to the drop in estrogen levels by overacting to raise estrogen. This produces hot flashes and sweating, because the hypothalamus is also involved in temperature control. What's more, the hypothalamus controls appetite, sleep cycles, sex hormones, and overall body temperature, which is why related symptoms are also considered menopause symptoms.

When estrogen levels rise, however, menopausal symptoms caused by the overactive hypothalamus disappear. So if you are having hot flashes, it's a good indication that your hypothalamus is working hard to raise estrogen levels in your body. The great news is that herbs and essential oils with phytoestrogenic, or estrogen-mimicking, properties produce estrogenic activity and calm the hypothalamus. Excitingly, immature egg-producing cells in the ovaries, also known as oocytes, can be stimulated by increasing their cellular energy. This can actually delay the onset of menopause and may restore the menstrual cycle, even in menopausal women. Even if the latter does not occur, however, the approach yields multiple benefits because improved cellular function is powerfully anti-aging, and even partial stimulation of egg-producing cells can produce remarkable rejuvenation.

Though it sounds as if the menopausal hypothalamus has the potential to only cause you worries, it's encouraging to know that this gland is also exquisitely sensitive to the blood levels of B vitamins circulating in your body. Raising your B vitamin status is an effective way to increase the levels of sex hormones in your body, alleviate hormonal problems, and even boost fertility. Low blood levels of vitamin B hugely compromise the hypothalamus's activity, so B vitamins are important to help you cope with most anxiety and stress, because the hypothalamus also controls the adrenals, which produce stress hormones. A depletion of B vitamins makes the hypothalamus less effective at controlling the output of these stress hormones. Adrenaline raises the heart rate and constricts blood vessels—two factors that get more dangerous as you age. High doses of folic acid have pronounced estrogenic effects, too, and have been shown to delay and even reverse menopause. For one, folic acid, applied topically or taken internally, enhances collagen levels in the skin to smooth wrinkles and thicken skin.

How Are Natural Treatments Different From Synthetic Hormones?

It is essential to remember that there is a huge difference between the synthetic and bio-identical hormonal preparations that may state that they use plants as their starting point and the truly natural preparations that I'm suggesting. Synthetic hormones, used in conventional hormone therapy, differ from our own natural hormones in significant ways that lead to a range of unpleasant side effects. They are also prescribed in very high doses, and their biological action is very powerful. All of this can lead to dangerous blood clots, continuous heavy bleeding, and hormone-sensitive cancers. Even though bio-identical hormones are considered to be similar to our own, natural hormones, they still produce powerful side effects, because it is difficult to determine the correct dose for any individual at any one time, and because supplying ready-made hormones to the body causes the natural hormone-producing glands to shut down, and even atrophy, as we shall see in a moment. All hormones in your body have a natural daily cycle, and this is impossible to mimic. The herbs, essential oils, foods, and supplements recommended in this chapter, and throughout this book, on the other hand, work safely and gently with your body to bring about the desired effects.

The problems that occur with the use of synthetic hormone preparations have produced a deep fear of *all* hormone treatments, as if natural preparations were synonymous with the synthetic ones that have been found to cause cancer. It is essential to fully grasp the enormous difference between the approach to hormonal function used in this book's program and the components of synthetic hormones that have produced serious health concerns and well-founded fears.

You may be familiar with synthetic hormones, which also go by the names of hormone replacement therapy (HRT) or estrogen replacement therapy (ERT). These therapies aim to replace the hormones that women lose after, or just before, the onset of the menopause. And while these hormones "resemble" a woman's hormones, they are not the same. Because they are similar to the hormones normally found in your body, they can produce some beneficial effects, but because they differ in significant ways from your natural hormones, they cause serious problems, too. Hormones are powerful, and at the same time extremely vulnerable to any imbalances. Problems can occur because the dose of one hormone is too high, which is a common issue for those who take pharmaceutical-grade hormones. But the range of problems increases when a woman takes only one or two hormones. This is because we know that *several* types of estrogens exist. The balance of essential hormones needed by your body in the correct amounts to stay young and reverse aging is impossible to achieve with pharmaceutical hormones.

As you saw a moment ago, bio-identical hormones are not the

answer, either. These are manufactured hormones whose shape is the same as those of the hormones found in a woman's body. The advantage over the earlier hormone preparations is that bio-identical hormones produce fewer side effects. But many of the problems that have been found to occur with the old-type hormones persist with bio-identical ones. Before anyone can even begin to use them, blood tests must determine the hormone levels for each particular person, and the task of getting the dosage right, from day to day, week to week, and month to month, is complicated, to say the least. In order to get this delicate balance right, a woman would need to have twenty-four-hour hormonal testing, including both salivary and blood measurements, and these tests would have to be performed during different seasons. Even then, a woman's ideal doses might still be unknown because her hormonal history would also need to be factored into this. What were her levels when she was thirty years old? When was she most fertile? These are all important questions that she may not be asked or know the answers to, yet this information is highly relevant when she's seeking the correct dose of a powerful pharmaceutical. This problem applies to all types of synthetic hormonal therapy, making the potential for imbalance with bio-identical hormones as serious as the situation that exists with the more conventional synthetic hormones. In addition, several different hormones may have to be taken to avoid a really gross imbalance here, too.

Melatonin: The Master Hormone

Melatonin is a hormone produced in the brain by the pineal gland and is closely involved with the regulation of the circadian (twenty-four-hour) rhythm of the body, governing sleep and wakefulness. It is essential to a healthy body at any stage of life, but particularly after menopause. Melatonin levels decline rapidly as we get older, which makes a good night's rest and consistent energy hard to come by. Some people may not realize that melatonin is a hormone. When using a synthetic melatonin in a study, researchers found it could restore the menstrual cycle in elderly women in a matter of days! Of course, I don't recommend synthetic hormones. The melatonin supplements on sale at health food stores in the United States and Canada, and used indiscriminately by people wishing to avoid jet lag or to get a good night's sleep, contain one of the most powerful hormones in the human body. So when you buy melatonin in the belief that it is harmless, and natural, the truth is that you are, in fact, purchasing a synthetic hormone with powerful, far-reaching, potentially hugely unbalancing effects. The pineal gland, which secretes melatonin, can atrophy significantly as a result of melatonin supplementation. You will be pleased to learn that this does not happen with the natural methods of raising melatonin recommended in this chapter and in this book.

Melatonin is actually found in more natural substances than you might expect. The most potent melatonin-stimulating food is tart cherry juice. Obtain a good helping of your chosen fruit or juice every day, and consume it after 4 p.m. to improve your sleep cycle. Delicious tropical fruit juices and fruits such as mango, banana, and orange produce significant measurable increases in melatonin levels safely and naturally. Adding a daily glass of pineapple juice to your diet is a great way to improve your sleep cycles and boost energy, with the added estrogenic benefits of enhanced ovulation, lubrication, and magnetic sex appeal. Walnuts, tomato paste, and oats also very effectively raise melatonin levels. Cedarwood Atlas essential oil stimulates melatonin synthesis when it's applied directly to the wrists at bedtime or in a base oil and used on the face or hair at night. Kudzu starch possesses potent estrogenic activity, and when added to pineapple juice, it can also increase melatonin activity. Kudzu can also add shine and length to your hair, add firmness to your breasts, and plump your face when it is taken internally. It can also be used externally when dissolved in water. Recent research has discovered high levels of melatonin in beer. Since beer also contains barley and hops, this drink can contribute to overall hormonal benefits if taken in moderation. Hops, for instance, contain two powerful antioxidants, 8-prenylnaringenin and isoxanthohumol. Eight-prenylnaringenin (8-PN) possesses powerful estradiol activity, and isoxanthohumol is readily converted into 8-PN, so the estrogenic effects of hops and beer are quite pronounced.

Natural Estrogens in Whole Herbs and Oils Do Not Increase Cancer Risk

Some natural estrogens, such as those found in Panax ginseng, ashwagandha, CoQ10, vitamin E, and pomegranate, have significant estrogenic effects that yield fuller and firmer breasts, thicker hair, younger skin, and a youthful silhouette. But they should not increase breast cancer risk.

Estrogen has a bad reputation, which is the result of the side effects caused by *synthetic* estrogens. Misunderstanding beneficial supplements is nothing new—you read how this happened with vitamin E, you've learned about the unnecessary sun phobia, which has contributed to a widespread vitamin D deficiency across the Western world in recent years, and we are only just emerging from several decades of shunning all oils and fats, even those essential to our health. We had deeply misplaced fears in these cases, stemming from knee-jerk reactions concomitant with incomplete understanding. This is also the situation with estrogen.

Yes, estrogen is responsible for breast growth and cell proliferation. But you wouldn't want it any other way! Without estrogen, women wouldn't have breasts, their reproductive organs would fail to develop properly, and they would be sterile. Estrogen is also responsible for smooth, youthful skin, long, shiny hair, and a woman's sex appeal. Naturally occurring estrogen is a good thing.

Cell proliferation is an essential part of being healthy. Without it, a cut would not heal, and millions of essential life processes that occur every moment of your life would grind to a halt. You would not survive for long without healthy cell proliferation. But cancer is not simply cell proliferation. Cancer is *out-of-control* cell proliferation. There is a huge difference. Your body creates new cells every second of your life. Breathing, exercise, life itself produce free radicals. You may be shocked to learn that cancerous cells are created in your body every day in large numbers. A healthy body, supplied by generous helpings of dietary antioxidants, easily copes with that.

The difference between this normal, very health state and cancer is control. An unhealthy body is easily overwhelmed by everyday life. Pollution, stress, exercise, breathing—all of these produce free radicals, but an unhealthy body loses the capacity to neutralize and control their effects. Cancer occurs when your body's defenses against the damaging effects of free radicals, in particular, are insufficient. This leads to out-of-control cell growth. When the body is healthy, it controls cell proliferation, or cell division, and keeps it within safe limits. Cell death, or apoptosis, is a vital stage in a healthy cell's life cycle that enables old cells to be cleared away and new ones to replace them. When this cellular mechanism fails, cells continue to divide and possibly result in a tumor. Cancer prevention and treatment are at their best when natural cell death is once more established, and the cells that should die do die, instead of forming cancer. Your body systems, including your immune system, and a wholesome diet rich in antioxidants keep cell growth within beneficial limits.

The link between estrogen and hormone-sensitive cancers is not as straightforward as it appears at first glance. Teenage girls have extremely high levels of estrogen as their breasts grow and their reproductive system develops very fast, but breast cancer is relatively rare in this age group. If high levels of estrogen and the resulting stimulation of breast cell growth were the causal factors in breast cancer, then teenage girls would have the highest breast cancer rate of all. It is true, however, that the rates of cancer, including hormonally sensitive cancers such as breast cancers, have risen alarmingly in the past twenty years, and younger women are succumbing to these diseases. But to jump to the conclusion that natural estrogen is responsible for this rise is an error. Synthetic estrogens, however, whether from plastics, environmental factors, or synthetic hormonal preparations, have been implicated. The truth is that natural estrogen, whether created by your body or eaten in plant form as part of a healthy diet rich in all kinds of plant factors, produces impressive anti-aging properties. When cancer is considered in terms of cellular dysfunction, it becomes less frightening, because natural substances are effective at restoring correct cellular function.

Cancer of all kinds is caused by inadequate antioxidant protection. If antioxidant levels in your body are too low to maintain peak cellular functioning, your cells are extremely vulnerable to damage. Restoring that all-important antioxidant protection, and thereby restoring healthy cellular function, prevents the formation of cancerous cells.

Let's take a look at some of the exciting anti-cancer findings that demonstrate the benefits and anti-cancer protection of natural estrogenic substances. This confirms their use as real, and very safe, alternatives to hormone and estrogen replacement therapies.

✳ Safe Estrogen Spotlight: Panax Ginseng

Ginseng is one of the most powerful natural substances the world has ever seen. Chinese emperors monopolized the right to harvest this herb, and wars were fought between the Tartars and the Chinese over ginseng territory. There were special ginseng collectors in China who faced death unless they delivered their harvested ginseng roots to the emperor. These collectors were often attacked by bandits because ginseng was so valuable. Armed guards were used to protect the stores. In 2012 the most expensive single *ounce* of this root ever was sold for 1.57 *million* U.S. dollars! It was wild crafted, and therefore extremely rare and potent. Its shape distinguishes it from the more common commercially grown variety—the wild root is small and round, unlike the large commercially produced specimens. Clearly, ginseng is a special plant, highly revered by those who know.

And when it comes to anti-aging and anti-cancer, ginseng continues to wow me and my clients. For instance, American ginseng, a very close relative of Panax ginseng, helps inhibit the growth of human breast cancer cells. Panax ginseng itself possesses impressive anti-cancer properties. More than three decades ago, one of my clients had been menopausal for many years until she took a high-quality Panax ginseng extract for two weeks and was amazed to see her periods return!

In Chinese medicine, Panax ginseng, or ren shen, is classed as one of the royal herbs. This is an esteemed category of herbs that don't have highly specific and limited actions in the body, but prolong life and balance in the body to make it function better than before. Royal herbs anti-age the human body in significant and visible ways. For starters, ginseng improves cellular function. Among its many varied gifts, it is a powerful SIRT1 activator. Ginseng also improves hormonal function effectively in women *and* men.

As my client demonstrated, ginseng restores ovarian activity, which is absolutely the best news any woman could hope for. Even if you hate the idea of ongoing periods and have no wish to conceive a child, the restoration of ovarian function after menopause is the holy grail of anti-aging, because when it is achieved, your estrogen levels are restored to those of a young woman.

However, even if your ovaries do not return to complete functionality, Panax ginseng still produces highly beneficial estrogenic effects on ovaries, vaginal tissue, and the uterus. In one study ginseng activated estrogen receptors in female rats that had had their ovaries removed. An ovariectomy is the surgical removal of a laboratory animal's ovaries, thus mimicking human menopause for scientific research. A substance that produces estrogenic effects in an ovariectomized animal will have the same effects in a menopausal woman. In a test tube study, researchers used a variety of Panax ginseng, also known as Korean red ginseng, and observed an estrogenic effect on ovarian estrogen receptors. Similarly, a case report from London concerning a sixty-two-year-old woman who had never taken estrogens documented a very strong estrogenic effect from ginseng that was evidenced by tight and lubricated vaginal tissue. Menopause produces marked vaginal atrophy, leading to significant thinning of vaginal walls and an absence of vaginal secretions. In this case study, ginseng prevented these changes from happening.

Ginseng's beneficial estrogenic effects on vaginal tissue are impressive and dramatic, and you can actually test these effects for yourself. After a few days of taking the ginseng treatment described at the end of this chapter, try testing the health of your vaginal tissues by inserting a finger into your vagina and noticing that the vaginal walls are more spongy, thick, soft, and moist. This is ginseng's estrogenic effect at work.

Estrogen decrease during menopause leads to a shortening of

the vaginal canal. Ginseng is able to lengthen it again by raising the cervix once more to its youthful position. This indicates a return to a biologically younger age of the entire reproductive system. As the vagina lengthens, the muscles supporting the uterus firm up and the symptoms of prolapse may well disappear. This is all the result of the powerful anti-aging estrogenic stimulation by ginseng on these hormonally sensitive tissues.

Panax ginseng may help protect against all kinds of cancers, including breast cancer, a shining example of the fact that estrogenic activity does not produce hormone-sensitive cancers if antioxidant activity is also present. In case you are worried about endometriosis or polycystic ovary syndrome (PCOS), ginseng is beneficial in these conditions, too. While it stimulates cell growth that has been depleted by a lack of estrogen in menopause, Panax ginseng actually normalizes the overstimulation of ovaries seen in endometriosis and PCOS, again exhibiting the balancing property that makes it such a highly valued and revered herb.

PCOS is one of the most common hormonal disorders suffered by women. It is characterized by a sex hormone imbalance that produces irregular, painful periods, an increase in facial hair, scalp hair thinning, and dramatically reduced fertility. Because ginseng has estrogenic activity, a valid concern would be that it would make PCOS much worse, since this condition appears to be associated, at least in part and in some cases, with an increased sensitivity to estrogen, with a consequent overstimulation of the ovaries. Instead, ginseng has been shown to be highly beneficial for this condition—reversing the disorder, producing healthy ovaries, and restoring fertility.

Panax ginseng may be able to help revitalize ovaries, restore fertility, improve the structure of the reproductive organs, and protect against cancer. If you would like to further enhance the vaginal changes brought about by ginseng, which works its magic from inside out, you can use pure vitamin E oil or lanolin directly in your vagina. They are messy, so use a thin panty liner as well, but the results are worth it. In only a few days, you should notice dramatic improvement. Urinary difficulties, such as exercise or stress incontinence (involuntary loss of urine when laughing or jumping), a weak urinary stream, and even urinary tract infections, which worsen during menopause, can also improve.

✳ Safe Estrogen Spotlight: Ashwagandha

The Sanskrit name of the herb ashwagandha translates to "the scent of a stallion." You may not agree—but the herb does have a unique scent. Ashwagandha is known in Latin as *Withania sominfera*. It was given mostly to men, because it was noticed that males who took ashwagandha were more sexually active. Researchers have since learned, however, that while ashwagandha raises testosterone in men, it *also* leads to increased levels of estrogen in women. Astonishingly, those increased levels of testosterone and estrogen appear to be produced by an indirect mechanism, as ashwagandha itself doesn't appear to possess direct hormonal activity. This herb has been shown to enhance female fertility, which is a sure sign that it has significant estrogenic effects. (However, ashwagandha also increases male fertility!) This amazing herb also boosts energy, restores pigment to graying hair, and improves brain function significantly—all highly welcome improvements whether you are menopausal or not. Ashwagandha can also help improve sleep and helps protect against ovarian cancer. In fact, a compound isolated from ashwagandha blocks vimentin, a pro-metastatic protein, meaning ashwagandha may help prevent the occurrence of metastases, the most dangerous cancerous changes.

Moreover, ashwagandha stimulates gonadotrophins, hormones released by the pituitary, which then go on to stimulate the sex glands. This may account for ashwagandha's remarkable effects on the sex hormones and explain why this effect is not directly estrogenic or testosterogenic. The pituitary is controlled by the hypothalamus and constitutes the second step in the sequence that begins in the hypothalamus and leads to the release of sex hormones in the human body. The first step is the activation of the hypothalamus by low circulating levels of a hormone, for example estradiol in women and testosterone in men. The hypothalamus then acts on the pituitary gland, and the pituitary in turn stimulates the ovaries or the testes to release estradiol or testosterone. The pituitary accomplishes its task via gonadotrophins, hormones that act in both sexes to increase the appropriate sex hormones. Now you can see how ashwagandha is able to benefit both men and women.

Ashwagandha actually bypasses the hypothalamus and directly stimulates the pituitary. In this way it helps increase ovarian weight and the numbers of mature follicles in the ovaries, which, for your *Bio-Young* purposes, means anti-aging. Follicles are densely packed cells that form a shell around the immature egg, or oocyte. The maturing follicles lead to ovulation and ready the egg for fertilization. Mature follicles are absent in menopause, and there is no ovulation, therefore no possibility of pregnancy. By increasing the number of maturing follicles in the ovary, ashwagandha may help reverse infertility and menopause. This amounts to a hugely positive situation for any woman wishing to rewind the clock safely, and with cancer-protective effects to boot!

✳ Safe Estrogen Spotlight: CoQ10

CoQ10 may increase the number of eggs in your ovaries, reverse your eggs' aging process so they're young again, help increase egg activity, and may significantly increase follicle count, which dramatically stimulates your ovaries and transforms them to their youthful selves.

In an aging woman, menstrual cessation for more than a year is said to be the marker of menopause. Even in the complete absence of hormonal testing, every woman knows what it means to miss her periods for that long. Even if she hated worrying about unwanted pregnancy, and the cramps and bother of monthly periods, it's a rare woman who welcomes this change without any regret, particularly since this absence is accompanied by a very sudden and fast deterioration in her looks.

It has been thought for many decades that a woman's ovaries stop functioning during menopause. They have been shutting down gradually for several years prior to the final shutdown, and with menopause, the process is complete. The ovaries have stopped producing eggs. And they never will again. That was the scientific teaching on menopause, at least until researchers looked at the effects of CoQ10. This natural substance, involved in the energy production of every one of your cells, is an extraordinary example of the interaction between cellular and hormonal function. By revving up the mitochondria, the tiny energy factories in your cells, CoQ10 makes every one of your cells younger. The oocytes in the ovaries contain the highest concentration of mitochondria of any cell in the body, so when you bring back your ovaries' mitochondrial function, they produce more oocytes, and these immature eggs mature into estradiol-producing eggs. Your estradiol levels rise and you successfully reverse menopause. Your whole body is brought back to a youthful, vibrant state.

✳ Safe Estrogen Spotlight: Pomegranate

Pomegranate is a delicious dynamo that possesses estradiol while protecting you from cancer of all types, including the hormone-sensitive versions. Pomegranate juice has been studied extensively and may help prevent heart disease, clear plaque from arteries, and dissolve blood clots. These conditions, by the way, are typical complications associated with synthetic hormone use.

Pomegranate contains a compound with the same shape as human estradiol, producing the whole spectrum of anti-aging effects that this hormone is capable of. Pomegranate has been shown to lift depression and strengthen bone. Most people have noticed that they tend to gain weight in middle age, when hormones are declining, but pomegranate stops this weight gain in its tracks by restoring hormonal function to youthful levels. This is particularly exciting with respect to that impossible-to-shift abdominal fat that signals the development of serious conditions such as heart disease and diabetes. Pomegranate also protects you against breast cancer and prevents metastases.

Pomegranate has significant beneficial effects on the female reproductive system. Pomegranate extract and oil reverse vaginal atrophy, and directly applying these to vaginal tissues further enhances the effect. It can also lift and firm your breasts! Just as hormones kept your breasts firm and lifted at thirty years old, they should do so again when you reverse hormonal aging with the right herbs and nutrients. You didn't need to do special exercises when you were thirty to keep the youthful outline of your breasts, and you don't need to now, when you reverse your hormonal aging. But exercise can speed up the process and increase the benefits of the natural substances you use, so I still recommend you do. Exercise has many benefits, including better cellular respiration and function.

☀ Safe Estrogen Spotlight: Vitamin E

As long ago as 1948, vitamin E was shown to reverse menopause. Rita S. Finkler was one of the earliest researchers to study vitamin E's relationship to menopause. She and her colleagues investigated vitamin E's effect on the uteri of aged rats and found that while normal chronological aging led to the uterus's atrophy and darkening, vitamin E administration reversed this atrophy and produced a youthful pink uterus again. These de-aged rats were even able to bear offspring! This astonishing research was largely forgotten and ignored until very recently, when research groups all over the world began carrying out new studies examining the effects of natural substances such as herbs and vitamins on menopausal models. And more recent research is confirming Finkler's initial findings. Vitamin E has beneficial estrogenic properties, restoring the uterus to its youthful functioning and increasing its weight, thereby reversing uterine atrophy. In one study, thanks to vitamin E, uterine weight increased 9.6 times—this is major, because such atrophy is the hallmark of menopause, so you are seeing an actual reversal of the condition here. Again, ovariectomy, or the removal of ovaries, is used as an animal model for human menopause. Since scientists can't measure uterine weight while a woman is still alive, animal models are sometimes used.

Some studies have created confusion and unnecessary fear in the general public about using antioxidants such as vitamin E. But perceived issues truly stem from a misunderstanding of basic organic chemistry and the fact that the vitamin E molecule can assume different shapes. A molecule's ability to take on different shapes is known in chemistry as stereoisometry, and the different shapes themselves are stereoisomers. Special isomers known as enantiomers also exist. Enantiomers are mirror images of one another. The difficulties produced by using the incorrect enantiomer can be illustrated if you imagine a right-handed glove and its mirror image, the left-handed glove. The right-handed glove is the natural vitamin E in this case, and the mirror image is the synthetic vitamin E. Vitamin E acts on receptors in your cells.

Imagine that these receptors are right hands, designed to work when the right-handed glove fits over them. It's obvious that the left-handed glove will not fit over the right hand, the receptor. The synthetic vitamin E (the left-handed glove) will never work—which once again goes to show that natural solutions are always your best bet.

The ability of a compound to exist in these different shapes is called chirality. Many natural substances are strongly chiral, with vitamin E among them. Synthetically made vitamins, amino acids, and so on, are formed as a mixture of the possible shapes, which is why synthetic vitamins often produce negative results. The thing is, this problem does not only exist in the field of vitamins and other supplements. It is of vital importance in drug design and can have serious consequences.

All this is to say that you should always use *natural* vitamin E for safe and healthy results. You will recognize it by the name *d*-alpha tocopherol. Do *not* use the synthetic, or unnatural, vitamin E, which you will recognize by the name *dl*-tocopherol, *dl*-tocopheryl acetate, or *all-rac* tocopheryl acetate. *All-rac* means that the vitamin E contains a racemic mixture of vitamin E compounds. *Racemic* means that all the possible shapes of vitamin E are included. Imagine a mixture of left-handed gloves, right-handed gloves, and all kinds in between, with some, but not all, the fingers in the correct place.

Here's a terrific example of how vitamin E can achieve antiaging benefits against all odds. In one study, researchers examined vitamin E's effects on ovary atrophy due to lead-related damage. We know that lead is a powerful disruptor of the hypothalamic-pituitary axis and can cause drastically reduced levels of gonadotropin. This produces terrible disturbances to the reproductive organs—the ovaries', fallopian tubes', and uterus's weight all drastically decrease, which indicates significant atrophy. This atrophy is further observed in the greatly reduced follicle numbers and size. In practice, this means that lead reduces fertility in women and increases miscarriage. However, when vitamin E was given together with lead acetate in an animal model of this scenario, every one of these terrible effects was prevented! Yes, you read that right—the entire reproductive system's function, which would have been seriously damaged by lead, was protected by vitamin E in its natural form.

As I've said, vitamin E can also help with vaginal atrophy, which is a condition associated with menopause and post-breast-cancer treatment because both are affected by lowered estrogen levels. Yet natural vitamin E, either taken internally or applied directly, has been shown to restore vaginal tissue to its youthful state, plus produce the thickening and sponginess that characterize biologically youthful vaginas. Significantly, researchers have found that women who experience vaginal atrophy also have low levels of vitamin D, because of its close hormonal interactions.

There are other compounds, called tocotrienols, that act in similar ways to vitamin E, a tocopherol. Tocotrienols stop hot flashes, for example. In many ways, tocotrienols appear even more potent than the tocopherols when it comes to anti-aging benefits. Tocotrienols clear arteries and stimulate fibroblasts to produce collagen. The richest sources of tocotrienols are rice bran oil and red palm oil. Rice bran oil contains gamma oryzanol, which possesses estrogenic activity and powerfully protects your skin against sun damage. Red palm oil, as you can tell from its beautiful orange color, is rich in natural carotenoids and also guards your skin against sun damage. Red palm oil also has the extraordinary ability to protect your telomeres and so produces a whole range of anti-aging effects.

And as for any cancer concerns, natural vitamin E is strongly protective against all kinds of cancer, including the hormonally sensitive types. In fact, women whose diets contain the highest concentration of tocopherols and tocotrienols enjoy significant protection from breast cancer.

✳ Safe Estrogen Spotlight: Royal Jelly

Worker bees live six weeks. Queen bees live five years. The difference is royal jelly! The queen begins life as any normal, short-lived bee. With one major, life-changing difference: once she has been selected to be the queen, she is fed only royal jelly. She is completely transformed. She becomes the only bee in the hive with developed ovaries, and lays up to two thousand eggs per day. This is an extraordinary effect, and, hardly surprisingly, it has inspired many women, and men, to add the amazing royal jelly to their anti-aging program.

So can it work for you? Absolutely. Royal jelly does stimulate hormonal function in a woman, and it does make her look and function like a woman who is decades younger. And much like the case of the queen bee, royal jelly increases the rate and number of mature eggs in a woman's ovaries and makes them more viable—that is, younger. What's more, research carried out in Japan has shown that royal jelly has highly potent and beneficial estrogenic properties in the human body, and is able to thicken the uterine lining. A thin uterine lining is yet another consequence of the low estrogen levels in menopause. A thick, healthy uterus is essential for fertility, reproductive health, and youthfulness.

So what are you waiting for? Become the queen bee—turn the clock back by decades!

BIO-YOUNG TREATMENTS

Please choose preparations based on ease of availability, cost, and personal preference. One is sufficient for treating this anti-aging mechanism, but two or more can speed improvements or improve a particularly neglected situation. Each one uses an ingredient discussed in this chapter. Enjoy!

Panax ginseng, also known as Korean red ginseng: Do not substitute Siberian, American, or any other type of ginseng. This root works in any form—take it in capsules, powdered, or as a liquid extract or tincture (alcoholic extract). With capsules, take ten to twenty a day. If you are using powder, take three teaspoons, three times a day. Take six teaspoons of a tincture's liquid extract three times a day.

CoQ10: Take 250 mg CoQ10 capsules, three times a day, with some form of fat or oil because it is oil-soluble. Most capsules contain some kind of oil already, but if you buy CoQ10 in powder form, just mix half a teaspoon in olive oil once a day.

Folic acid: Take two 400 mcg (micrograms) of folic acid once a day.

Ashwagandha: Take ten capsules of ashwagandha twice a day. In tincture form, take two teaspoons twice a day.

Royal jelly: Buy fresh royal jelly or capsules that contain the fresh preparation. Take six capsules a day. Freeze-dried royal jelly has many benefits, too, but it may not give quite as good results as the fresh kind, so take ten a day here. If you are allergic to bee products, do not use royal jelly.

Vitamin E oil or lanolin (external use): Apply half a teaspoon or less of these two products, once or twice a day, directly to the vagina to restore vaginal tissues by thickening them and making them spongy and moist. Vitamin E oil and lanolin, mixed together in a ratio of 1:1, make a wonderful preparation. At first, it will look as if they won't easily mix, but keep stirring until you get a spreadable cream. You don't need to use heat.

Vitamin E (internal use): Take 800 IU of a natural vitamin E daily. You can also buy wheat germ oil that's suitable for internal use and take two to six teaspoons per day. You can divide this dose up, so that you take one dessert-spoonful three times a day rather than three all at once. Rice bran oil or red palm oil can be taken for their tocotrienols at a dose of four teaspoons a day.

Pomegranate: Buy pomegranate powder in 500 gram or 1 kg lots and take ten teaspoons a day. Buy unsweetened and unflavored pomegranate juice and drink 100 ml a day. Pomegranate seed oil is available but expensive, so consider the powder or juice instead.

Melatonin: Raise melatonin levels with one of these foods, twice a day, every day: 200 ml of pineapple juice, 200 ml of orange juice, a handful of walnuts, three bananas, eight teaspoons of tomato paste, 100 ml of tart cherry juice, 15 grams of oats, or 150 ml of beer. Use 30 drops of cedarwood atlas essential oil to 100 ml of coconut base oil on your wrists at bedtime.

Kudzu starch: Pour four teaspoons of the starch into a mug, add pineapple juice, stir well, and drink it as soon as you prepare it, since kudzu may thicken the juice.

CHAPTER 11

Rev Your Sex Appeal

ANTI-AGING MECHANISM: Simulating the effects of ovulation

USE: Enhancing sexual attractiveness

STARRING: Evening primrose oil, fennel, fenugreek, mango butter, sandalwood essential oil

'd like to send you off with uplifting news about your libido and sex appeal. You are already alluring, delightful, and beautiful in every way, but this chapter will add a few finishing touches to your anti-aging regimen to make you truly enchanting. Consider it the chocolate frosting on an already gooey, sticky, gorgeous cupcake! Yes, you need to have all your bases covered. Yes, you should be stimulating fibroblasts, activating SIRT1, stimulating stem cells, elongating those telomeres, and reversing menopausal changes. But with a few more special plants, oils, supplements, nutraceuticals, and bioceuticals, you will be as irresistible as you can be in every possible way. *Va-va-va-voom.*

Get the Allure of Ovulation, Even If You're Not Ovulating

When women ovulate, it gives them an instant magnetism that men can't resist. Guys are very sensitive to this. They pick up on tiny, almost invisible cues that tell them everything they need to know about a woman, things she may not even be aware of herself. Of course, they don't *know* that they know. But they do. I call this the Lap Dancer Factor, because the study that brought this to the public's attention was carried out on lap dancers. The researchers found that lap dancers receive bigger tips when they are ovulating. Can you imagine?

Ovulation makes you super-alluring because you are fertile, feeling randy, and possibly even acting in an enticing way that sends men this signal. It also makes you very productive on every level—intellectually, physically, emotionally. But let me be clear—*you do not have to actually ovulate to experience this surge in beauty and energy.* This chapter introduces you to some very special herbs and oils that create an "as if" situation in your body that safely gives you the magnetism of a fertile, ovulating, young woman at her best time of the month.

Both men and women respond to ovulation—men are powerfully attracted to a fertile, youthful female, while a woman who is ovulating feels sexier, more sexual, and more turned on than at any other time. During this time, the two genders are in perfect harmony. But it seems a pity to have this scenario last only once a month. By using completely safe herbs and oils, it is easy to create the type of libido that ovulation gives you every day of the month, for the rest of your life.

We can do this by zeroing in on an essential fact. When you ovulate, progesterone levels are at the lowest point of your entire menstrual cycle. But your estrogen levels? They're at the highest level they'll ever reach! Mimicking this situation produces the surge of energy, sexuality, and allure that men respond to and you're driven to initiate. By increasing your estrogen to Lap Dancer Factor levels, the estrogen may stimulate pheomelanin in your skin, which helps make your complexion rosy and add oomph to hair follicles for a rich and vibrant result. You can experience the joy, energy, optimism, and flirty playfulness that come so easily when a woman is at her most fertile.

If you consider the role of biology in the survival of our species, and the part estrogen plays, this hormone is a must. The biological imperative for any species is survival, dependent on successful reproduction. A fertile, ovulating woman is at her alluring, bewitching best because estrogen makes her so. Biology demands it and helps her every step of the way. Perhaps that's why many things happen when you use natural substances to raise your estrogen, just as when you ovulate. Your skin can glow and produce feminine pink tones in your complexion. It will help make your breasts fuller. It can increase your energy to its most productive, creative level. It can help make you, obviously and visibly, the most gorgeous version of yourself. You may also be more attracted to men with chiseled chins, low voices, broad shoulders, and muscular thighs. This is especially fun when you consider a study that says you'll find yourself more likely to wear revealing clothing. Your own voice might also sound more attractive to both men and women when you are ovulating—or we can surmise, when your body's estrogen levels are restored to a comparable level. As women age, their voices can become deeper and rougher. This age-associated change can be prevented or reversed when you follow the program outlined in this book, and include the suggestions given in this chapter.

Appreciate Your Prostaglandins

The term *prostaglandin* is derived from the prostate gland, because prostaglandins were first isolated from semen. But prostaglandins are hormones that are not produced by glands. Rather, they are synthesized in situ—directly in the tissue where they are needed, as needed. Prostaglandins are involved in the contraction and relaxation of smooth muscle, such as the uterus. Certain prostaglandins are responsible for painful periods. And they are absolutely essential for ovulation to occur. They stimulate the release of estrogen, which then sets off the entire ovulation series of events.

Estrogen is essential for ovulation. It affects the ovaries directly by stimulating them. Prostaglandins enable this to occur. The way they enable estrogen to produce its effects on hormonally sensitive tissue is not yet entirely understood, but it is clear that prostaglandins are essential for estrogenic effects on the ovaries. This has implications for fertility, since the role of prostaglandins in female infertility has been largely ignored. Prostaglandins most likely play a very important controlling role, keeping estrogenic effects within safe limits. Obviously, this also has implications for breast cancer and other hormonally sensitive cancers. Further, the interaction between prostaglandins and estrogen explains why some herbs, oils, and supplements do not possess direct estrogenic properties yet display estrogenic activity—they may be exerting their activity via prostaglandins.

Prostaglandins act via cyclic adenosine monophosphate, or cAMP. The cAMP enables biological molecules, hormones, or neurotransmitters to produce their effects. Prostaglandins depend on cAMP for their activity. In turn, sex hormones such as testosterone or estrogen sometimes depend on prostaglandins for their activity. Forskolin, an herbal extract from a plant in the mint family, is a very powerful inducer of ovulation and works by stimulating cAMP. However, it can also raise testosterone, and some women suffer a masculinizing effect as a result. It depends on a woman's own testosterone levels. A woman whose levels are high already will suffer unwanted side effects, such as facial hair or a lowering of the voice, whereas a woman who has lower testosterone levels will not.

Because ovulation is a prostaglandin-dependent process, evening primrose oil simulates its effects. It is a very rich source of gamma-linolenic acid, or GLA, which acts as a precursor to one of the prostaglandins but works one step further along the activity pathway than cAMP, and so does not produce excess facial hair or a lowering of the voice. Evening primrose oil has quite substantial prostaglandin E1 (PGE1) activity, too. By acting via PGE1 rather than directly on sex hormones, it improves sexual functioning and sex hormone effects in women.

Evening primrose oil's benefits, whether the oil is taken internally or applied externally, are seemingly endless. It leads to smoother skin, a lessening of facial hair, increased fertile mucus, and a happy disposition. Women who experience breast pain during their periods find great relief when they use evening primrose oil. It increases breast size without the risk of cancer by increasing fat and glandular tissue in this area and thus lends bounce and lift. Judy Graham, one of the first authors to bring evening primrose oil to the public's attention, described its benefits for multiple sclerosis and admitted that a positive "side effect" of this oil was impressive, fast-growing breasts (and they stay this way even after you stop taking it). It is highly effective against eczema, producing smooth, pretty skin all over. It irons out wrinkles and sags and gives your skin softness and glow. Applied to the hair or taken daily as a supplement, evening primrose encourages shiny, long, healthy hair, too. And all of this because it stimulates ovulation, and acts in an "as if" manner for any woman, at any age, at any time of the month! It also stops hot flashes during menopause with impressive speed.

To Up Your Sexy, Lower Your DHT

As we discussed in earlier chapters, DHT, or dihydrotestosterone, is a male hormone responsible for many of the male aging processes, including baldness and prostate issues, but women suffer from DHT effects as they get older, too. In women, DHT produces thinning hair, unwanted facial and body hair growth, a gaunt face, visible veins on the arms and neck, ovulation difficulties, urinary problems, and shrinking breasts. I don't think I'm going out on a limb here by saying that none of these traits will make you feel particularly self-confident or desirable. Fortunately, all can be corrected and reversed.

One of the fastest ways to help lower DHT is to include pumpkin seed oil in your regimen. This delicious oil, usually sold lightly toasted, can be poured over salads or added to smoothies (though it is savory and may not blend well with banana!). Because of its anti-DHT activity, pumpkin seed oil can be very effective for hair regrowth on the scalp while abolishing hair growth on the face. Since DHT interferes with ovulation, pumpkin seed oil can amp up allure and lend your face a lovely roundness.

Lowering DHT is of huge importance for some women. Not every woman experiences its startling effects as she gets older, but many do, and these effects can be very distressing. Women feel unfeminine when DHT exerts its masculinizing outcomes, so it's good to know that natural substances are so helpful at inhibiting this hormone. Shaving, waxing, and other direct methods of hair removal can work locally to decrease unwanted hair, but the underlying hormonal imbalance will continue if you don't correct it. All the

DHT-related symptoms I mentioned earlier involve falling estrogen levels. Kudzu, also known as kuzu, is Japanese arrowroot, known in Latin as *Pueraria montana*. It is a close relative of *Pueraria mirifica*, which has powerful estrogenic Lap Dancer Factor activity. Kudzu shares this activity, and, like *Pueraria mirifica*, kudzu is very effective at lowering DHT.

Mango butter is also a wonderful facial and hair treatment if you have unwanted facial hair or thinning hair on your head. You can use this butter on your breasts, too, with very good results!

Who Needs Perfume? You Have Your Own Sexy Smell!

You might think that the way you smell can't possibly make a difference to how you look in a Facebook profile or online dating site picture. And it's true that you can't actually smell anyone through an image. But you can see the effect of pheromones very clearly. And certain herbs are so rich in plant pheromones that they are capable of making you the most sexual version of yourself, ever. Much of this is attributed to how natural plant scents affect your hormones, in terms of their effects on your skin's texture and bloom, as well as your sexuality via receptors found in your skin.

Copulins are sex pheromones found in vaginal secretions. To put it poetically, copulins are "the scent of a woman," and they turn men on. Don't take my word for it—scientists measured it and found that men's testosterone increased when they were exposed to copulins. The study showed that men exposed to copulins showed a significant increase in risk taking and displayed much higher levels of aggression and dominance than men who were not exposed to copulins. A woman releases copulins during ovulation, and they increase sexual desire in any man in her proximity. So you can see that an ovulating woman—or one who uses naturally estrogenic means to return her body to a similar state—sends out sexual signals on every level. In addition to all the changes she undergoes during this time—from fuller lips to an inclination to wear revealing clothes—you now know her physical scent changes, too. A youthful biology really is on your side when it comes to sex appeal!

What's more, new research also finds that your nasal passage isn't the only smell receptor in your body. Recent data show that your skin contains scent receptors that can "smell" a compound isolated from sandalwood oil when it is applied directly to the skin. Plus, when your scent receptors are activated in the skin, it stimulates keratinocyte activity that makes your skin younger as a result. And wouldn't you know, this happens even more during ovulation. The compound used in this study was just one active compound isolated from sandalwood oil, and the version the researchers used was synthetic, known as Sandalore. But you can do even better, and give your skin a whole symphony of active sandalwood compounds, by applying this gorgeous oil in its natural form, in a suitable oil base, to your face and body, because sandalwood acts as an aphrodisiac for women and raises copulins.

If you are wondering what real, live copulins actually smell like, the two main components are acetic and butyric acids. That means plain old distilled vinegar and slightly rancid butter are also a good approximation of a sexy, beguiling scent that tantalizes all men. Hard to believe, isn't it? I definitely prefer sandalwood, and I think you will, too! Unfortunately, sandalwood oil is native to India and was once primarily sourced from Indian trees until they were named an endangered species. Fortunately, it is still abundant in Australia. Patchouli is a wonderful oil to use as an alternative, because it has similar properties to sandalwood; you can easily substitute one for the other.

And while we're speaking of Eastern traditions that can rev your sex appeal, I suggest you add breast massage to your regimen, because direct stimulation of breast tissue and blood flow can cause breasts to grow. You may also want to invest in geisha balls, or ben wa balls as they're called in China, to strengthen pelvic floor muscles. Make sure to carefully read the instructions and consult with your gynecologist first. You can choose from many versions, including weighted ones, which provide a very good workout. These are much more fun than Kegel exercises and will help protect you against, and may even reverse, vaginal atrophy, womb prolapse, and urinary incontinence.

Now I'd like to move on to the natural substances that can improve your sex appeal—particularly fenugreek and fennel, pineapple juice, safflower oil, ylang-ylang essential oil, dang gui, and shatavari. And as you know, treatments that use all of these ingredients are found at the end of the chapter.

✳ Get Sexy Spotlight: Fenugreek and Fennel

Fennel possesses significant estrogenic properties, and with respect to ovulation, it has been shown to promote folliculogenesis and an increased number of growing ovarian follicles; it is also thought that fennel accomplishes this via the compound diosgenin, as well. Diosgenin was originally isolated from wild yam, or in Latin *Dioscorea villosa*, which gave the compound its name. Other plants contain diosgenin, with sarsaparilla among them, but neither wild yam nor sarsaparilla produces quite the same feminine allure as fennel and fenugreek do, most likely because they also contain compounds that interfere with this inviting effect. Even better, fennel essential oil, known as sweet fennel, enhances the effect of taking fennel powder. And because your skin and hair possess estrogen receptors, this wonderful oil will produce anti-aging effects on your face, arms, breasts, and hair when it is directly applied to these areas. If you apply fennel essential oil diluted in a base oil, or a treatment containing licorice, directly to your vagina, let's just say that your G-spot may find you. You just might discover a highly charged sensitivity of a level that you may have never known before. Fenugreek also contains diosgenin and shares fennel's wonderful properties. Though not as effective as evening primrose oil, both fennel and fenugreek may enhance the breast's look and roundness. In fact, harem women used fenugreek exactly for this purpose, and they knew a thing or two about womanly allure.

☀ Get Sexy Spotlight: Ylang-Ylang Essential Oil

Based on my own and my clients' experiences, I can attest to the fact that this oil acts in ways that are similar to fenugreek and fennel oils. Being an essential oil, ylang-ylang must be used externally only. Mix it with a primrose oil base and use on your face, breasts, and stomach to bring out your inner allure and outer beauty. If you mix it into your hair, your locks can shine and have blond undertones.

☀ Get Sexy Spotlight: Dang Gui

I have never come across a woman who didn't love this herb. It possesses a distinct, strong scent that's quite attractive, but its effects are what make this herb truly memorable. The Latin name for dang gui, also known as dong quai, is *Angelica sinensis,* which means Chinese angelica, and this herb is a relative of our own angelica that was once eaten candied and used for decorating cakes! Dang gui possesses estrogenic activity. It helps increase uterine weight and can reverse vaginal atrophy in an animal model of menopause. Because of this, it can make you feel turned on to life and love. It may also protect you against breast cancer and stops hot flashes in their tracks.

✳ Get Sexy Spotlight: Shatavari

The root of this herb, *Asparagus racemosus* or *Asparagus adscendens*, is a relative of our own asparagus and has been used in Ayurvedic medicine as a very special treatment for more than a thousand years. The Taoist masters used shatavari, known as tian men dong in Chinese medicine, as a royal herb to increase longevity and it was reputed to bestow a cheerfulness and sweet disposition on anyone who took it. The root was sold in whole pieces that jellified on storage and offered a chewy, slightly sweet treat. I particularly love the herb's reputation in the Ayurvedic system. Its name, *shatavari*, means "she who possesses a hundred husbands." If that's not sex appeal in action, I don't know what is.

Shatavari displaces estrogen at estrogen receptors, which means it has direct estrogenic activity. It increases breast growth and uterus weight. Since your body has estrogen receptors everywhere, including the brain, you will find with shatavari, exactly as with all of the natural substances recommended in this chapter, that these special herbs and oils reach multiple body systems. It will help you feel playful, optimistic, energetic, and of course, sexually magnetic as well.

BIO-YOUNG TREATMENTS

Please choose preparations based on ease of availability, cost, and personal preference. One is sufficient for treating this anti-aging mechanism, but two or more can speed improvements or improve a particularly neglected situation. Each one uses an ingredient discussed in this chapter. Enjoy!

Evening primrose oil: Buy two bottles, keep one in the fridge to take internally, and take three teaspoons, divided into three doses, a day. Use the other bottle for external use as a base.

Sweet fennel essential oil: Add 30 drops of this to 100 ml of evening primrose oil and use this preparation on your face, body, breasts, and hair before shampooing once or twice a day.

Ylang-ylang essential oil: If you choose to use both sweet fennel and ylang-ylang, then halve the quantity given above. Use 15 drops of sweet fennel oil and 15 drops of ylang-ylang oil in 100 ml of evening primrose oil. Apply all over. Use more frequently on your face, if possible.

Fenugreek powder and fennel seed powder: Take six teaspoons of each herb powder every day. Divide the dose into three lots. Make sure you mix the dry powder with the water very well. Let it stand for a few moments if necessary, then stir again. If you find them easier to take singly, do that. Six spoonfuls each daily will bring the best, and fastest, results, but if you only manage four, that will certainly work, too. Just take as much of these powders as you can!

Shatavari: Simmer two teaspoons of shatavari powder in a cup of milk and drink while still warm. Add honey to sweeten, if you'd like. Delicious! My favorite supplier for this is Pukka Herbs.

Dang gui: Buy a dang gui tincture online and take four teaspoons a day.

Pumpkin seed oil: I love the taste of this oil and take it straight from the spoon, but you can sprinkle this over your salads if you prefer. Use four to six teaspoons a day.

Kudzu: Dissolve four teaspoons in a half cup of water and drink. Don't let this stand too long, as it will thicken. You can also make a lovely, simple pudding by bringing kudzu to a boil with juice or water, simmering gently, stirring all the time. Add honey to make it a dessert.

Mango butter: Buy a tub of this wonderful, rich butter online and use on your face as a moisturizer. You can use it on your hair before you wash it, too.

Sandalwood essential oil: Try this on its own or use 15 drops in 100 ml of base oil such as evening primrose. You can mix and match with ylang-ylang and sweet fennel, making sure your total number of drops of essential oils does not rise above 50 in 100 ml of base oil.

Part III

THE *BIO-YOUNG* PROGRAMS

CHAPTER 12

Roxy's Ultimate *Bio-Young* Plan and My Personal Plan

Thus far, you've done all you can to learn about the incredible natural solutions that can help make you biologically younger on cellular and hormonal levels. You are armed with enough information to try and slow down and reverse the aging process, and I hope that after trying a few *Bio-Young* treatments, you are realizing that age really is just a number. There is a huge body of scientific research that proves anti-aging is possible, and you're the living and breathing proof. Are you ready to take this a step further?

In the next five chapters, I'll present various plans that you can follow for whatever purpose you might wish to achieve. You can choose to follow just one plan for the rest of your life, change plans as your needs change, or mix and match to address where you are in the aging process.

Following is the Ultimate *Bio-Young* Plan, which I use most often for my anti-aging clients, as well as My Personal Plan, which I use every day on myself.

Roxy's Ultimate *Bio-Young* Plan

Maca: Four teaspoons for curves and bone strength.

Fennel and/or fenugreek powder: Four teaspoons.

Ashwagandha and shatavari: Four teaspoons.

Boron: 9 mg.

Natural vitamin E: 800 IU per day.

Folic acid: 800 mcg per day.

Evening primrose oil (internally): Four teaspoons.

Avocado oil: Six teaspoons.

Fennel, dill seed, ylang-ylang, and aniseed essential oils for the whole body: Add 50–100 drops each of these essential oils to 250 ml of unrefined, organic if possible, avocado oil, goose fat, emu oil, or lard, and use this twice a day all over. This addresses aging on your face, body, and hair. Use it everywhere but the eye area; here use the same oils, but reduce the essential oil concentration to 10 drops each and use 150 ml of avocado oil. If you're sensitive, reduce essential oils to 30 drops each.

Jojoba oil: Apply a thin layer every day for skin rescue, particularly around the eyes and as a makeup remover.

Amla, gotu kola, and coconut oil treatment: Apply a thin layer every day.

Sodium lactate liquid (60 percent): Apply a thin layer every day.

Rosemary and eucalyptus globulus essential oils: Use 20–30 drops every day before shampooing hair. In addition, use a pre-shampoo treatment of 50 drops of fennel essential oil to 100 grams of goose fat or lard, or 100 ml of jojoba oil or avocado oil.

Frozen blueberries or cherries: Eat at least 250 grams every day.

My Personal Daily Basic Plan

Royal jelly: Six to ten capsules (Regina is a good make) in three doses. This can be taken all at once if this is more convenient *or* two large spoonfuls of fresh royal jelly.

Rice bran oil: Three tablespoons (in three doses).

Evening primrose oil: Two teaspoons (or 6–8 capsules) a day.

Pomegranate oil: Two to three teaspoons (or 6–8 capsules).

Panax ginseng powder: Two large spoonfuls.

Resveratrol skin treatment: I use a fruit juice rich in resveratrol such as pure, unsweetened pomegranate juice and apply it to my face, neck, and arms at least twice a day. I leave this on for as long as possible, but at least five minutes, before rinsing off and following with amla and gotu kola cream.

Amla and gotu kola cream: I apply this twice a day on my face, neck, and arms.

Avocado oil with fennel and ylang-ylang essential oils: I use this treatment all over my body before I shower or bathe, and on my hair before I shampoo. I leave this treatment on for thirty minutes.

CHAPTER 13

Mini Programs for Fast Results

This chapter will calm your panic and boost your beauty for a special event that looms on the horizon. A first date coming up this weekend, a romantic getaway with your partner, the school reunion, a vacation by the sea, or a ski break—all of these present special challenges, and a great deal of stress if you don't feel or look good. It's important to note that the major problem that all of the situations in this section share is *time*—specifically, not enough! I hope it goes without saying, then, that these plans are terrific for any occasion that demands you look your best in a pinch. Short and sweet, my Mini Programs for Fast Results address as many issues as possible, as fast as possible, while using the smallest number of products available. And while all the programs here can be used by women of any age, they do not aim to repair every possible aging problem; instead, they address most of the issues very well, and are not too heavy for young skins or too light for older skins.

These programs are designed to be followed exactly, but it is absolutely fine as you become more familiar with natural substances and their revolutionary anti-aging effects to mix and match, and add more items from various chapters in this book to suit your needs.

The First Date Mini Program

You've just met someone special who gets your heart racing and makes you smile for no reason, or rather, for the best reason of all—you are happy. So much so that you can't sleep, you don't feel hungry, and you're counting the moments until that magical first date. But then you wake up midweek with bags under your eyes (from thinking about your night out), pale and drawn (from not eating), and looking twice your age (from not using my program yet). That is not ideal! But help is at hand. Follow steps 1–3 below for instant radiance. In a day or two, you'll be ready to go!

Clarify. When you have only a day or so to look great, you want a clear, fresh complexion as fast as possible, which is where proteasome activators come in. Baking yeast granules are amazing. Place two teaspoons of baking yeast from the baking section of the grocery store into a container, add enough warm water to make a spreadable paste, wait until you get bubbles, then apply to your face and neck. If you would like to extend the treatment to your arms and décolletage, please do so, but do it in the shower or the bath! Leave the yeast on your skin for five to ten minutes to work its magic, then rinse off. If you have substantial photo damage, use tomato paste instead. Spread it on your face, neck, arms, and breasts in the shower or the bath for clear, bright, radiant skin. Leave on for five minutes, then rinse off. Both of these treatments will help leave your skin soft, radiant, refreshed, and looking young!

Plump up with squalene. Apply a thin layer of this skin smoother, three times a day, to enhance your glowing skin so that on the day of that date, you will look gorgeous!

Treat your hair. Give your crowning glory a deep conditioning treatment to make it silky to the touch by the weekend. Lard may sound unusual but it is one of the most effective treats you can give your hair. It helps your hair grow and stops breakage, and helps enhance your natural hair color without disturbing any tints or dyes; and once it's washed off, your hair should gleam so that everyone notices. Smooth one to two teaspoons on your hair, depending on its thickness and length. To enhance effects, add 30 drops each of rosemary and eucalyptus globulus essential oils for every 100 grams of lard, and use that as your pre-shampoo treatment. Lard is solid, but you can heat it gently in a saucepan, take it off the heat, add the essential oils, let it cool, and store. And lard, by the way, washes out very easily. You may shampoo twice if you wish, but you don't need to. If you don't have lard on hand, or would like an alternative, then choose from any of these, which can be combined, if you like: one to two teaspoons of olive oil, avocado oil, red palm oil, or coconut oil, depending on hair thickness and length.

The Romantic Getaway Mini Program

You want to look young and enchanting but you absolutely don't want the process of becoming the most enticing version of yourself to take you away from your lover for long! The trick is to concentrate on maximizing your sex appeal. Everything you pack for this special time should enhance your extraordinary allure. We can do that here in only four steps. Long-term, I suggest you revisit chapter 11 and mix and match until you find your favorite and most effective remedies.

Honey: Use a thin layer in the shower for soft, dewy skin and on hair before you shampoo; as a moisturizing, anti-aging treatment when your face is makeup-free (be sure to wash off after five minutes); and at breakfast, when you can add two teaspoons to your hot tea or yogurt. Applying honey directly to your breasts will instantly help perk them up and make them seem fuller and firmer.

Sandalwood or ylang-ylang scent: This is a very individual preference, but adding 30 drops of either essential oil (or both, if you use 15 drops each) to 100 ml of coconut oil and using this as your moisturizer throughout your romantic getaway will help keep your sex appeal at its peak and make your skin look stunningly young and beautiful, without the slightest danger of under-eye bags. Keep in mind that under-eye bags result from decreased elastin synthesis, but they can be exacerbated by eating animal fats. Choose a chicken breast for dinner, for example, and eat only low-fat dairy. In addition to its significant anti-aging effects, sandalwood will help make you feel sensual, so it's a win-win for you both!

Berries: They are so easy to add to your romantic menu, and their beauty potential is so huge, you should nibble them at every opportunity. It will help your eyes look clear, your skin to glow, and you should feel energized and ready to have fun at any time of day or night! Add 100–200 grams of blueberries, raspberries, or strawberries or 100–200 ml of pomegranate juice to as many meals as you can.

Fennel: Take two teaspoons of this three times a day or more while you're away.

The School Reunion Mini Program

I'm going to assume that even though you will probably know the date of your reunion for some time, about three weeks out you'll be gripped with panic. There seems to be all the time in the world, then suddenly none. The key to this program is that the turnaround time is three weeks, so if you want to anti-age for a job interview or special event in that same window, this program works for those occasions, too!

Red palm oil: This will help give you a beta-carotene glow on your skin, longer telomeres, and skin protection from the sun. Take four tablespoons of red palm oil each day and use a 500 gram pot as a base for an external treatment to which you add 30 drops each of myrrh, fennel, ylang-ylang, and dill seed essential oils. This will help increase elastin (dill seed) in, firm up (myrrh), and visibly anti-age (fennel and ylang-ylang) your skin. Use this mix on your face and body. If you prefer a colorless alternative to red palm oil to use externally, substitute coconut oil in the above skin treatment. Avocado oil is my absolute favorite and may be substituted for red palm oil. Avocado oil helps increase collagen and elastin synthesis and is astonishingly hydrating, and can smooth out wrinkles and lines. I find it more hydrating than coconut or red palm oil, so if your skin is very dry, switch to avocado oil. In that case, use 100 ml of avocado oil as your base and add 20 drops of the essential oils mentioned here. Dill weed (also known as dill) essential oil is fine to use as a substitute for dill seed essential oil.

Lard: Smooth one to two teaspoons on your hair, depending on its thickness and length. This treatment alone should make your hair brighter, and amazingly soft. Even better, add 30 drops of fennel, rosemary, and eucalyptus globulus essential oils to 250 grams of melted lard, store in a wide-mouthed container, and use in the same way as plain lard. (Used regularly, this can make your hair grow faster. But you need to use the treatment at least three times a week, for at least six months, to see appreciable gains in length.) If you would rather use a vegetarian treatment, avocado oil is an excellent alternative. Use the same essential oils as for the lard treatment, in the same proportions, and apply before you shampoo.

Gelatin: Stir four teaspoons of gelatin into pineapple juice or water three times a day. In three weeks' time, your skin should be firmer, your muscles more taut, your hair thicker and shinier, and even your eyes can benefit. As we age, hyaluronic acid production decreases everywhere in our bodies, including our eyes, which can lead to primary open-angle glaucoma, a type of blindness with no known cause. Gelatin has been found to restore levels of hyaluronic acid and reverse the mechanism involved in this condition.

Ashwagandha: This herb will help you radiate youthful gorgeousness. Take two teaspoons twice a day in the three weeks leading up to the reunion. If you prefer ashwagandha capsules, take six capsules twice a day. If you have the tincture, take two teaspoons twice a day. Add it to some juice if you like.

Bee pollen: Take four teaspoons of bee pollen granules twice a day for a golden youthful glow.

Apple cider vinegar: Three weeks is not enough time for substantial weight loss if you are to retain your health and good looks and not end up looking drained. But taking apple cider vinegar, four teaspoons in the morning and at night, can help your body look toned on your big day.

The Sunshine Holiday Mini Program

This program is a little bit less "mini" than the others since sun damage accelerates skin aging so rapidly, but once you are familiar with the steps, it is very easy to follow and highly protective. Of course, as with all suggestions in this chapter, you may consult the appropriate chapter in the book and mix and match as you wish.

Gelatin: This increases collagen in the skin, even after sun exposure. Take two teaspoons of gelatin powder in juice three times a day.

Red palm oil: Carotenoids help protect your skin against sun damage. Take two teaspoons of red palm oil in the morning, at noon, and in the evening for all-day sun protection. You can use red palm oil externally, but you don't need to. It does give skin an orange tint, and there are external treatments that provide excellent sun protection without adding color to your skin.

Tomato paste: Fortunately, this is easy to eat at almost every meal, since tomato-based sauces are very popular. It's enough if you include this skin protector in at least one meal every day.

Cocoa: Use at least four teaspoons of pure cocoa powder as a sun-protecting supplement every day while exposed to the sun. You can add it to hot milk, tea, or coffee.

Squalene: Apply a thin layer of this oil to your skin three times a day.

Amla, gotu kola, and coconut oil: This preparation is for external use, so make it at home and bring it with you. The instructions are given at the end of chapter 4. You can use rice bran oil instead of coconut oil for an added boost of sun protection from the ferulic acid contained in rice bran oil, and you can use amla and gotu kola tinctures instead of the powder. When using tinctures, there is no herb sediment to filter out, but you need to heat the base oil you are using, in this case coconut or rice bran oil, enough to boil off the alcohol that is contained in the tinctures. Take great care when doing this as you could cause a fire or a serious burn. It's best to heat the oil on the back burner of your stove. Leave the lid off and let the alcohol evaporate from the tinctures. The process should be complete after fifteen minutes. Remember to leave the saucepan lid off, so the alcohol can escape!

Rosehip and chamomile oil: In the evening after sunbathing, apply this treatment to take away redness and repair photodamage. To 50 ml of rosehip oil, add 40 drops of German chamomile essential oil. German chamomile oil is soothing.

Estrogenic tonic: It's not a good idea to use essential oils on your skin when you are in the sun, but you don't want to miss out on estrogenic power while on vacation, so make a tonic to take internally. Mix fennel and fenugreek tinctures in a 1:1 ratio, which means if you have 500 ml of fenugreek, you add 500 ml of fennel, mix it, bottle it, and pack it in your suitcase. Take two teaspoons three times a day. You can take this tonic at any age, as long as you are over the legal age limit; if you are trying to conceive, however, you should check everything you plan to take with your doctor. Herbs with estrogenic activity could prevent you from becoming or staying pregnant, so do not use them.

Ski Vacation Mini Program

Being out in the crisp, cold air is an exhilarating experience, but it can wreak havoc on your skin. Cracked, dry skin can bleed and hurt, and certainly needs special care.

Squalene: Apply a thin layer three times a day to keep your skin smooth and soft.

Red palm oil: Take two teaspoons morning, noon, and evening to protect you against the sun damage that snow glare causes. Even your eyes are protected when you take red palm oil internally.

Avocado oil: Use it on your face, hair, and all over your body before a shower. Take two teaspoons a day to keep your skin cold-resistant. Or try an avocado and licorice preparation. Heat 250 ml of avocado oil with three large spoonfuls of licorice root powder for twenty minutes. Let it cool, strain, and bottle, then use all over your body for amazing anti-aging, hair-growing, and skin-smoothing effects. Almond oil is a superb alternative, as it's easily available wherever you are in the world.

Fenugreek and fennel: Mix these two tinctures half-and-half and take six teaspoons a day, divided into three doses.

CHAPTER 14

Treatments by Age

Every suggestion in this book is applicable to you, no matter what age you are. You can't hurt your skin, hair, or any part of your body with the suggestions in this book. But your needs at each age can be different and varied, and they most certainly can change. This section takes those scenarios into account. So what I'll do here is first describe the primary concerns of each age group, and then you can match your age to the specific treatments I suggest for your age group in the chart that follows.

To speak in broad strokes, I like to split anti-aging into three categories: before you're thirty years old, after you're thirty years old, and after you're seventy years old. Until the age of thirty, keeping cellular function optimal is the most important aspect of your anti-aging program, but after thirty, and with accelerating urgency, hormonal activity becomes your most pressing anti-aging strategy. To help you minimize the number of supplements and herbs you need to take every day, you'll focus on those that possess significant hormonal benefits but also possess estradiol-like activity to dramatically improve both cellular and hormonal function. After the age of forty-five, the focus is on using animal fats to improve your skin, wound healing, preventing and reversing sun damage, and repairing the skin barrier, which becomes more prone to damage with age. The skin barrier is easily damaged by drying skin products, harsh washing, sunbathing, and cold weather. After the age of seventy, it's important to remember that it took decades to accumulate the damage that may show on your face, hair, and body, so I ask that you stick with the regime for at least three months before you assess the results. It takes that long for scalp hair regrowth to show, for example. And while skin benefits should be obvious sooner, they will increase the longer you remain on the program.

Ages 18–30

This is the peak of natural health and beauty, although it may not feel like it. Most women are not fortunate enough to have the confidence to enjoy the time when their cellular and hormonal functions are in their prime. It's also typically coupled with late nights, fast food, and perhaps hormonal contraception, which sets the stage for a rather fraught time. Pollution and an unhealthy lifestyle cause significant disruption to health and beauty, which is why smoothies are so popular. Nothing restores cellular energy as fast as raw fruits and vegetables. Some women do, unfortunately, suffer hormonal disturbances even at this age, and I'll address this to some extent in the chart that follows. The good news is, your body should respond fast to even the smallest improvements you make.

Until the age of thirty, the most important aspect of aging that needs to be addressed is cellular function. As we age, cellular function continues to decline, but hormonal decline is added to the problems, until hormonal dysfunction becomes overwhelming in the fifty-and-above age group. After this age, good health and good looks become impossible to achieve without restoring both cellular and hormonal function. Your priorities for now are to activate SIRT1, the longevity gene that turns your youth factor to its maximum potential and dramatically slows the rate at which you age now and for decades to come. The best way to activate SIRT1 is to take advantage of the smoothies and berries available everywhere you go. You must also moisturize lightly and take care of your hair. Your hair should be growing very well at this stage, though if you have recently stopped taking hormonal contraception, or have given birth, your hair might be experiencing slowed growth. Hair loss that occurs postpartum is simply the shedding of hair that didn't fall out during pregnancy, and it is nothing to worry about. But hair loss that follows the cessation of hormonal contraceptives can be more serious. Pay particular attention to any thinning or slow-growing areas. Finally, you will want to activate your proteasomes. Most issues during this time involve inflammation, blocked pores, or breakouts. Proteasome activation is gentle and effective in the treatment of these conditions.

Ages 30–45

This is the time when serious aging begins, and yet most of us are too busy to pay attention. We're so caught up in building homes and careers that it's like one day we wake up and don't recognize the face staring back from the mirror! During these fifteen years, hormones begin to decline quite steeply, yet very few of us realize that our problems are caused by hormonal dysfunction, because the menopausal years haven't begun in earnest. But the truth is that menopause is beginning during this time, and the hormonal decline accelerates as we edge toward forty. So keeping hormonal activity high during this period should significantly slow down and prevent aging. You can keep firm, thick, elastic skin and luxurious hair all your life if you begin to take steps to keep your hormonal levels high at this stage. It doesn't matter if you're at one or the other end of this fifteen-year span. Your skin, muscles, hair, and bones—all parts of you—are beautifully responsive to anti-aging intervention, so enjoy the improvements! You'll want to focus on increasing elastin and collagen levels in your skin, preventing the atrophying of the pretty, plump fat layer, and stopping unwanted hair growth on your face and body by lowering male hormones. SIRT1 activation is also very important at this age. Before thirty, late nights and an inadequate diet didn't hit you too hard, but bad health choices after thirty have a pronounced effect.

Ages 45–55

Hormonal levels take a very serious hit during this time, and it shows. Fine lines deepen into wrinkles, and sagging becomes obvious around the jawline and neck. Upper arms lose their definition, hair becomes thinner, and unwanted hair turns into horrible bristle. There are more upsetting changes, but you don't need me to list them all. At this age, you can't neglect your dipping hormones, because if you do, you will look terrible very quickly and experience a

Age	Skin Clarity (avoid eye area)	Skin Elasticity	Skin Thickness
18–30	Tomato paste, baker's yeast, sake, apple cider vinegar	Internally: gotu kola, vitamin C Externally: vitamin C and glycerin serum (see skin discoloration section in chapter 15)	Internally: coconut oil, evening primrose oil, red palm oil, jojoba oil, tomato paste Externally: rosemary essential oil in a coconut oil base
30–40	Externally: tomato paste, quercetin (oak bark or onion), apple cider vinegar (not on eye area), yogurt	Internally: vitamin C, rosemary herb Externally: dill seed essential oil in a coconut oil base	Internally: tomato paste, gotu kola, cocoa, avocado oil Externally: squalene, red palm oil, aniseed essential oil in a coconut oil base

"crash" in your energy and productivity that won't be corrected until you correct your hormones. Don't forget SIRT1 activation at this age, too, to keep your energy at youthful levels. Pay attention to skin and scalp treatments as well.

Ages 55 and Over

Most women are either going through or have just completed menopause at this age, so hormonal care is crucial. Sleep is a huge issue at this age, which means it's vital to activate melatonin activity. Boost your natural hormone replacement therapy to help keep your face plump and gorgeous, especially in the delicate under-eye area, which is so very prone to looking saggy and wrinkled. Your hair is also thinning here, and you'll want to pay attention to teeth and bones, too, by eating the right foods and using natural substances.

To help you design your own program, the table here provides you with a great starting point. Use it to find the best choice out of every chapter for your age group.

Hair	Cellular Function	Hormonal Function
Pre-shampoo: coconut oil with rosemary and eucalyptus essential oils	Internally: Blueberries, pomegranate juice, tomato paste, gotu kola Externally: gotu kola, amla, rosemary essential oil in a coconut oil base	Internally: evening primrose oil, fenugreek, bee pollen Externally: evening primrose oil
Pre-shampoo: coconut oil with rosemary and eucalyptus essential oils	Internally: blueberries, pomegranate juice, green powder such as spinach, gotu kola, red palm oil, avocado oil Externally: baker's yeast	Internally: fenugreek, kudzu, shatavari Externally: ylang-ylang in evening primrose oil base

Age	Skin Clarity (avoid eye area)	Skin Elasticity	Skin Thickness
40–50	Externally: soy protein or genistein mixed in water or aloe vera gel, hyaluronic acid or related compounds, sodium lactate liquid, or yogurt	Internally: vitamin C, rosemary herb, evening primrose oil Externally: dill seed essential oil, avocado oil, licorice, soy protein or genistein, black cumin oil	Internally: gelatin, tomato paste, cocoa powder Externally: animal fats, sarsaparilla, aniseed essential oil, avocado oil, almond oil, squalene, licorice in lard, comfrey, vitamin E, jojoba oil, rice bran oil
50–60	Externally: rice bran oil, soy protein, genistein, sodium lactate liquid, or yogurt	Internally: vitamin C, rosemary herb, evening primrose oil Externally: rosehip oil, dill seed essential oil in coconut oil base for eye area	Internally: gelatin, tomato paste, cocoa, whey protein Externally: animal fats, sarsaparilla, vitamin E oil, avocado oil, almond oil, squalene, licorice in lard, or in avocado oil, mango butter, jojoba oil, rice bran oil
60–70	Externally: kudzu in aloe vera gel, sodium lactate liquid, or yogurt	Internally: vitamin C, rosemary herb, evening primrose oil Externally: licorice in rosehip oil, with dill seed essential oil added, rice bran oil, black cumin oil	Internally: gelatin, tomato paste, cocoa powder, avocado oil, evening primrose oil Externally: animal fats, sarsaparilla, avocado oil, vitamin E oil, olive squalene, licorice in lard or in avocado oil, comfrey, mango butter, cocoa butter, jojoba oil, rice bran oil
70 and above	Externally: gotu kola in aloe vera gel, sodium lactate, or yogurt	Internally: vitamin C, rosemary herb, evening primrose oil Externally: soy protein or genistein, licorice, and dill seed essential oil in rosehip oil base, black cumin oil	Internally: gelatin, tomato paste, cocoa, avocado oil, evening primrose oil Externally: animal fats, licorice in lard or in avocado oil, almond oil, squalene, sarsaparilla, mango butter, black cumin oil, jojoba oil, rice bran oil

Hair	Cellular Function	Hormonal Function
Pre-shampoo: rosemary and eucalyptus oils in avocado oil	Internally: berries, pomegranate juice, amla, gotu kola, avocado oil, CoQ10 Externally: baker's yeast, red palm oil, rice bran oil, amla, gotu kola, comfrey, myrrh essential oil in a coconut oil base	Internally: vitamin E, maca, ashwagandha, fenugreek, fennel, shatavari Externally: aniseed, fennel, ylang-ylang essential oils in evening primrose oil base
Pre-shampoo: onion blended in avocado oil and strained, rosemary and eucalyptus essential oils, lard, avocado oil Shampoo: add calcium pantothenate to shampoo	Internally: ginkgo, gotu kola, CoQ10, apple cider vinegar, honey, bee pollen, cocoa Externally: rosemary, myrrh, and frankincense essential oils in an avocado oil base	Internally: vitamin E, boron, folic acid, Panax ginseng, ashwagandha, maca, fennel, fenugreek, hops, shatavari Externally: sandalwood, ylang-ylang, aniseed, fennel, cedarwood atlas essential oils in 50:50 evening primrose/avocado oil base
Pre-shampoo mask: soy protein mixed with avocado oil, rosemary, ylang-ylang and eucalyptus essential oils, lard, or avocado oil Shampoo: add calcium pantothenate	Internally: CoQ10, honey, bee pollen, gotu kola, cocoa, apple cider vinegar, amla, avocado oil, walnut oil Externally: amla and gotu kola in a coconut or avocado oil base, red palm oil, avocado oil	Internally: royal jelly, rice bran oil, vitamin E, boron, maca, ashwagandha, Panax ginseng, fennel, fenugreek, folic acid, hops, shatavari Externally: fennel, aniseed, and cedarwood essential oils in 50:50 evening primrose/avocado oil base
Pre-shampoo: rosemary, ylang-ylang and eucalyptus essential oils in lard or avocado oil base Shampoo: add calcium pantothenate	Internally: ginkgo, pomegranate juice or powder, gotu kola, amla, CoQ10, blueberries, cherries or cherry juice, pineapple juice, walnut oil Externally: amla and gotu kola in coconut oil, myrrh and frankincense essential oils in avocado oil	Internally: royal jelly, vitamin E, bee pollen, honey, fennel, fenugreek, maca, boron, folic acid, hops, shatavari Externally: ylang-ylang, fennel, aniseed, and cedarwood atlas essential oils in 50:50 evening primrose/avocado oil base

Top Ten Most Common Concerns—and Their Solutions!

T his chapter provides you with a quick guide to the top ten problems I most often see occur in myself and in my clients as we grow older—along with some fast, effective solutions. For more solutions to age-related concerns, please consult the index.

1. *Acne.* Acne is, in fact, caused by the male hormones, or androgens. It is possible to lower androgenic activity in your body by taking one teaspoon of turmeric powder in water twice a day or drinking three cups of spearmint tea a day. A dab of peppermint essential oil can be applied directly to outbreaks to help dry them up, but be very careful around your eye area, because peppermint makes your eyes sting. If you do get peppermint oil in your eyes, rinse with cool water or apply a little low-fat yogurt and then rinse. Aloe vera is very effective, too—apply a thin layer to your face, massage gently, then rinse with cool water and pat dry. Pure, unsweetened cocoa powder clears acne if you take at least one tablespoon of this—you can mix it with water, milk, or juice. Cocoa powder can also be stirred into yogurt.

2. *Dark circles.* Dark circles are capillaries seen through the thin skin that's under your eyes. Drinking a green juice once a day can

help. Two daily teaspoons of any of the following stirred into juice or water should result in a huge improvement, too: spinach powder, chlorella powder, spirulina, or barley grass. The priority in this condition is to thicken the skin and improve its elasticity. Thirty drops of dill seed essential oil to 100 grams of coconut oil makes a perfect nightly treatment for the eye area, reducing puffiness and dark shadows thanks to dill seed's estrogenic properties, which increase skin thickness and elasticity. The amla, gotu kola, and coconut oil treatment that I refer to a lot is great for this, too. You can also apply pure almond oil as often as you are able, but particularly at bedtime. Licorice and avocado oil can increase elastin and collagen, which makes it very effective for under-eye bags. Simmer four teaspoons of licorice powder (or 10–20 licorice tea bags) in 200 ml of avocado oil, let it cool, strain, and pat on the affected area. It's great for your face, hair, and whole body.

3. *Skin discoloration.* Vitamin C and glycerin serum are very effective for evening out your complexion and fading skin discoloration. Dissolve two teaspoons of pure vitamin C (ascorbic acid) powder in 100 ml of vegetable glycerin. You can do this by adding the vitamin C powder directly to a small bottle of glycerin (I use plastic bottles and jars for safety). Shake well. Add a little water if you can see crystals of vitamin C. Use this lotion at night, on makeup-free skin. Apply all over your face, neck, hands, and any other problem area, leave on for five minutes, and then rinse off and pat your skin dry. Follow this with the amla, gotu kola, and coconut treatment. Onion lotion, prepared by blending half an onion in half a pint of water and straining the liquid, is fantastic for clarifying the skin, fading any dark spots, and making the skin youthful and radiant. Leave the lotion on for five minutes before rinsing off. The onion scent should evaporate, but if not, apply apple cider vinegar to reinforce the effects of the onion and remove the aroma. You can use the apple cider vinegar on

its own, too, omitting the onion lotion. A thin layer of tomato paste is also effective. Rinse off after five minutes. A licorice and avocado oil preparation also fades skin and evens the complexion.

4. *Cellulite.* The easiest way to help tone up limbs and break up cellulite is to use apple cider vinegar every day as a lotion. Apply it neat and use a massage glove afterward to enhance the effect. Instant coffee and horse chestnut tincture are excellent when they are used as a lotion, too.

5. *Gray hair.* Melanocytes, the cells that produce hair color, are stimulated by onion, eucalyptus globulus, red palm oil, avocado oil, and lard. You can use onion juice, which you can make by blending chopped onion with water in a blender, and then straining out the bits. Store this in the refrigerator and use at night or before you shampoo your hair. If you choose eucalyptus, red palm oil, or lard, apply a thin layer and leave them as long as possible before you shampoo. Leave any of these treatments on your hair for half an hour before you shampoo.

6. *Hair loss.* This is easily treated with rosemary and eucalyptus globulus essential oils. Use them straight from the bottle. Apply a few drops of rosemary to your scalp and follow with a few drops of eucalyptus. Do this every night for three months for new growth!

7. *Large pores.* Tomato paste is excellent for reducing pore size. Apply a thin layer to your problem area, leave on for five minutes, and rinse with tepid water. Repeat up to three times a day. This is a wonderful preparation to use before bed, after removing makeup and before your night treatment. Tomato paste is anti-inflammatory, which means it shouldn't irritate your skin, but do not use it on the delicate eye area, just in case. If you do find any discomfort, discontinue use.

8. *Under-eye bags*. Under-eye bags result from slack skin, muscle atrophy, and fat deposits beneath the skin. The amla, gotu kola, and coconut oil treatment mentioned earlier is brilliant for fading the area under your eyes and shrinking any swelling or bags. Use pure coconut or jojoba oil to remove eye makeup. Choose SIRT1 activators to increase collagen and elastin. Two hundred fifty grams of blueberries or other berries daily will help increase the skin's elasticity. These fruits will also prevent excessive fat deposits on your body, including the area under your eyes. Gelatin, whey protein, pea, or brown rice protein, taken internally, increase skin thickness and muscle, and restore and support your face and body, including the delicate under-eye area. Cut animal fats from your diet, and do not use animal fats around your eyes.

9. *Varicose veins*. Veins bulge because they lack elastin. Elastin can be increased directly by applying 30 drops of dill seed essential oil in 100 ml of a coconut oil base on the affected area. Continue the treatment for at least three months. Bee pollen, taken at a dose of four tablespoons a day, strengthens the vein walls significantly.

10. *Wrinkles on forehead and around the mouth*. A thin layer of jojoba oil can be astonishingly effective for deep lines on your face and neck. It's brilliant yet gentle enough to use around the eyes, too! Sodium lactate lotion (60 percent) can work miracles on these lines and creases as well. Apply the lotion, leave on for at least five minutes, and then rinse off.

CHAPTER 16

Customize Your Own Anti-Aging Plan

M any of the substances in this book activate several anti-aging mechanisms at once, often benefiting both cellular and hormonal mechanisms. This makes it possible to use the same natural substance for several purposes, which makes designing your own DIY treatment program easier. You can add several essential oils to a base oil, for example, and use the resulting treatment to help anti-age your under-eye area, your hair, and your body. I frequently use the same formulation for my face, neck, body, and hair, and even my eye area. You can create your own program using your favorite treatments from specialized chapters, *Bio-Young* Treatment boxes at the end of each chapter, or any of the more specific programs in chapters 12 through 14. You know your body better than anyone, so I welcome your interest in creating a custom program that is made entirely for you and by you.

When designing a program, the most important point to remember is the central thesis of this book: aging is the result of the decline in the two essential life processes of the human body—cellular and hormonal function. Keep this in mind, and make sure you use treatments that address these two all-important instigators of aging. Your reward can be fast, visible anti-aging results. Until the age of thirty, the most important anti-aging mechanisms to concentrate on involve cellular function. After this age, and particularly after forty, hormones decline very rapidly, and restoring hormonal function should be your primary focus, while of course keeping cellular function optimal. As you have seen in this book, when you raise hormonal activity in your body, skin, and hair, cellular function should improve, too. You never want to neglect either one of these two vital aspects of anti-aging.

I hope you are excited and encouraged by the range of possibilities that are now available for you to plan your own anti-aging strategies. Just as millions of books are written using only the letters of the alphabet, many possible programs can be designed using the information in this book.

Here are some general guidelines to keep in mind as you make your choices. These are the general areas of concern that bother most women, so I hope they will provide you with useful starting points when you come to design your own program.

• When treating the eye area, make sure that the treatments you apply around your eyes contain a lower concentration of essential oils than your body and hair treatments, and apply them with a gentle touch. Use a third of the essential oil dose recommended for your face, body, or hair when preparing treatments for the delicate area around your eyes.

• Dull, flaky skin benefits from proteasome activation using instant yeast granules (chapter 3) and aquaporin balancing using apple cider vinegar (chapter 7).

• Sagging skin needs fibroblast-stimulating help, provided by elastin synthesis enhancers such as dill essential oil (chapter 2).

• Sun damage is treated with amla, gotu kola, rice bran oil, and rosehip oil (chapter 4).

• The thinning skin that comes with declining levels of estrogen responds amazingly well to fennel, sandalwood, or ylang-ylang essential oils, mixed into an oil base (chapter 11).

• Get rid of flab with ginkgo and apple cider vinegar (chapter 7).

• Make your skin smooth, young, and dewy by stimulating skin stem cells with comfrey (chapter 5).

• Make sure your bone structure provides your face and body with youthful support (chapter 6).

• Grow your hair and make it gorgeous with rosemary and eucalyptus essential oils (chapter 8).

Have fun!

ACKNOWLEDGMENTS

Huge hugs and kisses to my wonderful agent, Dorie Simmonds.

Many thanks to all the lovely people at Atria.

Love and kisses to my hun, Matilda.

Thank you for you, MK. Always.

Love, and everything, forever, to D, D, and O.

REFERENCES

INTRODUCTION

Azzi, Lamia, M. El-Alfy, Celine Martel, and F. Labrie. "Gender differences in mouse skin morphology and specific effects of sex steroids and dehydroepiandosterone." *Journal of Investigative Dermatology* 124 (2005): 22–27.

Babu, P. V., et al. "Therapeutic effect of green tea extract on advanced glycation and cross-linking of tail-tendon collagen in streptozotocin induced diabetic rats." *Food and Chemical Toxicology* 46, no. 1 (2006): 280–85.

Cameron, D. "New study validates longevity pathway." 2013. http://hms.harvard.edu/news/new-study-validates-longevity-pathway-3-7-13.

Carlson, J. R., et al. "Reading the tea leaves: Anticarcinogenic properties of (-)-epigallocatechin-3-gallate." *Mayo Clinic Proceedings* 82, no. 6 (June 2007): 724–32.

Chwan-Li Shen, James K. Yeh, Jay J. Cao, Ming Chien Chyu, and Jia Sheng Wang. "Green tea and bone health: Evidence from laboratory studies." *Pharmacological Research* 64, no. 2 (August 2011): 155–61.

Hyun Chul Goo, Yu-Shik Hwang, Yon Rak Choi, Hyun Nam Cho, and Hwal Suh. "Development of collagenase-resistant collagen and its interaction with adult human dermal fibroblasts." *Biomaterials* 24, no. 28 (2003): 5099–5113.

Kin, J., J. S. Hwang, Y. K. Cho, Y. Han, Y.-J. Jeon, and K.-H. Yang. "Protective Effects of (-)–epigallocatechin–3-gallate on UVA and UVB-induced skin damage." *Skin Pharmacology and Physiology* 14, no. 1 (2001): 11–19.

References

Kwon, O. S., et al. "Human hair growth enhancement in vitro by green tea epigallocatechin-3-gallate (EGCG)." *Phytomedicine* 14, nos. 7–8 (August 2007): 551–55.

Lee, Mak-Soon, Chong-Tain Kim, In-Hwan Kim, and Yangha Kim. "Inhibitory effects of green tea catechin on the lipid accumulation in 3 T3-L1 adipocytes." *Phytotherapy Research* 23, no. 8 (2009): 1088–91.

Lu, Y.P., et al. "Tumorigenic effect of some commonly used moisturising creams when applied topically to UVB-pretreated high-risk mice." *Journal of Investigative Dermatology* 129, no. 2 (2009): 468–75.

Luo, G., Z. Z. Xie, F. Y. Liu, and G. B. Zhang. "Effect of vitamin C on myocardial mitochondrial function and ATP content in hypoxic rats." *Zhongguo Yao Li Xue Bao* 19, no. 4 (July 1998): 351–55.

PhytoCellTec Symphytum. "Speed up your cell renewal through stem cell activation." http://tri-k.com/sites/default/files/PhytoCellTec%20Symphytum%20-%20Brochure%20April%202013.pdf.

Sheng, R., Z. L. Gu, and M. L. Xie. "Epigallocatechin gallate, the major component of polyphenols in green tea, inhibits telomere attrition mediated cardiomyocyte apoptosis in cardiac hypertrophy." *International Journal of Cardiology* 162, no. 3 (January 2013): 199–209.

Twort, C. C., and C. J. M. Twort. "The utility of lanolin as a protective measure against mineral-oil and tar dermatitis and cancer." *Journal of Hygiene* 35, no. 1 (1935): 130–49.

Weinreb, O., et al. "Neurological mechanisms in green tea polyphenols in Alzheimer's and Parkinson's diseases." *Journal of Nutritional Biochemistry* 15, no. 9 (September 2004): 506–16.

Wolfram, S. "Effects of green tea and EGCG on cardiovascular and metabolic health." *Journal of the American College of Nutrition* 26, no. 4 (August 2007): 3735–3885.

Wu, A., Z. Ying, D. Schubert, and F. Gomez-Pinilla. "Brain and spinal cord interaction: A dietary curcumin derivative counteracts locomotor and cognitive deficits after brain trauma." *Neurorehabilitation and Neural Repair* 25, no. 4 (May 2011): 332–42.

Xie, W., C. Sun, and S. Liu. "The effect of hawthorn flavanone on blood-fat and expression of lipogenesis and lipolysis genes of hyperlipidemia model mouse." *Zhongguo Zhong Yao Za Zhi* 34, no. 2 (2009): 224–29.

CHAPTER 1: SUPER SIRTUINS! OR, HOW TO LOOK GREAT ON YOUR 256TH BIRTHDAY

Baur, J. A., et al. "Resveratrol improves health and survival of mice on a high-calorie diet." *Nature* 444, no. 7117 (November 2006): 337–42.

Biodyne TRF Laboratories. Luzerne, Switzerland. http://www.luzern-labs.com/ingredients/

Bonte, F., et al. "Influence of Asiatic acid, madecassic acid and asiaticoside on human collagen I synthesis." *Planta Medica* 60, no. 2 (April 1994): 133–35.

Crowe, M. J., et al. "Topical application of yeast extract accelerates the wound healing of diabetic mice." *Journal of Burn Care and Rehabilitation* 20, no. 2 (March–April 1999): 155–62.

Gohill, Kashmira J., et al. "Pharmacological review on *Centella asiatica*: A potential herbal cure-all." *Indian Journal of Pharmaceutical Sciences* 72, no. 5 (September–October 2010): 546–56.

Guerente, L. "Calorie restriction and sirtuins revisited." *Cold Spring Harbor Symposia on Quantitative Biology* 27 (2013): 2072–85.

———. "Sirtuins in aging and disease." *Cold Spring Harbor Symposia on Quantitative Biology* 72 (2007): 483–88.

Howitz, K. T., et al. "Small molecular activators of sirtuins extend *Saccharomyces cerivisiae* lifespan." *Nature* 425 (2003): 191–96.

"Li Ching-Yun Dead; Gave His Age as 197." *New York Times,* May 6, 1933, p. 13.

Liu, C., et al. "Effect of the root of Polygonum multiflorum Thunb. and its processed products on fat accumulation in the liver of mice." *Zhongguo Zhon Yao Za Zhi* 17, no. 10 (October 1992): 595–96, 639.

Markus, Andrea, and B. J. Morris. "Resveratrol in prevention and treatment of common clinical conditions of aging." *Clinical Interventions in Aging* 3, no. 2 (June 2008): 331–39.

Moreau, M., et al. "Enhancing cell longevity for cosmetic application:

References

A complementary approach." *Journal of Drugs in Dermatology* 6 Suppl. (2007): 14–18.

Mortiboys, H., et al. "Ursocholanic acid rescues mitochondrial function in common forms of familial Parkinson's disease." *Brain* 136, no. 10 (2013): 3038–50.

Pannacci, M., et al. "The extract of G115 of Panax ginseng C.A Meyer enhance [*sic*] energy production in mammals." *Planta Medica* 78 (2012).

SOFW. http://www.sofw.com/index/sofw_en/sofw_en_product_launch_pad.html?naid=5498.

Xu, M. F., et al. "Asiatic acid, a pentacyclic triterpene, in *Centella asiatica*, attenuates glutamate-induced cognitive deficits in mice and apoptosis in SH-SY5Y cells." *Acta Pharmacologica Sinica* 33, no. 5 (May 2012): 578–87.

CHAPTER 2: FIBROBLASTS, ANTIOXIDANTS, AND FREE RADICALS—OH MY!

Adil, M. D., et al. "Effect of Emblica officinalis (fruit) against UVB-induced photo-aging in human skin fibroblasts." *Journal of Ethnopharmacology* 132, no. 1 (October 2010): 109–14.

Aslam, M. N., E. P. Lansky, and J. Varani. "Pomegranate as a cosmeceutical source: Pomegranate fractions promote proliferation and procollagen synthesis and inhibit matrix metalloproteinase-1 production in human skin cells." *Journal of Ethnopharmacology* 103, no. 3 (February 2006): 311–18.

Bae, J. Y., et al. "Dietary compound ellagic acid alleviates skin wrinkle and inflammation induced by UVB irradiation." *Experimental Dermatology* 19, no. 8 (August 2010): 182–90.

Bergo, Martin, Per Lindahl, and Peter Campbell. News briefing with Martin Bergo, MD, PhD, codirector, Sahlgrenska Cancer Center, University of Gothenburg, Sweden; Per Lindahl, professor of biochemistry and cell biology, University of Gothenburg; and Peter Campbell, PhD, director, Tumor Repository, American Cancer Society, January 29, 2014. *Science Translational Medicine*.

Cenizo, V., et al. "LOXL as a target to increase the elastin content in adult skin: a dill extract induces the LOXL gene expression." *Experimental Dermatology* 15, no. 8 (August 2006): 574–81.

Chace, K. V., et al. "Effect of oxygen free radicals on corneal collagen." *Free Radical Research Communications* 12–13, no. 2 (1991): 591–94.

Chen, K.-C., et al. "UV-induced damages eliminated by arbutin and ursolic acid in cell model of human dermal fibroblast WS-1 cells." *Egyptian Dermatology Online Journal* 5, no. 1 (June 2009).

Chuarienthong, P., N. Lourith, and P. Leelapornpisid. "Clinical efficacy comparison of anti-wrinkle cosmetics containing herbal flavonoids." *International Journal of Cosmetic Science* 32, no. 2 (April 2010): 99–106.

Feng, B., et al. "Protective effect of oat bran extracts on human dermal fibroblast injury by hydrogen peroxide." *Journal of Zhejian University Science B* 14, no. 2 (February 2013): 97–105.

Fujii, T., et al. "Amla (Emblica officinalis Gaertn.) extract promotes procollagen production and inhibits matrix metalloproteinase-1 in human skin fibroblasts." *Journal of Ethnopharmacology* 119, no. 1 (September 2008): 53–57.

Hausenloy, D., and D. Yellon. "Time to take myocardial reperfusion injury seriously." *New England Journal of Medicine* 359, no. 5 (2008): 518–20.

Houck, J. C., et al. "Induction of collagenolytic and proteolytic activities by anti-inflammatory drugs in the skin and fibroblast." *Biochemical Pharmacology* 17, no. 10 (1968): 1081–90.

Lee, Y. S., et al. "Inhibition of ultraviolet-A-modulated signaling pathways by Asiatic acid and ursolic acid in HaCaT human keratinocytes." *European Journal of Pharmacology* 476, no. 3 (2003): 173–78.

Makpol, Suzana, et al. "Modulation of collagen synthesis and its gene expression in human skin fibroblasts by tocotrienol-rich fraction." *Archives of Medical Science* 7, no. 5 (2011): 889–95.

Martin, R., et al. "Photoprotective effect of a water-soluble extract of Rosmarinus officinalis L. against UV-induced matrix metalloproteinase-1 in human dermal fibroblasts and reconstructed skin." *European Journal of Dermatology* 18, no. 20 (2008): 128–35.

References

McDougall, A. "Kao demonstrates therapeutic effect of eucalyptus extract on skin's outer layer functions." 2012. http://www.cosmeticsdesign-europe.com/Formulation-Science/Kao-demonstrates-therapeutic-effect-of-eucalyptus-extract-on-skin-s-outer-layer-functions.

Nevin, K. J., and T. Rajamohan. "Effect of topical application of virgin coconut oil on skin components and antioxidant status during dermal wound healing in young rats." *Skin Pharmacology and Physiology* 23, no. 6 (2010): 290–97.

Newport, Mary. "Treatment chart: Coconut oil for Alzheimer's." 2013. http://www.eat2think.com/2013/07/research-benefits-coconut-oil-alzheimers.html.

Offord, E. A., et al. "Photoprotective potential of lycopene, carotene, vitamin E, vitamin C and carnosic acid in UVA-irradiated human skin fibroblasts." *Free Radical Biology and Medicine* 32, no. 12 (June 2002): 1293–1303.

Pacheco-Palencia, L. A., et al. "Protective effects of standardized pomegranate (Punica granatum L.) polyphenolic extract in ultraviolet-irradiated human skin fibroblasts." *Journal of Agricultural and Food Chemistry* 56, no. 18 (September 2008): 8434–41.

Park, M., et al. "Carnosic acid, a phenolic diterpene from rosemary, prevents UV-induced expression of matrix metalloproteinases in human skin fibroblasts and keratinocytes." *Experimental Dermatology* 22, no. 5 (2013): 336–41.

Ress, A. M., et al. "Free radical damage in acute nerve compression." *Annals of Plastic Surgery* 34, no. 4 (April 1995): 388–95.

Sang, T. K., et al. "The effect of ursolic acid and all-trans-retinoic acid on ultraviolet a [*sic*] radiation induced elastin mRNA expression in cultured dermal fibroblasts." *Journal of Dermatological Science* 12, no. 2 (1996): 208–208(1).

Shanmugam, M. K., et al. "Inhibition of CXCR4/CXCL12 signaling axis by ursolic acid leads to suppression of metastasis on transgenic adenocarcinoma of mouse prostate model." *International Journal of Cancer* 129, no. 7 (2011): 1552–63.

Zhao, P. W., et al. "The antioxidant effect of carnosol on bovine aortic endothelial cells is mainly mediated via estrogen receptor alpha pathway." *Biological and Pharmaceutical Bulletin* 35, no. 11 (2012): 1947–55.

CHAPTER 3: POWERFUL PROTEASOMES FOR SKIN AND BODY

Arnold, J., and T. Grune. "PARP-mediated proteasome activation: A coordination of DNA repair and protein degradation?" *Bioessays* 24, no. 11 (November 2002): 1060–65.

Bakondi, E. "Age-related stress-induced loss of nuclear proteasome activation is due to low PARP-1 activity." *Free Radical Biology and Medicine* 50, no. 1 (January 2011): 86–92

Bonoli, M., A. Bendini, "Qualitative and semi-quantitative analysis of phenolic compounds in extra virgin olive oils as a function of the ripening degree of olive fruits by different analytical techniques." *Journal of Agricultural and Food Chemistry* 52 (2004): 7026–32.

Chondrogianni, N., et al. "Fibroblast cultures from healthy centenarians have an active proteasome." *Experimental Gerontology* 35 (2000): 721–28.

———. "Identification of natural compounds that promote proteasome and confer lifespan extension." *Planta Medica* (2009): 75.

Das, S., et al. "Cardioprotection with palm oil tocotrienols: Comparison of different isomers." *American Journal of Physiology—Heart and Circulatory Physiology* 294, no. 2 (February 2008): H970–78.

Delcros, J. G., et al. "Proteasome inhibitors as therapeutic agents: Current and future strategies." *Current Medicinal Chemistry* 10 (2003): 479–503.

Deocaris, C. C., et al. "Glycerol stimulates innate chaperoning, proteasomal and stress-resistance functions: Implications for gerontomanipulation." *Biogerontology* 9, no. 4 (August 2008): 269–82.

Donohue, T. M. Jr., et al. "Decreased proteasome activity is associated with increased liver pathology and oxidative stress in experimental liver pathology." *Alcoholism: Clinical and Experimental Research* 28, no. 8 (August 2004): 1257–63.

Katsiki, M., et al. "The olive constituent leuropein exhibits proteasome stimulatory properties in vitro and confers life span extension of human embryonic fibroblasts." *Rejuvenation Research* 10 (2007): 157–72.

References

Korres.com. Quercetin and oak antiaging and antiwrinkle day cream. http://www.korres.com/default.aspx?page_id=729.

Kozie, R., et al. "Functional interplay between mitochondrial and proteasome activity in skin aging." *Journal of Investigative Dermatology* 131, no. 3 (March 2010): 594–603.

Kwak, M. K., et al. "Antioxidants enhance mammalian proteasome expression through the Keap1Nrf2 signaling pathway." *Molecular and Cellular Biology* 23 (2003): 8786–94.

Nevin, K. J., and T. Rajamohan. "Effect of topical application of virgin coconut oil on skin components and antioxidant status during dermal wound healing in young rats." *Skin Pharmacology and Physiology* 23, no. 6 (2010): 290–97.

Wang, D., et al. "Proteome dynamics and proteome function of cardiac 19S proteasomes." *Molecular and Cellular Proteomics* 1, no. 10 (May 2011).

Zhang, Q., et al. "Green tea extract and (-)-epigallocatechin-3-gallate inhibit apoxia and serum-induced HIF-1alpha protein accumulation and VGEF expression in human cervical carcinoma and hepatoma cells." *Molecular Cancer Therapeutics* 5, no. 5 (2006): 1227–38.

CHAPTER 4: HERE COMES THE SUN—EMBRACE IT!

Adil, M. D., et al. "Effect of *Emblica officinalis* (fruit) against UVB-induced photoaging in human skin fibroblasts." *Journal of Ethnopharmacology* 132, no. 1 (2010): 109–14.

Afnan, Q., et al. "Glycyrrhizic acid (GA), a triterpenoid saponin glycoside alleviates ultraviolet-B irradiation induced photoaging in human dermal fibroblasts." *Phytomedicine* 19, no. 7 (May 2012): 658–64.

Al-Waili, L., et al. "Honey for wound healing, ulcers and burns: Data supporting its use in clinical practice." *Scientific World Journal* 11 (April 2011): 766–87.

Aquilera, Y., et al. "The protective role of squalene in eye damage in the chick embryo retina." *Experimental Eye Research* 80, no. 4 (April 2005): 535–43.

Chen, L., et al. "Honeys from different floral sources as inhibitors of enzymatic browning in fruit and vegetable homogenates." *Journal of Agricultural and Food Chemistry* 48, no. 10 (October 2000): 4997–5000.

Engleman, Nancy, et al. "Nutritional aspects of phytoene and phytofluene, carotenoid precursors to lycopene." *Advances in Nutrition* 2 (January 2011): 51–62.

Erejuwa, O. O., et al. "Hypoglycemic and antioxidant effects of honey supplementation in streptozotocin-induced diabetic rats." *International Journal for Vitamin and Nutrition Research* 80, no. 10 (January 2010): 74–82.

Heinrich, U., et al. "Long-term ingestion of high-flavanol cocoa provides photoprotection against UV-induced erythema and improves skin condition in women." *Journal of Nutrition* 136, no. 6 (June 2006): 1565–69.

Ihmad, I., et al. "Tualang honey protects keratinocytes from ultraviolet radiation induced inflammation and DNA damage." *Photochemistry and Photobiology* 88, no. 5 (September 2012): 1198–1204.

Jeyam, M., et al. "Validating nutraceuticals to alleviate progeria using molecular docking studies." *Journal of Pharmaceutical and Biomedical Sciences* 13 (2011): 1–7.

Kamimura, H., et al. "Enhanced elimination of theophylline, phenobarbital and strychnine from the bodies of rats and mice by squalene treatment." *Journal of Pharmacobio-Dynamics* 15, no. 5 (1992): 215–22.

Lin, X.-F., et al. "Anticarcinogenic effect of ferulic acid on ultraviolet-B irradiated human keratinocytes HaCaT cells." *Journal of Medicinal Plants Research* 4, no. 16 (2010): 1686–94.

Pareja, B., and L. Kehl. "Contribution to the identification of Rosa aff rubiginosa L. oil rose active principles." *Anales de La Real Academia Nacional de Farmacia* 56, no. 2 (1999): 283–94.

Richter, E., et al. "Effects of dietary paraffin, squalene and sucrose polyester on residue disposition and elimination of hexachlorobenzene in rats." *Chemico-Biological Interactions* 40 (1982): 335–44.

Silvan, J. M., et al. "Control of the Maillard reaction by ferulic acid." *Food Chemistry* 128, no. 1 (2011): 208–13.

Staniforth, Vasinree, et al. "Ferulic acid, a phenolic phytochemical, inhibits UVB-induced matrix metalloproteinases in mouse skin via posttranslational mechanisms." *Journal of Nutritional Biochemistry* 23, no. 5 (May 2012): 443–51.

Sun, X., et al. "Lipid peroxidation and DNA adduct formation in lymphocytes of premenopausal women: Role of estrogen metabolites and fatty acid intake." *International Journal of Cancer* 131, no. 9 (November 2012): 1983–90.

Tourna, J. A., et al. "Ubiquinone, idebenone and kinetin provide ineffective photoprotection to skin when compared to a topical antioxidant combination of vitamin C and E and ferulic acid." *Journal of Investigative Dermatology* 126 (2006): 185–87.

Yamada, Y., et al. "Dietary tocotrienol reduces UVB-induced skin damage and sesamin enhances tocotrienols effects in hairless mice." *Journal of Nutritional Science and Vitaminology* 54, no. 2 (2008): 117–23.

Yan, J.-J., et al. "Protection against beta-amyloid peptide toxicity in vivo with long-term administration of ferulic acid." *British Journal of Pharmacology* 133, no. 1 (May 2001): 89–96.

CHAPTER 5: DIY STEM CELL THERAPY

Ashcroft, Gillian S., et al. "Topical estrogen accelerates cutaneous wound healing in aged humans associated with an altered inflammatory response." *American Journal of Pathology* 155, no. 4 (October 1999): 1137–46.

De Oliviera, Ana Paula, et al. "Effect of semisolid formulation of Persea Americana Mill (Avocado) Oil on wound healing in rats." *Evidence Based Complementary and Alternative Medicine* (2013), Article ID 472382.

Esteban, M. A., and D. Pei. "Vitamin C improves the quality of stem cell reprogramming." *Nature Genetics* 44 (2012): 366–67.

Kuo, S.-M., et al. "Cellular phenotype-dependent and -independent effects of vitamin C on the renewal and gene expression of mouse embryonic fibroblast." *PLoS One* (March 2012).

Lee, D.-C., et al. "Effect of long-term hormone therapy on telomere length in post-menopausal women." *Yonsei Medical Journal* 46, no. 4 (August 2005): 471–79.

Ranzato, E., S. Martinotti, and B. Burlando. "Honey exposure stimulates wound repair of human dermal fibroblasts." *Burn Trauma* 1 (2013): 32–38.

Schmid, D., et al. "Stem cell activation for smoother and more even skin." *Mibelle Biochemistry, Switzerland* (2013).

Skyberg, J. A., et al. "Apple polyphenols require T cells to ameliorate dextran sulfate sodium-induced colitis and dampen proinflammatory cytokine." *Journal of Leukocyte Biology* 90, no. 6 (2011): 1043.

Uma, H.-J., et al. "Withafarin A inhibits JAK/STAT3 signaling and induces apoptosis of human renal carcinoma Caki cells." *Biochemical and Biophysical Research Communications* 427, no. 1 (October 2012): 24–29.

Yang, Z., et al. "Withania somnifera root extract inhibits mammary cancer metastasis and epithelial to mesenchymal transition." *PLoS One* (September 2013).

CHAPTER 6: GOOD TO THE BONE

Alcantara, E. H., et al. "Diosgenin stimulates osteogenic activity by increasing bone matrix protein synthesis and bone-specific transcription factor Runx2 in osteoblastic MC3 T3-E1 cells." *Journal of Nutritional Biochemistry* 22, no. 11 (November 2011): 1055–63.

Bogani, P., et al. "Lepidium meyenii (Maca) does not exert direct androgenic activities." *Journal of Ethnopharmacology* 104, no. 3 (2006): 415–17.

Braun, K. F., et al. "Quercetin protects primary human osteoblasts exposed to cigarette smoke through activation of the antioxidative enzymes HO-1 and SOD-1." *Science World Journal* 11 (2011): 2348–57.

Bu, S. Y., et al. "Dried plum polyphenols attenuate the detrimental effects of TNF-alpha on osteoblast function coincident with up-regulation of Runx2, Osterix and IGF-I." *Journal of Nutritional Biochemistry* 20, no. 1 (January 2009): 31–44.

Effendy, M. Nadia, et al. "The effects of Tulang honey on bone metabolism in postmenopausal women." *Evidence-Based Complementary and Alternative Medicine* (2012).

References

Gonzales, G. F., et al. "Effect of Lepidium meyenii (Maca) on spermatogenesis in male rats acutely exposed to high altitude (4340 m)." *Journal of Endocrinology* 180, no. 1 (2004): 87–95.

Hooshmand, S., et al. "Comparative effects of dried plum and dried apple on bone in postmenopausal women." *British Journal of Nutrition* 106 (2011): 923–30.

Prouillet, C., et al. "Stimulatory effect of naturally occurring flavonols quercetin and kaempferol on alkaline phosphatase activity in MG-63 human osteoblasts through ERK and estrogen receptor pathway." *Biochemical Pharmacology* 67, no. 7 (April 2004): 1307–13.

Puel, C., et al. "Prevention of bone loss by phloridzin, an apple polyphenol, in ovariectomized rats under inflammation conditions." *Calcified Tissue International* 77, no. 5 (November 2005): 311–18.

Rubio, J., et al. "Effect of three different cultivars of Lepidium meyenii (Maca) on learning and depression in ovariectomized mice." *BMC Complementary and Alternative Medicine* 6, no. 1 (2006): 23.

Tang, C. H., et al. "Water solution of onion crude powder inhibits RANKL-induced osteoclastogenesis through ERK, p38 and NF-kappaB pathways." *Osteoporosis International* 20, no. 1 (January 2009): 93–103.

Yamaguchi, M., and E. Sugimoto. "Stimulatory effect of genistein and daidzein on protein synthesis in osteoblastic MC3T3-E1 cells: Activation of aminoacyl-tRNA synthetase." *Molecular and Cellular Biochemistry* 214, no. 1 (2000): 97–102.

Yen, M. L., et al. "Diosgenin induces hypoxia-induced Factor-1 activation and angiogenesis through estrogen receptor-related phosphatidylinositol 3-kinase/Akt and p38 mitogen-activated protein kinase pathways in osteoblasts." *Molecular Pharmacology* 68 (2005): 1061–73.

Zhang, M. Y., et al. "In vitro and in vivo effects of puerarin on promotion of osteoblast bone formation." *Chinese Journal of Integrative Medicine* 18, no. 4 (April 2012): 276–82.

Zhang, Y., et al. "Effect of ethanol extract of Lepidium meyenii Walp. on osteoporosis in ovariectomized rat." *Journal of Ethnopharmacology* 105, nos. 1–2 (2006): 274–79.

CHAPTER 7: TURN FAT TO MUSCLE

Arner, P., and J. Ostman. "Relationship between the tissue level of cyclic AMP and the fat cell size of human adipose tissue." *Journal of Lipid Research* 19 (1978): 613–18.

Bidon, C., et al. "The extract of Ginkgo biloba EGb 761 reactivates a juvenile profile in the skeletal muscle of sarcopenic rats by transcriptional reprogramming." *PLoS One* 4, no. 11 (November 2009).

Boque, N., et al. "Prevention of diet-induced obesity by apple polyphenols in Wistar rats through regulation of adipose gene expression and DNA methylation patterns." *Molecular Nutrition and Food Research* 57, no. 8 (August 2013): 1473–78.

Carls-Grierson, M. M. "Modulation of activity of the adipocyte aquaglyceroporin channel by plant extracts." *International Journal of Cosmetic Science* 29, no. 1 (February 2007): 7–14.

Facino, R. M., et al. "Anti-elastase and anti-hyaluronidase activities of saponins and sapogenins from *Hedera helix*, *Aesculus hippocastanum* and *Ruscus aculeatus:* Factors contributing to their efficacy in the treatment of venous insufficiency." *Archiv der Pharmazie* 328, no. 10 (October 1995): 720–24.

Fasshauer, M., et al. "Suppression of aquaporin adipose gene expression by isoproterenol, TNFalpha and dexamethasone." *Hormone and Metabolic Research* 35, no. 4 (2003): 222–27.

Hara-Chicuma, Mariko, et al. "Progressive adipocyte hypertrophy in aquaporin-7-deficient mice: Adipocyte permeability as a novel regulator of fat accumulation." *Journal of Biological Chemistry* 280, no. 16 (April 2005): 15493–96.

Kunkel, S. D., et al. "Ursolic acid increases skeletal muscle and brown fat and decreases diet-induced obesity, glucose intolerance and fatty liver disease." *PLoS One* (June 20, 2012).

Ohta, Y., et al. "Gene expression analysis of the anti-obesity effects of apple polyphenols in rats fed a high-fat diet and a normal diet." *Journal of Oleo Science* 55, no. 6 (2006): 305–14.

Roy, S., et al. "Transcriptome of primary adipocytes from obese women in response to a novel hydroxycitric acid-based dietary supplement." *DNA and Cell Biology* 26, no. 9 (September 2007): 627–39.

References

Saponara, R., and Enrica Bosisio. "Inhibition of cAMP-phosphodiesterase by biflavones of ginkgo in rat adipose tissue." *Journal of Natural Products* 61, no. 11 (1998): 1386–87.

Shahat, A. A., et al. "Regulation of obesity and lipid disorders by *Foeniculum vulgare* extracts and *Plantago ovata* in high-fat diet induced obese rats." *American Journal of Food Technology* (2012).

CHAPTER 8: HAIR TO REMEMBER

Camargo, F. B. Jr., et al. "Skin moisturizing effects of panthenol-based formulations." *Journal of Cosmetic Science* 62, no. 4 (July–August 2011): 361–70.

Fischer, T. W., et al. "Effect of caffeine and testosterone on the proliferation of human hair follicles in vitro." *International Journal of Dermatology* 46, no. 1 (January 2007): 2735.

Shabani, Fatemeh, and Reyhaneh Sarir. "Increase of melanogenesis in the presence of fatty acids." *Pharmacologyonline* 1 (2010): 314–23.

Ventura-Martinez, Rosa, et al. "Spasmolytic activity of Rosmarinus officinalis L. involves calcium channels in guinea pig ileum." *Journal of Ethnopharmacology* 127 (2011): 1528–32.

CHAPTER 9: A NATURAL APPROACH TO FACIAL CONTOURING

Al-Waili, N. S. "Natural honey lowers plasma glucose, C-reactive protein, homocysteine and blood lipids in healthy, diabetic and hyperlipidemic subjects: Comparison with dextrose and sucrose." *Journal of Medicinal Food* 7, no. 1 (2004): 100–107.

Cho, S., et al. "High dose squalene ingestion increases type 1 procollagen and decreases ultraviolet-induced DNA damage in human skin in vivo but is associated with transient adverse effects." *Clinical and Experimental Dermatology* 34, no. 4 (June 2009): 500–508.

Fernandez-Cabezudo, Maria, J., et al. "Intravenous administration of manuka honey inhibits tumor growth and improves host survival when used in combination with chemotherapy in a melanoma mouse model." *PLoS One* (February 2013), w.plosone.org/article/info%3Adoi%2F10.1371%2Fjournal.pone.0055993.

References

Finkler, R. S. "The effect of vitamin E in the menopause." *Journal of Clinical Endocrinology and Metabolism* 9 (1948): 89–90.

Gaylor, J. L. "Biosynthesis of skin sterols. III. Conversion of squalene to sterols by rat skin." *Journal of Biological Chemistry* 238 (June 1963): 1643–55.

Larson-Meyer, Enette D., et al. "Effect of honey versus sucrose on appetite, appetite-regulating hormones and postmeal thermogenesis." *Journal of the American College of Nutrition* 29, no. 5 (October 2010): 482–93.

Nemoseck, Tricia M., et al. "Honey promotes lower weight gain, adiposity and triglycerides than sucrose in rats." *Nutrition Research* 31, no. 1 (January 2011): 55–60.

Shekterle, Linda M., et al. "Dermal benefits of topical D-ribose." *Clinical, Cosmetic and Investigational Dermatology* 2 (2009): 151–52.

"Volufiline Grow Breasts Naturally." http://www.growbreastsnaturally. com/volufiline-for-breast-enhancement.

Zaid, Siti, et al. "The effects of Tualang honey on female reproductive organs, tibia bone and hormonal profile on ovariectomised rats—animal model for menopause." *BMC Complementary and Alternative Medicine* 10, no. 82 (December 2010): 1472.

CHAPTER 10: THE SECRET TO REVERSING MENOPAUSE

Al-Quarawi, A. A., et al. "The effect of extracts of *Cynomorium coccinium* and *Withania somnifera* on gonadotrophins and ovarian follicles of immature Wistar rats." *Phytotherapy Research* 14, no. 4 (June 2000): 288–90.

Barua, A., et al. "Dietary supplementation of Ashwagandha (*Withania somnifera* Dunal) enhances NK cell in ovarian tumors in the laying hen model of spontaneous ovarian cancer." *American Journal of Reproductive Immunology* 70, no. 6 (December 2013): 538–50.

Benton, Y., and R. F. Casper. "The aging oocyte—can mitochondrial function be improved?" *Fertility and Sterility* 99 (2013): 18–22.

Cunningham, J., et al. "Oestrogen-like effect of ginseng." Department of Nephrology, London Hospital, August 19, 1980.

References

Finkler, R. S., et al. "The effect of vitamin E in the menopause." *Journal of Clinical Endocrinology and Metabolism* 9 (1948): 89–90.

Fujiwara, T., et al. "Preliminary study on action of coenzyme Q10 in female reproductive system." www.senpu.jp/coq10/pdf/jp-039.pdf.

"Getting to the root of ginseng." *Smithsonian,* July 2002. http://www.smithsonianmag.com/science-nature/getting-to-the-root-of-ginseng-65654374/?no-ist.

Helms, S. "Cancer prevention and therapeutics: Panax Ginseng." *Alternative Medicine Review* 9, no. 3 (2004).

Houck, J. C., V. K. Sharma, Y. M. Patel, and J. A. Gladner. "Induction of collagenolytic and proteolytic activities by anti-inflammatory drugs in the skin and fibroblast." *Biochemical Pharmacology* 17, no. 10 (1968): 2081–90.

Jung, J. H., et al. "Therapeutic effect of Korean red ginseng extract on infertility caused by polycystic ovaries." *Archives of Pharmacal Research* 32, no. 3 (March 2009): 347–52.

Kuk, S. M., and Y. J. Lee. "Estrogen receptor is activated by Korean red ginseng *in vitro* but not *in vivo*." *Journal of Ginseng Research* 36, no. 2 (April 2012): 169–75.

Liu, L., et al. "Effects of ginsenosides on hypothalamus-pituitary-adrenal function and brain-derived neurotrophic factor in rats exposed to chronic unpredictable mild stress." *Zhongguo Zhong Yao Za Zhi* 36, no. 10 (May 2011): 1342–47.

Mori-Okamoto, J., et al. "Pomegranate extract improves a depressive state and bone properties in menopausal syndrome model ovariectomized mice." *Journal of Ethnopharmacology* 92 (2003): 93–101.

"Most expensive ounce of ginseng sold: $1.57 MILLION!" http://drinkmrpink.com/most-expensive-ounce-of-ginseng-sold-1-57-million/.

Raja Sankar, R. S., et al. "*Withania somnifera* root extract improves catecholamines and physiological abnormalities seen in a Parkinson's disease model mouse." *Journal of Ethnopharmacology* 125, no. 3 (2009): 369–73.

Rocha, A., et al. "Pomegranate juice and specific components inhibit cell and molecular processes critical to metastasis of breast cancer." *Breast Cancer Research and Treatment* 136, no. 3 (December 2012): 647–58.

Saber, M. A-A. "Effect of royal jelly on viability and *in vitro* maturation of Egyptian sheep oocytes in serum supplemented medium." *British Journal of Pharmacology and Toxicology* (2012).

Sharaf, A., and N. Gomaa. "Oestrogenicity of vitamins." *Qualitas Plantarum et Materiae Vegetabiles* 20, no. 4 (1971): 279–83.

Sharma, D. N., and L. Bhattacharya. "Role of vitamin E on antifolliculogenesis effects of lead acetate on diameter of follicles containing ovarian tissue of Swiss albino mice." *Global Journal of Biology, Agriculture, and Health Sciences*, Global Institute for Research and Education, www.gifre.org.

Sreeja, S., et al. "Pomegranate extract demonstrate a selective estrogen receptor modulator profile in human tumor cell lines and in vivo models of estrogen deprivation." *Journal of Nutritional Biochemistry* 23, no. 7 (July 2012): 725–32.

Takasaki, A., et al. "Endometrial growth and uterine blood flow: A pilot study for improving endometrial thickness in the patients with a thin endometrium." *Fertility and Sterility* 93, no. 6 (2010): 1851–58.

Yang, Z., et al. "*Withania sominfera* root extract inhibits mammary cancer metastasis and epithelial to mesenchymal transition." *PLoS One* (2013).

Zhong, S., et al. "Dietary carotenoids and vitamins A, C and E and risk of breast cancer." *Journal of the National Cancer Institute* (1999): 547–56.

CHAPTER 11: REV YOUR SEX APPEAL

Busse, Daniela., et al. "A synthetic sandalwood odorant induces wound healing processes in human keratinocytes via the olfactory receptor OR2AT4." *Journal of Investigative Dermatology* (July 2014).

Circosta, C., et al. "Estrogenic activity of standardized extract of *Angelica sinensis*." *Phytotherapy Research* 20, no. 8 (August 2006): 665–69.

Clark, K. E., and L. Myatt. "Prostaglandins and the reproductive cycle." (2008) Glob Libr Women's Med. DOI 10.3843/ GLOWM.10314.

Cousins, A. J. "Changes in women's mate preferences across the ovulatory cycle." *Journal of Personality and Social Psychology* 92, no. 1 (2007): 151–63.

References

Durante, K. M., et al. "Changes in women's choice of dress across the ovulatory cycle: Naturalistic and laboratory task-based evidence." *Personality and Social Psychology Bulletin* 34 (2008): 1451–60.

Goh, S. Y., and K. C. Loh. "Gynecomastia and the herbal tonic 'Dong Quai.'" *Singapore Medical Journal* 42, no. 3 (March 2001): 115–16.

Khazaei, M., et al. "Study of *Feoniculum vulgare* effect on folliculogenesis in female mice." *International Journal of Fertility and Sterility* 5, no. 3 (November 2011): 122–27.

Park, Y., et al. "Effect of conjugated linoleic acid on body composition in mice." *Lipids* 32, no. 8 (August 1997): 853–58.

Pipitone, R. N., and G. G. Gallup. "Women's voice attractiveness varies across the menstrual cycle." *Evolution and Human Behavior* 29 (2008): 268–74.

Sharma, S. C., et al. "Steroidal saponins of *Asparagus adscendens*." *Phytochemistry* 21 (1982): 2075–78.

INDEX

Index

Index

Index

cancer (*cont.*)
  stem cell treatments and, 87–88, 90, 92
  synthetic antioxidants and, 39–40
  UVA and UVB radiation and, 57, 58, 59, 66
capers, 53, 114
cardiovascular disease, 35, 68
carnosic acid, 42–43
carnosol, 43, 59
carotenes, 66. *See also* beta-carotene
carotenoids, 67, 147, 189
carrots, 44, 66
carvacol, 78
castor oil, 147
catabolism, 48–49, 130
cataracts, 60, 65
cedarwood essential oil, 142, 176, 192, 227
cellular function
  age-related plans and, 221, 222–23, 225, 227
  aging process and, 18–19, 59
  antioxidant foods for, 66
  bone loss and, 105
  energy levels and, 50
  free radical damage to, 36
  green tea compounds and, 27
  hormonal interaction with, 36, 39
  isoprenoids and squalene and, 63
  melatonin and, 60
  menopause and, 171
  Panax ginseng for, 29
  progerin inhibitors and, 68
  proteasomes in protein breakdown and, 48, 49–50

  sirtuin-activating compounds and, 24, 27, 29
  sun protection and, 57, 59
  vitamin D and, 60–61
cellulite
  causes of, 128
  massage glove for, 128–29, 135, 231
  natural substances for, 124, 129–32, 133, 135, 136, 231
ceramides, 19, 143
chalcones, 24
chamomile oil, 5, 74–75, 81, 148, 219
chamomile tea, 75
cheese, 97
chemical peels, 51
cherries, 24, 176, 192, 211, 227
chicken protein, 72, 96, 216
chicory, 108, 112
chili peppers, 114
chlorogenic acid, 127
chocolate, 80, 114. *See also* cocoa powder
cholesterol-containing fats, 78–79, 82, 163
cholesterol levels, 2, 162–63
cinnamon, 62, 116
circadian clock, 61, 175
cocoa butter, 2, 3, 163, 164, 166, 168, 226
cocoa powder, 24, 66, 80, 100, 114, 219, 226, 229
coconut oil, 30, 34, 37–38, 41, 45, 46, 54, 129–30, 192, 210, 215, 216, 217, 219, 224, 225, 226
coffee, 16. *See also* caffeine
  cellulite and skin care with, 69, 130, 131, 132, 136, 140

Index

Index

hyaluronic acid serums, 72, 81, 226
hyaluronidase, 71
hydrogen peroxide, 34, 36, 37, 45, 46
hydroxycitric acid (HCA), 124, 127
hydroxytyrosol, 134
hyperthyroidism, 107
hypodermis, 38, 163, 166
hypothalamus, 172–73, 184, 188
hypothyroidism, 107

I

immune system, 28, 60, 97, 125, 178
incontinence, 183, 201
Indian gooseberry. *See* amla
infections, 27, 28, 36
insomnia, 130, 170
instant coffee, 70, 130, 136, 142,
    149, 231
insulin, 60, 115
insulin sensitivity, 23, 133
iodine, 108
isoprenoids, 62–63
isoxanthohumol, 177

J

Janus kinase (JAK) inhibitors, 87–88
jojoba oil, 73, 164, 210, 211, 224,
    226, 232
juniper essential oil, 129–30, 135

K

kale, 52, 147
Kegel exercises, 201
keratin, 37, 38, 42, 43, 143
keratinocytes, 42, 43, 88, 90, 200
kidney disease, 122
knee joints, 116
Korean red ginseng. *See* Panax
    ginseng

kudzu, 114–15, 117, 177, 199, 205,
    225, 226
kudzu starch, 117, 176–77, 192, 205

L

lanolin, 148, 150, 163, 164, 183, 191
lard, 3, 79, 82, 143, 146–47, 149,
    150, 163, 210, 211, 214–15,
    217, 226, 227, 231
large pores, 231
lavender, 126
lavender oil, 142
LDL (low-density lipoprotein)
    cholesterol, 163
lemon juice, 90–91, 148
lemon oil, 79
leukemia, 27
Li Ching-Yuen, 15
licorice, 3, 40, 76, 81, 99, 100, 128,
    148, 150, 202, 220, 226, 230, 231
licorice tea, 100, 150, 230
lime oil, 79
lipid peroxidation, 63–64
lipolysis, 27, 123
liver cancer, 88, 92
liver disease, 26, 122
liver protection, 33, 54, 110
longevity genes. *See* sirtuins
lung cancer, 39, 122
luteolin, 66
lycopene, 44, 66, 67

M

maca, 106, 109–10, 117, 210, 227
Macassar oil, 142
macular degeneration, 35
madecassoside, 70–71, 131
magnesium, 108, 115, 118
magnesium citrate, 130

Index

Index

Index

Printed in the United States
By Bookmasters

VISIONS

What the Preacher Saw

Dianne Chatman

WESTBOW
PRESS®
A DIVISION OF THOMAS NELSON
& ZONDERVAN

Scriptures marked KJV are taken from the KING JAMES VERSION (KJV): KING JAMES VERSION, public domain.

Scripture quotations marked (NLT) are taken from the Holy Bible, New Living Translation, copyright © 1996, 2004, 2007 by Tyndale House Foundation. Used by permission of Tyndale House Publishers, Inc., Carol Stream, Illinois 60188. All rights reserved.

WestBow Press books may be ordered through booksellers or by contacting:

WestBow Press
A Division of Thomas Nelson & Zondervan
1663 Liberty Drive
Bloomington, IN 47403
www.westbowpress.com
1 (866) 928-1240

ISBN: 978-1-5127-7296-8 (sc)
ISBN: 978-1-5127-7297-5 (hc)
ISBN: 978-1-5127-7295-1 (e)

Library of Congress Control Number: 2017900924

Print information available on the last page.

WestBow Press rev. date: 01/27/2017

CONTENTS

Acknowledgements

First, I would like to thank The Father for giving us His only begotten Son, our Lord and Savior Jesus Christ, who without Him, none this would have been possible, and The Holy Spirit for giving me, these wonderful visions, and experiences, and pressing it into my spirit, that it was time, to share visions, that I will be sharing with you, the reader today. May the Lord bless you. I also would like to thank my friend, Portia Bowman, truly an anointed woman of God, for being an ear for me to share this portion of my story with. Whose anointed prayers and witness, have blessed my soul, and increased my courage in the Lord, May God bless and keep you, my sister

in the Lord, and a true woman of God. I also would like

thank my sister, Ramonia Joiner, for allowing me to come

into her home, and use her computer, while continuing to

work in, this next calling in my life, and to all of those, whose

prayers and encouragements, have kept me lifted up before

Lord. Thank you for inspiring confidence in me to write.

Thank you, and may the Lord continue to bless and favor

you in this life.

- Dianne Chatman

INTRODUCTION

In the year that King Uzziah died I saw also the
Lord sitting upon a throne, high and lifted up, and
his train filled the temple.

- Isaiah 6:1, (KJV)

When God wanted to get a particular message across unto
men, he would often give them visions allowing them to
see things heavenly, spiritually, physically and prophetically.
These visions either foretold of upcoming events, or revealed
a more clearer and truthful picture of present events that were
not known. One example of this was in the book of Ezekiel
in the seventh chapter. God wanted to show Ezekiel what the

elders of Judah were doing at that present time that provoked causing Him to bring judgment upon Judah, for idolatry. The Lord wanted Ezekiel to see what was going on right then that He did not know about.

> "And He put forth the form of a hand, and took me by a lock of mine head; and the spirit lifted me up between the earth and the heaven, and brought me in the visions of God to Jerusalem, to the door of the inner gate, that looketh toward the north; where was the seat of the image of jealousy, which provoketh to jealousy."
>
> - Ezekiel 8: 3, (KJV)

So he would have an even better understanding as to the Lord's displeasure with Judah.

In Isaiah's vision, the Lord wanted to let Isaiah know who the true ruler over Israel was, and He was not dead, He was very much alive! God wanted Isaiah to understand that He was still Soveriegn over Israel. No doubt the vision gave great comfort and peace to Isaiah after king Uzziah died and

it seemed like the nation was left without Godly leadership, and things seemed to be slipping back the way that they were before Uzziah had become king. With the people falling back into old sinful ways and habits, a state of self indulgence and moral decline.

God's reassurance to Isaiah, was a sign of hope. That all was not lost and He was still on the throne and his presence was very much there with the nation of Israel. God will bring his people back to him. So the vision that the Lord God gave to Isaiah filled him with the assurance that God was still with them overseeing the affairs of the people of Israel. Just as He is today, God is still overseeing the affairs of man. Watching all that we do, carefully leading and guiding us from day to day.

As you read in the book of Isaiah, you will find that God gave many visions unto Isaiah. Many which have already come to past, some that are yet to come to past. So you see visions are real, especially when they come from God.

"And it shall come to pass afterward, That I will pour out my spirit upon all flesh; and your sons and

your daughters shall prophesy, your old men shall

dream dreams, your young men shall see visions:"

- Joel 2:2, (KJV)

God chooses whom he will to receive certain gifts, and callings upon their lives, even if the one that is called and blessed so with an assignment from the Lord, feels that they are the least likely one to be chosen, but everyone has a gift or gifts of something that can be used of the Lord. Sometimes we do not become aware of our gifts till after we are saved, and experience being born again. Our eyes, and our hearts, become open to God, and all that He has for us. Then there are those who are aware of certain spiritual gifts in operation in them even before the born again experience, but just don't understand what it is. They may not understand the what and the why, but they are aware that there is a gift.

For the gifts and calling of God are without repentance

- Romans 11: 29, (KJV)

In other words, God does not take them back, they are irrevocable. Will they save you? No, they are just spiritual tools which the Holy Spirit gives us to help make our ministry more effective in reaching the lost, strengthening the weak and establishing the message of the gospel of Christ, Salvation for all.

In the following text, I am going to share some of the visions that the Holy Spirit shared with me over the years and some more recent. It is my prayer that you will find hope direction and courage in them just as I did when they were given to me. May you be blessed.

> "And the Lord answered me, and said, Write the
> vision, and make it plain upon the tables, that he
> may run that readeth it."
>
> - Habakkuk 2: 2, (KJV)

Often times when I have shared my visions with others, I was told I should write them down so that others could be encouraged by them too. For a long time I was not willing to do this, for fear of being rejected. That has since changed. I am

seeing now that more and more people are becoming bolder about what God has shown them or given them, without fear of being talked about or rejected. this has made me more confident about sharing what the Lord revealed unto me.

I have never thought of myself as no great person, just someone who loves the Lord with all her heart. Have I been the greatest Christian? No, but like David I believe in getting back up after I have been knocked down. Whether it has been by my own doing or someone, or something else's. I do consider myself blessed.

Just to bring a little clarity to the matter before I share these particular visions. I would like to share with you the first time I began to notice that something was different. I noticed that I could see things that my other siblings could not see(or either they just did not let on that they could see), around me when I was a child. I knew things, that by all rights, I should not have known.

Once while we were living in Massachusetts, my stepfather often took us to New Hampshire, it was his favorite place

to go. I enjoyed the trips, because it was a chance to see something I had never seen before. I always enjoyed looking at nature and its beauty, even as a child. It never ceased to amaze me. During one of those times, as I was starring out the window from the back seat, I saw a little white house sitting at the base of the mountain. I immediately got excited and yelled out to my mother, " There goes that little white house sitting at the base of the mountain!" My mother instantly replied, "what little white house?" Now, even more excited than before, because she did not seem to remember it, cried out, "There to the right, sitting back off the road!" From there I began to describe everything about the house and the mountain, and what we going to see further down the road. My mother quickly replied back, that we had never been this way before. I couldn't understand why she was denying seeing the little white house before and the mountain that it sat at the base of. That was when my step father chimed in and said, that we had never been there before.

By this time I was really getting excited about it, I just

knew we had been there before. I thought they were just picking at me and trying to make me feel bad, as if I were telling a lie. I told them of the black and white road sign that we were about to see on the side of the road perched on an old piece of wood that was leaning. The sign had the name of the next city that was coming up, and how there was going to be a fork in the road and we were going to go in the direction of that city because the map we were following. By that time my mother and my stepfather were both telling me to be quiet and to sit still or they were going to turn around and smack me. I was hurt. With tears rolling down my face, I sat quietly after that, convinced they were lying to me.

After we got home, my mother told me again how we had never been there before, and she could not understand how I knew about it and could describe the house and the area with such great detail. I was a child I did not know either. I just knew this, that I did not dream it. It was after that event I started paying attention to everything that seemed unusual. It is always amazing to me what the Lord will show you when

you open yourself to him. Even as a child I had a very strong awareness of the Lord. I might not have been saved or born again then, but I always accepted that there was a God.

How often the Lord has tried to talk to us or show us something that could be of a help or warning to us and we have quietly ignored him like he just those not exist. I have found that even among the members of the body of Christ, there is still an element of unbelief when it comes to the workings of the Holy Spirit

It is because of the very prophetic visions in the Bible that we have hope today.

The revelations revealed in the visions that Jesus Christ gave John on the Isle of Patmos and the very descriptive visions that were given to Daniel, are the reasons why we know what is to take place in these last days for this world and the church. They were given so we would be well prepared for what is going to be happening in this world, and the more I study the Word of God, the more it reads like a newspaper.

This is just what the prophet Isaiah needed to see at that

time to comfort him and reassure him, that God was seated on the throne over Israel and to that effect, all mankind. These visions that were given me by the Holy Spirit have given me hope and encouragement where my faith is concerned in God and my Savior Jesus Christ, confirmation in my spirit where His written word is concerned, and opened my heart and my mind to a better understanding of who God is, how He sees us, and His deep love and compassion for His children.

> "It is He that sitteth upon the circle of the earth. He giveth power to the faint; and to them that have no might he increaseth strength. That they may see, and know, and consider, that the hand of the LORD hath done this, and the Holy One of Israel hath created it".
>
> - Isaiah 40: 22, 29, 41: 20, (KJV)

CHAPTER ONE

The Vision of the Two Suns

I have found that sincere prayer opens communications between us and the Father, especially when you are calling on Him in the mighty name of Jesus, and in sincere worship and praise for who He is and who He is to you. He will always show up.

One night during the winter, a few friends, guests, and I were gathered together in my home for our weekly prayer meeting. The Lord had laid it in my spirit to start having prayer and Bible study in my home every Friday night. As it began to grow, others opened up their homes for us to come

and have prayer and Bible study in their homes as well. This particular night, the meeting was being held in my home. I lived in a small one floor, two bedroom house in Akron Ohio. My living room was not very big, but we managed to get everybody in who wanted to join us for prayer. We prayed for various needs and conditions and the Lord never failed to meet us there in prayer. One time, one of the members of our prayer group, came straight there from the emergency room of the hospital. She volunteered at a clothing charity, and they were handing out winter coats to those who couldn't afford them.

While we were in the midst of praying, I heard someone knocking. I got up and opened the door. The woman immediately started to speaking so excitedly that we could hardly understand what she was saying! When we finally calmed her down so that we could understand her, she explained how she had just come from the emergency room and how they had just finished examining her. She told how she had slipped on some ice that she hadn't noticed before

on the steps. As she limped inside, we hurried and got her a chair, and a pillow for leg. Her knee, right shoulder, and arm was swollen and bruised. We asked her if she wanted someone to drive her home, or even back to the hospital. She quickly said no, and that she had specifically left there, to come and get prayer! She went on to say, that she knew, if she could just get to prayer, everything would be alright. By this time I noticed that not only was the knee swollen, but her whole leg had swollen as well. She asked me if I would pray for her. I knew that the Lord had performed miracles in the past for me, because of the prayers of the saints and my own. I trusted in the Lord, that if all of us came together in prayer on one accord, that Christ would show up in the midst of us! There is strength in numbers.

> "For where two or three are gathered together in my
> name, there am I in the midst of them."
>
> -Matthews 18:20, (KJV)

I quickly gathered everyone around her and told everyone to call on the name of Jesus. I anointed her knee, leg and

shoulder with praying oil and asked the Lord Jesus to heal

her knee and to take the swelling down that was in her body

and to touch her and heal her where she was injured. I knew

that if anyone could help her, Jesus could! We watched as the

swelling went down in her leg, and around her knee, and the

bruises that were on her body from the fall, clear up before

our eyes! It was truly wonderful to see. I am always excited at

the miracles I see my Lord do, it always amazes me.

She told us that she felt much better and the knee was no

longer hurting. We were all excited and thanking the Lord Jesus

Christ for what He was doing in our prayer group and for what

He was blessing us to see Him do. It so encouraged our little

prayer group; that it soon began to include various ministers

and their wives from around the city as word got out about

the meetings and how the Spirit of the Lord was moving in

them. Each meeting, the Holy Spirit seemed to move more and

more. It was during one of those meetings in my home, while

we were in prayer, I was on my knees at the end of the sofa. I

was giving thanks unto the Lord for all that He had been to

me and all that he was yet doing in my life. While in the midst of prayer, the Holy Spirit gave me a vision of the suns. In this vision, I was lifted up between heaven and earth. I saw myself standing above the earth to the side. As if I was suspended in mid air. I saw the sun, it was shining brightly. Its rays were shining down upon every city and country around the world. Everything was green and beautiful with a lovely blue sky just like it would be on a nice sunny summer day. The thing that interested me the most though, was that the sun's rays were individual lights. It was not the overall light that we would see shining around us on a sunny day, but these were single rays of light that were just shining a little brighter than the regular light we see from the sun. I watched as these individual lights began to rise and go into the sun, as the sun itself, began to rise higher in the sky. As it rose, it took the single lights with it, drawing them into itself. They rose from every place under the sun, and from every corner of the earth. From the east, west, north, and south till the sun and it's rays, rose higher and higher, till they were out of sight! By then, I understood

what I was being shown. I knew I was being allowed to witness something wonderful. As I remained suspended in mid air, I kept silent, watching, not wanting to miss nothing that was going on. Then the scene changed. Just as the bright sun rose out of sight, there appeared another sun rising up from the earth. This one blood red, surrounded by dark and foreboding clouds. It rose midway in the sky just above the earth. It did not sit high at all. I watched as the dark clouds began to spread out over the face of the earth. Even the sky was reddened by this second sun. I felt myself, having a feeling despair and great sadness at what I was witnessing. It was as if all the joy of the first sun was leaving out of the earth, and in its place, a feeling of trouble, dark times, and despair. I wrapped my arms around myself as the tears began rolling down my face.

The once beautiful, and bright scene that was there before, was now being replaced by a much darker and troubling one, even the land was blackened by the darkness of the sky and the clouds. As I looked downward towards the earth, there in the midst of the darkness where a few broken rays

of light left behind by the first sun! Just bits and pieces, but there nonetheless. Some were laying on the ground as if fallen, and some were standing up. There was a grayish smoke everywhere. The lights were surrounded by the darkness that was in the land. Some of the broken rays of light that were on the ground seemed to be shine just a little weaker than the light of those that were standing up, but they were still very visible in the dark. As I looked up in the sky to the right, I saw the first sun once again appear in the sky. It was coming down from up above shining brightly just as it did before. I saw the broken pieces of light, that were left in the earth before, began to rise and be gathered to the first sun as it came down closer and closer to the earth. I remember feeling joy at seeing the first sun returning in the sky again. As it was coming down in the sky towards the earth, the darkness that was in the land, started breaking up, and disappearing.

As I was watching this, I felt myself being pulled back from what I was seeing in the vision. It was so real! It felt like it had just happened, right there around me. I felt the air on

my face. I could feel the warmth coming from the first sun on my skin, and the despair and the coldness of the second sun, in my spirit. The vision was real. It left me feeling somewhat shaken inside, and disturbed, because I had never had a vision like that before. When I realized that I was back in my living room. I noticed that my hands were red and sweating and my face was too. I felt great grief, and sorrow for the rays of lights that that had become broken off from the first sun, and were left behind. By this time, I had come to completely understand, what I had seen in the vision. Those that had been left behind were subjected to great grief and sorrow, and had to endure the trouble and the trials that were coming under the red sun, and the darkness it was going to spread over the land. My heart went out for them, having to go through and suffer what was going to happen to the world. Yes, I understood greatly.

I was grateful for the first sun and its rays, those that were able to rise with it, but the sorrow of the second sun lingered with me well after prayer. I shared what I had seen with the others in the prayer group. We all agreed on what the vision was revealing.

Being a person who loves the study of God's Word, I knew that what the Holy Spirit was showing me was a portion of the rapture, the catching away, as you may call it, and a portion of what was going to be happening afterwards. From what the Lord was showing me, it is going to be a dark time. Full of bloodshed and misery, thus - the red sun. Those that came to believe in Christ after the rising of the first sun were going to be surrounded by those who did not believe, and did not care. Trouble was going to be in the land, which explains the darkness that I was seeing. Some of the lights that were left in the land, were going to be slain, but their light, or their lives, were still going to stand as a witness for others. Those that were still standing, or alive when Christ returns, they, like the first ones who rose, would be gathered together with Him, but they were going to have to go through many trials, and great sorrows, from being left behind.

The experience of seeing the vision of the two suns and what was going to come to pass, was encouraging and frightening. There are those that say, if you are saved, you should not be

afraid. The emotion that I was feeling, was not for myself, but for those that were going to be lost. Yes, it made me want to all the more, be sure of my walk with Christ as well. I don't believe anyone can say, with any surety, that they have a seat in God's kingdom, until they are at that last hour of their life, like Paul, in his last letter to Timothy. -

> "I have fought a good fight, I have finished my course, I have kept the faith:
>
> Henceforth there is laid up for me a crown of righteousness, which the Lord, the righteous judge, shall give me at that day: and not to me only, but unto all them also that love his appearing."
>
> - II Timothy 4: 7-8, (KJV)

This is a faith walk, one that we have to keep until the end, if we are going to see, Christ's face in peace. It is not a matter of, will I serve Him or not, but it is a matter of enduring to the end. Like Christ said in Matthew 10: 22, when talking to

the disciples, about the persecutions and the trials, that they were going to face:

"And ye shall be hated of all men for my names sake: but he that endureth to the end shall be saved."
- Matthew 10: 22, (KJV)

Those that were watching me in my prayer group, shared with me how my face began to be change while I was praying. They told me how my face began to look flushed and red. Those who had came over and touched me, to see if I was alright, said my skin felt hot and that I was perspiring, as if my body was heating up. They told me, they could hear me praying at first, Then I just became very still. I was not aware of any of this. I felt as if I had just been taken somewhere else, and was being allowed to view something, that no else, or, at least, know one that I knew, had ever seen. No, I was not in a trance, nor was I meditating, I was praying, quite verbally to be exact, because there were things that were pressing in my spirit, I wanted to talk to Christ about, and also, give thanks to Him about. We were all, praying quite vocally in my small

living room. Because I could hear others praying that were kneeled down beside me, in various spots and places, in my living room. This vision, brought to reality to me, the words that Christ spoke to the disciples, when sharing with them the events that were going to be taking place during and after the rapture. It was very reaffirming and establishing. Bringing to light, the truths of God's Word. This is the first, of these kind of visions that I had during the period of years, since I was first saved! The other vision of this type, I had in the year 2009, after I had moved to Atlanta, Georgia.

Now you see why it was so hard to share these particular visions that the Holy Spirit was giving me, outside of the few I knew would receive them. There is so much skepticism in the world and even in some of our churches. I found it hard to share what I had seen, for fear of being ridiculed. In my mind, I would often, go back to what my mother said to me when I was very young, and was just becoming aware of this particular gifting that the Lord had given me. I didn't know, at that time, it was a spiritual gift. I just knew that it

was something, that often, happened to me. As Paul said in
1 Corinthians, -

> "When I was a child, I spake as a child, I understood
> as a child: but when I became a man, I put away
> childish things."
>
> > - 1 Corinthians 13: 11, (KJV)

He said this in reference to our spiritual maturity, and
the understanding that we receive thereof, from the Holy
Ghost, as we grow in grace, wisdom and knowledge, in things
pertaining to the Spirit of the Lord.

My mother told me, not to speak of things I saw, because
people would think I was strange and would not want to
have anything to do with me. She shared an experience with
me, of when she was child. She told me, how, while out one
day with others, cutting down trees, on some property that
they were clearing, she was standing and looking at the truck
that they were placing some logs on. She told me that her job
was to pick up the loose twigs and small branches that were
laying on the ground and bundle them up to be burned.

While looking at the truck, she suddenly saw the ropes that were holding the logs in place, brake, causing the logs to roll off the truck, crushing a family member beneath them, that was trying to secure them to the truck. Because the incident hadn't happened yet, when she told a family member about what she had seen, they didn't believe her. Three days later, the incident occurred, just as it was revealed to her, the ropes that had been placed around the logs, broke. The owner of the truck, at the time, decided that he would cut costs, and buy cheaper ropes to save money. The ropes were weak and not very strong, unable to hold the weight of the logs, they broke. She told me, how, that after that, the family member that she had told what she had seen, began to treat her very nasty, and spread unkind rumors and lies about her to others, saying that she caused the incident to happen, which in fact, if they had only listened to her, a man's life, might have been spared. It hurt her, and she never spoke again about what she saw. What she told me, left a lasting impression in my mind, and created fears in me, that I have had to battle through,

to overcome, to share what the Lord has given me. I had full intentions of never sharing what the Lord was revealing to me in my visions, with anybody, except, but with the few, whom I knew would understand. I have since come to realize, that my intentions, were not the Lord's intentions. He wasn't giving me these visions, just to keep them to myself, they were meant to be shared. Since then, the Holy Spirit has given me many confirmations and witnesses to this fact, and has continually, pressed it into my spirit, that it was time share the visions He was giving me, with the world. It brings to my mind, what Christ said in the book of Revelations:

> "He that hath and ear, let him hear what the Spirit
> saith unto the churches".
>
> -Revelation 2:6, (KJV)

I believe with all surety, that these things will be. The times and what is happening in the world today, is its own proof and evidence, that what the Word of God, and the Spirit of God are saying, is, indeed, truth. So let us hear what what the Spirit is saying unto the church.

The Throne Room Of Jesus

During the year 2004, during a Jurisdictional meeting held in Columbus Ohio, where I had just received my Missionary license, I was given another vision by the Holy Spirit, of the throne room of Jesus. One of the many visions that were given to me after that very great and highly anointed women's meeting that was held in Columbus, Ohio, during the state jurisdictional meetings. The speaker for the evening, was the wife of the Bishop, who was also an Evangelist, and a anointed woman of God. During the meeting she had shared with us her testimony about how she had been healed of terminal

cancer while in the hospital. She told us, how her doctor had told her and her family that there was nothing else they could do for her. That they had done all that they could do. She told us how she began to cry, the thought of leaving her husband and her family behind became too much for her to bear. She shared with us how she began to pray and call out to the Lord Jesus to heal her and to make her whole again so she could be with her family. She said that she told the Lord that if He would heal her totally and would make her cancer free, she would dedicate her whole life to Him and would let nothing stand in her way of serving him. Not her husband, not her children, not nobody. She would dedicate all to the Lord.

It brings to mind, to me, of the story of Hannah in the Bible and how she prayed in the book of 1 Samuel, when she petitioned the Lord for a son. After watching her husband, Elkanah and Peninnah, Elkanah's other wife,(multiple wives were allowed back then), have children. Hannah longed for a child herself. Peninnah taunted her severely about her being barren and not able to have children, causing her to despair

and to weep greatly. When it came time for them to take their yearly journey up to the temple of the Lord as was custom to do. Hannah went to the temple to pray:

> "So Hannah rose up after they had eaten in Shiloh, and after they had drunk. Now Eli the priest sat upon a seat by a post of the temple of the Lord. And she was in bitterness of soul, and wept sore. And she vowed a vow, and said, O lord of hosts, if thou wilt indeed look on the affliction of thine handmaid, and remember me, and not forget thine handmaid, but wilt give unto thine handmaid a man child, then I will give him unto the Lord all the days of his life, and there shall no razor come upon his head."
>
> -1 Samuel 1: 9-11, (KJV)

The Lord God answered her request of Him and she did bear a son and called him Samuel, meaning- Heard by God. Samuel, because of the prayer that Hannah prayed and because she did do as she promised the Lord, and brought the young boy to the temple and left him in the care of Eli who

was high priest at the time, to dedicate him to the service of the Lord.

> "For this child I prayed; and the Lord hath given me my petition which I asked of Him:
>
> Therefore also I have lent him to the Lord; as long as he liveth he shall be lent to the Lord. And he worshipped the Lord there."
>
> - 1 Samuel 1: 27, 28, (KJV)

> Samuel, through the divine call of the Lord God on his life, did go on to become a great priest, prophet, and judge over Israel.
>
> - (1 Samuel 3: 1-21, 7: 15-17)

The Bishop's wife, also, promised the Lord to dedicate her life totally to the will and the service of God for the rest of her life. Upon doing so, she shared with us; how that, suddenly all her pain subsided. She felt stronger and full of energy. She told us how the color had come back into her skin were she had been looking very pale. She told us how that even her appearance changed, whereas she was looking very

old because of the cancer, after she was miraculously healed, she now looked and felt years younger. A testimony that I can truly relate to myself, but that also is another testimony. Upon re-examination of her, stemming from her appearance and miraculous recovery, which indeed it was, because this happened within in minutes of her prayer, her doctors, baffled, had her returning time and time again, examining her just to make sure that what they had found upon re-examination of her while she was in the hospital was true. Every test came out the same. The cancer was gone! She kept her word. Later going on to become a powerful and anointed minister of God; and from what I have been told, went on to pastor over her own church as well. Powerful prayer, powerful anointing, true dedication!

This was the kind of anointing that we were experiencing in the room that day! We were praying about releasing everything that could possibly standing in the way of serving God with all our hearts, and rededicating ourselves to a stronger, and a more personal walk with Christ. It was during this prayer

as they were making the alter call, I began to walk towards the front of the room to get closer to the altar, but because of the press, for there were many coming forth for prayer; I was only able to make it about halfway. By this time many of the men had come in as well, being drawn in by the powerful preaching, prayer, and testimony of the Bishop's wife.

The Spirit of the Lord was moving greatly in the room, it was just awesome! It was as if the whole room was lit up with the fire of the Holy Ghost! The powerful preaching, witness and prayer of first lady - the Bishop's wife, had so inspired everyone in the room, we could hardly contain our praise! It was as if the Spirit of the Lord was just bouncing off the walls! When I could not make my way up front to the altar because of the press. I began praying right where I was. I started to releasing everything I thought could possibly stand in the way of me serving the Lord Jesus Christ.! It was a great outpouring, and spiritually uplifting time; everyone looked to be caught up in the Spirit of the Lord!

I remember weeping as I was pouring my heart out to

God, as I often did when the Spirit of the Lord was moving in me, tears would fall. It was then, all of a sudden, I saw what looked like a man whose lower half of his body was that of a lion, but the upper half of his body was of a man, coming down towards me. He took my hand, and then preceded to take me up higher. I saw myself passing through different levels as we went up. When we got to the third level, I was brought into a beautiful room. The room was made of all white marble, with strands of what looked like silver and gold minerals running through it. The whole room looked to be fashioned out of one solid piece of marble. There were no seems, and no dividing lines anywhere! The marble had a creamy, beautiful white appearance to it, and the whole room just glowed with light! It was marvelous!

There, in the midst of it, was this solid white throne. It was made of the same marble. In fact, It was a part of the marble! Carved out of it. On each side of me there stood an angel. One to the left, and one to the right, they had brought me before the throne.

I was trying to see who it was that was sitting on the throne, because I couldn't see his face. He was dressed in a long white robe that seemed to just shine with luminescent colors. Very pleasant to look at. I admit, I was somewhat nervous. I didn't know why I was there. My first thought was, had I did something wrong, as to the reason I was being brought before the throne? But at the same time, I could not shake the feeling of excitement and honor of just being there. Still, I was unable to make out who it was on the throne, light that was shining from their face kept me from being able to see who it was. Their feet and hands were covered by their robe at this time as well. Without speaking a word, I watched as they brought their right hand out of their robe. There in the midst of it, was an hole about the width of an nickel. Then they brought their foot out from under the bottom of the robe. It had the same piercing in it. I dropped to my knees, feeling strength, just leave my body. I knew who it was I was standing before! Feeling unworthy to be in His presence, I covered my face with my hands, crying uncontrollably,

because I all I could think of, was, that it was my sins that caused this, He died for me. In fact, He died for all our sins. He paid our price. He was crucified that we might live! When I saw the holes in His hand and in His foot, even though I now was a born again Christian, I still could not shake the blood guiltiness of the fact that He died on the cross for us, because we were not able to redeem ourselves; but now, because of Him, and what He had done for us, we now have the opportunity to be born again!

As the angels that were standing on each side of me, helped me back to my feet., I wondered why He did not speak. I turned to the angel standing to my right and asked him, why was He, Jesus, just staring at me? What was he looking at, and why doesn't he speak to me? The angel replied that Jesus, does not see our flesh, He looks beyond our flesh to our spirit where He resides. It was then that I saw my body separated into three different parts, or chambers. The first part, the flesh part of me, looked like a layer of thin dust formed into the shape of my body. The second part, was a layer of light. Through the

particles of dust of the first layer, you could see the light from the second layer, shining through,like pinpoints of light. The third part, was a chamber in which there was a washing action going on, like what you might see if your were looking into a washing machine as it was churning. The top part of the chamber was clean. The bottom part was of a grayish color, where the washing, was taking place.

I asked the angels what was this? He replied, The first layer, the layer of dust, was my flesh, and because the flesh was sinful, Christ did not look at it. The second layer, the layer of light, was my spirit. He told me that, that was where His spirit, the Spirit of Christ dwelled in me. He said that, the Lord Jesus does not see our flesh, he looks, to see His spirit within us.

The third part, he replied was my soul. It was being cleaned and purged by the Holy Spirit. He told me that I was half way there, and that when the washing was done, I would be clean, and that is when I would be with Jesus. As I looked at the grayish color of the water, I was disheartened, that I was still so dirty. I thought since I had given my life to Christ, that I

was clean, this unfortunately, is how many of us think when we are in Christ, that now, all our ways are clean, but life, and its experiences, teach us otherwise. One of the names of the Holy Spirit, is the Spirit of truth, and He allows us to see ourselves, as Christ sees us. I was somewhat disappointed that all that cleaning, was going to take the rest of my life before it was over, but I was encouraged to know that I was being cleaned by the Holy Spirit and that one day I would be with Jesus. It brings to light the scripture in Isaiah:

> "But we are all as an unclean thing, and all our righteousnesses are as filthy rags; and we all do fade as a leaf; and our iniquities, like the wind, have taken us away."
>
> - Isaiah 64: 7, (KJV)

Later on, I understood why this is so, because all our lives, we will be need to be constantly cleansed by the Spirit of the Lord, from something. Old ways, old habits, that try to creep in to cause us to fall back into a sinful life, words spoken wrongly, stubbornness, disobedience, anger. Thoughts, giving

place to our emotions, out of the will of God, and, so on. All these things, and more, have to be cleansed from our spirits, if we are to follow Christ in truth, and in righteousness. Unfortunately this is a mind set, many Christians embrace, that they no longer need to be cleansed of anything once they have been born again. This type of thinking, keeps us in bondage, because it keeps us from seeing the truth about ourselves. That is, that all our lives we are going to need to be cleaned, or washed by the Holy Spirit, so that we may be able, to one day stand before the Lord in peace, thus the work of the Holy Spirit in our lives. To make us presentable to Christ. The final cleansing comes from Christ, Himself, when we changed, from mortal, to immortal, from corrupt, to incorrupt:

> "In a moment, in the twinkling of an eye, at the last trump: for the trumpet shall sound, and the dead shall be raised incorruptible, and we shall be changed."
>
> - 1 Corinthians 15: 52, (KJV)

When we receive our spiritual bodies, all that was left of our flesh and its ways, will be gone. This is the final cleansing, when we are changed and we are with Christ.

It was almost more than I could bear! I just wanted to run to Jesus and fall at His feet and just wrap my arms around Him, and just thank Him for all that He had done for me! As I started to walk towards Him, they angels pulled me back. I didn't understand. I asked them, why couldn't I go to Him. The one on my right replied, that I was not worthy to touch Him. I was heartbroken, I started walking away. I began to pray in my heart, Lord Jesus, if I cannot touch you with my hands, I will touch you with my heart. I will touch you with my prayers, I will touch you with my song, I will touch you with my praise, I will touch you with my service, and I will touch you with my love and the honoring of your name. I will touch you with all that is in me. The angels lead me pass the right side of the throne. I started walking, I noticed that I was on the side of a mountain. The path leading down from the throne room was long and narrow as it winded down

the mountain. As I was walking I noticed someone coming towards me. Still saddened and a little upset by the fact that I could not touch My Lord and Savior, Jesus Christ, I just kept walking. I remember thinking how I did not want to harm Him, I just wanted lay at His feet and thank and praise him for all He had done for me, and all that He had been, and still was too me. I couldn't understand why the angels would not allow me to touch Him. As I looked up, I noticed the man I saw earlier walking towards me. He was clothed in a blue and purple robe, and a red scarf; which wrapped around his body and came up over his shoulder, and hung off his shoulder in the back. He was closer now.

I wondered who could this be walking towards me. I really did not want to talk to anybody at that time; I was still just so hurt from not being able to go to Jesus, and tell Him how much I loved Him. As the man was getting closer to me, I began to get afraid and somewhat agitated, because it seemed like he was determined to run into me. I was thinking that the path was already too narrow for one, and there was

nowhere else for me to step out of the way without falling off the mountain itself. I began to get nervous, I didn't know what to do. The man just kept coming closer and closer. He had a warm smile on His face. I wondered why was He smiling so. He came even closer. As He got right in front of me, He stopped.

I could see him better now. He smiled. I felt myself calming down, and the fear leaving me. He began to speak, "You could not come to me, and touch me, because of your sins. But I could come to you and touch you, to bring you back to me." At that moment, I knew who he was. I did not recognize him at first because he looked like a plain, and simple man from the distance. but when He spoke I knew who He was. He said again, "You could not come up to heaven, to touch me; but I could come down from heaven to touch you. I came down from Heaven to bring you back to me."

I wrapped my arms around His shoulders as I hugged Him and cried. He hugged me back. I felt all my fears and sorrows just leave away. I began to thank him for everything, and for

allowing me hold him and touch him. I thanked him for dying for me, for paying my price. I thanked Him for loving me, for saving me, and for saving my life. I thanked Him for not looking at my flesh, but looking at my heart and my spirit. For seeing how much I loved Him, despite the wretched life that I had lived before Him, and for dying for me on the cross, that I might live. I thanked Him for everything I could think of. It was just wonderful, that I could touch Him and thank Him personally for who and what He was and is to me, and for all that He had done for me.

This vision established in me, Christ's love for me, and not just for me, but for all who believe and accept His salvation. Jesus will forgive you if you ask, and truly seek salvation. He will come and see about you. The Lord has many ways of touching His people, of letting them to know that He loves them and wants to be with them. Sharing their life with them. I couldn't go to Him, because my sins had separated me from Him, so Christ came to me. Jesus gave up all that

He was in Heaven, to come and bring us salvation, and we did not know Him:

> "And, behold, two of them went that same day to a village called Emmaus, which was from Jerusalem about threescore furlongs,
>
> And they talked together of all things which had happened.
>
> And it came to pass, that, while they communed together and reasoned, Jesus himself drew near, and went with them.
>
> But their eyes were holden that they should not know Him. And He said unto them.
>
> And they drew nigh unto the village, whither they went: and he made as though he would have gone further.
>
> But they constrained Him, saying Abide with us: for it is toward evening, and the day is far spent. And He went in to tarry with them.

And it came to pass, as he sat at meat with them, he took bread, and blessed it, and brake, and gave to them.

And their eyes were opened, and they knew him; and he vanished out of their sight."

-Luke 24: 13-17, 28-30, (KJV)

Christ came to us, because we were unable to come to Him. Our sins separated us from having the meaningful relationship we so desperately needed with the Father. Through the acceptance of Christ, as Lord and Savior, and the forgiveness of sins, we are given the opportunity, to once again come into sweet fellowship with the Father.

"Behold, the Lord's hand is not shortened, that it cannot save; neither his ear heavy, that it cannot hear:

But your iniquities have separated between you and your God, and your sins have hid his face from you, that he will not hear".

- Isaiah 59: 1-2, (KJV)

Christ came to earth to save all who desire to be saved and have their relationship restored back to a most Holy and loving God. He volunteered to come and be the ultimate sacrifice for our sins.

"So Christ was once offered to bear the sins of many; and unto them that look for him shall he appear the second time without sin unto salvation.

Wherefore when he cometh into world, he saith, Sacrifice and offering thou wouldest not, but a body hast thou prepared me:

Then said I Lo, I come (In The Volume Of The Book It Is Written Of Me) To Do Thy Will, O God."

Hebrews 9: 28, 10: 5, 7, (KJV)

The Vision Of The Banquet Table

In 1993 during the month of August, I can't remember the exact day, I was laying down on my bed kind of half asleep, and half awake, not quite ready to get up. I was trying to get those extra few minutes before getting up, and starting the day. I remember laying there just praying quietly, about some things I was going through in my body at the time. I had been hurt on the job earlier, and it had set off some other health issues which I was later told that I was not suppose to have been bothered with until I was reached my 80's, God willing. I was often left feeling drained, very tired, weak, and mostly

in a lot of pain. Some years later, in the year 2005, The Lord God did miraculously heal, just as He had revealed to me five years before in 1995, but this is another wonderful testimony to tell at a different time.

This particular morning, I was feeling, just a little more drained than usual, and I thought if I could just rest in the bed for just a little while longer, and just talk with the Lord about it; the feeling would soon pass and I would be able to get about the day. Turning on my side, I remember looking at the clock and the time it was, then suddenly, it was as if a deep sleep just came over me. I remember feeling a cool breeze blow across my face, like someone had just breathed on me. One of those kind of breezes you feel on a nice summer's day, when it's not too hot and it's not too cold, but just right. It was so relaxing and calming.

When I opened my eyes, I was surprised to see where I was standing. I was standing in the midst of a great crowd, surrounded by people from all over the world. From adults to children, all ages, and sizes. We were all dressed in white Linen

robes. It was amazing! Everyone was smiling and looked to be very happy. It was wonderful to see. No one looked to be at odds with anybody, even though there was so many of us, all gathered together in one place. It was as if everyone was just so glad to be there and in the midst. All I could tell as far as I could see was we were without number! Everyone looked to be just glad to see one another! That amazed me more than anything at that particular moment. It was a rarity to see all the different races and no one upset with anyone.

As far as I could see from the front, the sides and behind me, people were standing close together, happy as happy can be, including me.

I looked all around, trying to see as much as possible. We all seemed to be crowded around someone standing in the middle of us. Everyone had made a circle around Him, and unfortunately, being short, I had to stand on my tiptoes, because those that were standing around me, were much taller than I. There were others short like myself, in the midst, we were all trying our best to see the person standing in the middle.

I could not see his face because the light that was illuminating from Him was so bright, I could not make out His facial features. He had on a white linen robe that seemed to move and flow easily as He moved. There was a gold sash or scarf that was wrapped around his waist and draped over his shoulder. He had hair that was wavy and was to his shoulders. It looked to be brown, and shown with gold streaks in it. He stood in the middle of us, and he looked to be just a head taller than the rest of us.

I watched as he held out his hand and said, "Welcome to the banqueting table." He told us to sit down and eat and that we could eat as much as we wanted. The table was beautiful! It was the longest table I have ever seen in my life. It seemed to have no end! I was fascinated! I have never seen so much food before! There was food and fruits of all kinds on the table. The table itself was covered in a bright white and luminous table cloth that had a beautiful pattern in it that matched the intricate carvings in the silverware. It reflected every color of the rainbow, it was beautiful! The plates looked

like they were made of mother of pearl, trimmed in a bright gold! The silverware was also made of the same beautiful bright gold, the purest form of gold I had ever seen! It was all so very beautiful to see! The intricate carving that I saw on the silverware handles, I noticed was carved into all the gold items on the table. From the bowls, to the stems of the drinking glasses, to the candlestick holders that were placed on the table between the bowls and the different platters of food. It was beyond words! Just absolutely gorgeous! The drinking glasses looked to be made of the clearest crystal you would ever want to see. The rims of the glasses were trimmed in the same beautiful bright gold as the plates were, and reflected the same luminous rainbow of colors.. What was so astonishing to me, was that when they reflected these colors, they all did it at the same time, as if they were moving in a pattern to the sound of the softly playing music that was playing in the air around us. The music had no distinct instrumental sound that I could pickup. All I know, is that it felt alive. As if having a sound of its own.

I noticed, from the plates, to the glasses to the bowls, to the tablecloth, and even to the silverware. The rainbow reflection of the luminous light was shining off of everything in the room, which by the way, looked to be a great hall room with no end in sight, that I could see. There were beautiful flower arraignments which consisted of every flower you could possibly think of. Some looked to be tropical, with beautiful shades of green leaves in them. Some were mixed with flowers I thought I recognized. Beside them stood the candle holders. Three beautiful luminous white, mother of pearl looking candles were in them. The tallest candle being in the middle. With one candle on each side of it, to the left and the right. All three were of equal size, but the one in the middle set highest. They had a soft creamy white flame glowing on the top of them. The flame never flickered as most candle flames do, they just softly flowed, as if moving together. I remember marveling at the sight of them. The candles reflected the same rainbow of luminous colors as everything else that was a part of the table set up. They too were moving in waves to

the same softly playing music that was in the air. Every wave of luminescent light shining off of the items that were on the table all moved together at the same time. It seemed as if the light, itself were alive!

As we were all invited to the banqueting table, we quickly found a chair to sit in. The chairs were a beautiful wood that had the same beautiful intricate pattern carved into it, that I saw carved in the gold items on the table. The seats and the backs where covered in a material I do not know. It was not rough, but it was not too soft either. It just kept us in place as we sat. It was not slippery as some chair cloths are. It kept us in place as we sat. It was comfortable. The arm rests on each side, were curved to the curvature of our arms from the elbows to the hands. The wood of the arm rests looked like a beautiful polished redwood.

I remember walking and putting my hands on top of the chair I wanted to sit in. I tried to get as close as I could to the chairs that I saw were placed mid ways the length of the table across from me. The chairs I saw sitting mid way, across from

me, were three thrones. The tallest being in the middle just like the three candlesticks that were placed in various places on the table.

The throne in the middle was covered in a beautiful intricate red pattern like material, a deep shade of red. The brocade looking pattern, and the carving in the wood of the thrones was the same as the carvings that was found in all the other items on and around the table. What this means I don't know. I don't know if it was a language or just a lovely design. All I know is that it was very beautiful to see. I know I have probably used the word beautiful too many times, but I don't know how else to describe it. It was just breath taking too me. I have always been a simple person. I can dress up when I want to, but mostly, I choose to keep it simple. To see something like this, was just amazing to me. What blessed me the most, was that I was standing amongst them. I remember being very happy and grateful, that I was not left out!

All around us there appeared to be a cloudy like mist, as if we were standing in the midst of clouds. I remember

questioning in my mind as to, how was it that we were we all able to stand, as if standing on solid ground, and not falling through? Just my limited thinking, trying to grasp, the nothing impossible in God. I remember looking at my feet, noticing that the slippers that I was wearing, were also made of a luminous, and iridescent type of material, kind of white and silvery looking. It all was just, too wonderful to me.

As with every vision that I received from the Lord, I always looked to see if I could find something pertaining to it in the Bible. Call me Gideon, if you like. It just confirmed all the more in me, that what I was seeing, was truly of the Spirit of the Lord. Not that I doubted the Lord, but that I doubted myself. Because of the type of visions that the Holy Spirit were revealing to me, I felt so unworthy to receive them, but for the grace of God.

As I stated before, I never was one to write down my visions as soon as I had them. Which is why I cannot remember the exact day the Holy Spirit has given me a vision, just the vision

itself, mainly. They, have always remained clear in my mind. Things like that, you do not forget, and who would want to?

"And I heard as it were the voice of a great multitude, and as the many waters, and as the voice of mighty thunderings, saying, Alleluia: for the Lord God omnipotent reigneth.

Let us be glad and rejoice, and give honor to Him: for the marriage supper of the Lamb is come, and his wife hath made herself ready.

And to her it was granted that she should be arrayed in fine linen, clean and white: for the fine linen is the righteousness of the saints.

And he saith unto me, write, Blessed are they which are called unto the marriage supper of the lamb. And he saith unto me, These sayings are true sayings of God.

And I fell at his feet to worship him, And he said unto me, See thou do it not: I am thy fellow servant,

and of thy brethren that have the testimony of Jesus: worship God: for the testimony of Jesus is the spirit of prophesy."

- Revelation 19: 6-10, (KJV)

Now here is the question, are we ready for the feast? Have we made ready for the banquet that is to come in heaven with Christ our Lord and King? Are we prepared to go into the Wedding feast?

"Then saith he to his servants, The wedding is ready, but they which were bidden were not worthy.

Go ye into the highways, and as many as ye shall find, bid to the marriage.

So those servants went out into the highways, and gathered together all as many as they found, both bad and good: and the wedding was furnished with guests.

And when the king came in to see the guests, he saw there a man which had not on a wedding garment:

And he saith unto him, Friend, how camest thou in hither not having a wedding garment? And he was speechless.

Then said the King to the servants, Bind him hand and foot, and take him away, and cast him into outer darkness; there shall be weeping and gnashing of teeth. For many are called, but few are chosen."

- Matthew 22: 8 - 14, (KJV)

How marvelous to know what awaits us in Heaven, and how wonderful it is to have Jesus Christ, the Son of the living God, in one's life.

The Prayers Of The Saints

After the prayer of releasing during that powerful women's day service in Columbus Ohio when the presence of the Lord was moving so powerfully in the room! The Holy Spirit began to give me a succession of visions pertaining to our Lord and Savior Jesus Christ, and to things heavenly.

This particular vision dealt with the prayers that we pray unto the Lord. I remember when I was five years old and my mother was putting me to bed. She told me for the first time, I'm going to teach you how to pray, and every night I want you to say this prayer before you go to bed. The prayer went

like this, " Now I lay me down to sleep, I pray the Lord my soul to keep. If I should die before I wake, I pray the Lord my soul to take."

Being only five years old, I was obedient, because I feared my mother, and didn't want to get spanked for not being obedient. Truth be told, it started an awareness in me that there just might actually be a God that was listening to our prayers. At that time and really for sometime after that, throughout my child hood, I wasn't sure, but I did believe or at least hoped that it was so. That one prayer, set off many prayers in my life that followed me into adulthood and eventually did cause me to come and give my life to Christ. I remember praying over and over in my early teen years for God to change my mind. I would all ways start my prayer off like this, " Lord, I don't know any, Thee's or Thou's; but they said if we prayed in your name, the name of Jesus, you would hear our prayer. Life was very stressful then, I wasn't saved. I didn't know the Lord as my personal Savior, and even though I attended church and said I believed, I still did not

know Him as my own personal Savior. I just knew of Him. Praying from my heart, I continued praying in that manner, hoping, that the Lord was listening to me; He was.

When I really began to notice that some of my prayers were actually being heard, was when I entered high school and the mind that I carried all through middle school, was gone! As if someone had just wiped the slate clean of all the bad thoughts that I was suffering from and in their place, put a mind of wanting to live and be happy instead. Where that mind came from? I could not tell you, only that it happened, and I believe it was God that did it; because I hadn't told no one else about what was going on in my young mind at that time. I did not have a relationship with the Lord then. To me, it was strange, but exciting at the same time. It was as if I just woke up one day, and that which had been plaguing me in my thoughts, and in my mind, for the past three years, was gone. I had never experienced that before, and for someone who had not a relationship with the Lord, for Him to move like that on my behalf, was something unexpected.

I was always taught, growing up in church, that God did not hear a sinner's prayer. I found that not to be true, at least not in the way it was explained to me, because if God did not hear our prayers when we are honestly seeking to know Him, though we are sinners, how would we become born again?

> "God is a Spirit: and they that worship him must worship him in spirit and in truth."
>
> - John 4:24, (KJV)

That's it, in spirit and in truth. We must be honest with God, and recognize, that He is a Spirit, though we cannot see Him, that doesn't mean, He is not there, and He is not listening. Also by not praying repetitive prayers that we really don't mean. Like the hypocrites, and the heathen were doing at the time, in the Bible, when Christ rebuked them for their phoniness. They would put ashes on their head and walk around in sackcloth before the people, making a show of things, trying to appear like they were so holy and dedicated to God, whereas inwardly they were not serving the Lord God at all with their heart!

"And when thou prayest, thou shalt not be as the hypocrites are: for they love to pray standing in the synagogues and in the corners of the streets, that they may be seen of men. Verily I say unto you, They have their reward.

But thou, when thou prayest, enter into thy closet, and when thou hast shut thy door, pray to thy Father which seeth in secret; and thy Father will reward thee openly.

But when ye pray, use not vain repetitions, as the heathen do: for thet think that they shall be heard for their much speaking.

For the Father knoweth what things ye have need of, before ye ask Him."

- Matthew 6: 5 - 8, (KJV)

God is looking for real, true, and sincere prayer from the heart, and the soul! At that time, I may had not have had a relationship with Him, but I all ways gave Him honor and

respect for who He was and is. I valued Him, I just didn't value myself at that particular time. To this day, I believe because I was praying from my heart, through His mercy and loving kindness, He chose to answer me, the sinner that I was! But for the Grace!

After that mighty prayer on the day of the women's meeting, this was one of the many visions the Holy Spirit had given to me.

After the service, my sister-in-law and I, at that time, went back to our hotel room. The meeting was held in Columbus Ohio. We had driven down from Akron to attend the meeting. The Jurisdictional meeting lasted three days. I had laid down on my bed, still feeling the presence of the Spirit of the Lord on me strongly. I tried to sleep, but sleep just would not come. I was still too caught up in the Spirit! I tried closing my eyes, trying to calm myself down, but the Spirit of the Lord, was still moving in me. I could not settle down. The way the Spirit of the Lord was moving in the meeting, to me, it was just awesome. As I closed my

eyes, The Spirit of the Lord, was revealing so many things to me, as I lay on the bed. My sister- in law later told me later, that as I was laying down on the bed, I started talking and describing things pertaining to what the Bible said about heaven. She told me, how that I was talking really fast, and she wanted to remember what I was saying. So she hurried and found a piece of paper so she could write down what I was saying. Afterwards, she told me, how that she picked up her Bible and began to look up what I was saying. She said she was not able to write it all down because I was talking so fast. All I knew, was that, me and the Lord was having a conversation and He was revealing many things to me. One of the visions I saw was this; I saw the throne room of Jesus, only this time, it was a little different. The throne sat in the forefront, in the middle of the room.

I watched, as I was once again standing to the side, and viewing what was taking place. I saw Christ Jesus sitting on the throne. Only this time, His throne sat in the middle of the forefront of the room. He was looking straight ahead, as

if intently focusing on something. After a moment or so, I smelled a sweet fragrance enter the room. The scent filled the room. I wondered where it was coming from. It had a light smoke that seem to flow with it, like the smoke that comes from burning incense. I looked to see where it was coming from in the room.

Then I noticed that I could hear voices speaking in the midst of the smoke, of what I thought, was just burning incense! They were prayers, and they were all coming up around the throne of Jesus Christ. They, were the fragrance, I was smelling in the room. Prayers of the saints, in all tongues! All languages! They were coming up and encircling Christ, like a cloud, and He was listening to every one of them! Even though there were many, many prayers, coming from all over the world, constantly rising up around the throne, flowing around Him; He did not miss a one.

I watched in amazement as He listened to every one of them, individually so, With much patience, while giving attention to every prayer, He sat very still, never moving,

not once. I thought to myself, there was no way I could do that and never get tired. I think I would have shut it down for a moment! Only Christ Jesus, could so patiently listen to all our prayers like that, without ever getting tired. Hearing each prayer, no matter how small, no matter how long, and no matter how many. I saw as these prayers like the smoke of incense just flowed up, encircled Him, and entered into His ears. His face, looking ever so concerned with every prayer. All I could think of, was that Jesus heard and was listening to all our prayers, every last one of them, that were prayed out of sincerity of heart. All of them mattered to Christ. Do you know how encouraging that is to know, that Jesus hears all our prayers that we pray from our heart? To know that Jesus is listening to all of your prayers to Him, at all times, from everywhere? You know sometimes we think He isn't listening, when we are pouring our heart out about whatever it is that we are praying to the Him about, well, just watching Him listening to all those that were praying to Him, gave me such a spiritual boost in my walk with Christ. It encouraged me not

to let myself get discouraged, and stop praying just because a prayer is not answered speedily, but to know that my prayer has been heard, and in God's time, He will answer it! Even now, when discouragement tries to creep in, and it will at times, when we are going through trials, or troubles. When it does, I remind myself of what was shown me in this vision, and encourage myself in the Lord. I hope that in the sharing of this beautiful vision that was given me by the Holy Spirit, about the prayers of the saints, and how they are received by Christ, that you will find the same hope and encouragement that I have found in it.

Now I understand even all the more why the Lord God had the Prophets of old to write the visions down that He was giving them, because He knew that one day, the world was going to need them! We would be needing them, the saints of God. So please be encouraged people! There is not a prayer that escapes our Lord's ears! He listens to them all, He hears us, when we call.

"And when he had opened the seventh seal, there was silence in heaven about the space of half an hour.

And I saw the seven angels which stood before God; and to them were given seven trumpets.

And another angel came and stood at the altar, having a golden censer; and there was given unto him much incense, that he should offer it with the prayers of all saints upon the golden altar which was before the throne,

And the smoke of the incense, which came with the prayers of the saints, ascended up before God out of the angel's hand."

- Revelation 8: 1-4, (KJV

The Voice Of God: Thunders And Lightning

I can only imagine how the Israelites must have felt. When they were all standing at the base of Mount Sinai. Watching Moses ascend up into the cloud that surrounded the mountain, to talk to God. Listening at the thunder boom, causing the ground to shake. Watching the lightening flashing as it went streaking through the sky and the clouds surrounding the top of the mountain. It must have been a frightening experience for them. Often when we think of God, for the most part; we imagine the lighter side of Him. We don't like to think of the terribleness

of Him, His power, might, and majesty. I have found since I have been born again, that dark clouds and their terribleness, does not always mean evil. It also represents the awesomeness of power and majesty, when it comes to God. He is omnipotent-all powerful. As a child, I used to be afraid of when I would see dark, thick, and brooding storm clouds, however, since I have been saved, I now think twice about them. In the natural sense, dark clouds may or may not be good. They could represent storms, in a bad way as pertaining to floods, or electrical power outages, or they could be lifesavers, as in pertaining to drought. The presence of dark looking storm clouds could mean that a needed rain, is about to fall, or in another sense, too much rain is about to fall. The same principle applies to spiritual matters as well. Dark and ominous clouds can represent the presence of the Almighty God, as it did for the children of Israel, when they were standing at the base of the mount. They could also represent a sign of judgment. They also represent a sign of dark, and troubling times ahead, as well. It depends on what context they are being used in.

"And Moses brought forth the people out of the camp to meet with God; and they stood at the nether part of the mount.

And mount Sinai was altogether on a smoke, because the Lord descended upon it in fire: and the smoke thereof ascended as the smoke of a furnace, and the whole mount quaked greatly

And all the people saw the thunderings, and the lightnings, and the noise of the trumpet, and the mountain smoking: and when the people saw it, they removed, and stood afar off.

And they said unto Moses, Speak thou with us, and we will hear: but let not God speak with us, lest we die.

And Moses said unto the people, Fear not: for God is come to prove you, and that His fear may be before your faces, that ye sin not.

And the people stood afar off, and Moses drew near

unto the thick darkness where God was." - ."

- Exodus 19: 17, 18, 20: 18-21, (KJV)

The mountain quaked, because of the power and majesty of God descended upon it. It was more than the natural mountain could bear. They had been in Egypt for four hundred years. The little knowledge that they had about the Lord God, being passed down from generation to generation, wasn't enough to prepare them for this.

Surely, they had seen the miracles and mighty wonders that God had did to deliver them from the hand of Pharaoh. They also, witnessed the wonders of God in the desert, where He caused water to flow from the rocks, and bread to fall from the sky, but even with all this; it still wasn't enough to prepare them for this. Which makes me wonder; Why not?

It wasn't that they hadn't prepared themselves physically. The men had stayed away from their wives. Keeping themselves clean. They had washed their bodies and their clothes. They had fasted, preparing for their meeting with God on the

mountain. What went wrong? Why were they so frightened when the presence of God showed up on the mountain? When the people saw what was happening on the mount, they quickly decided that they only wanted Moses to talk to them from that point on. Could it be, that no matter how much you clean and dress up the outside, if what's inside is not prepared to meet the Lord, like your heart, for instance, the presence of the Spirit of the Lord, might would be, a frightening experience? I have found, that too many, today, who have not come to Christ, the moving of the Spirit of the Lord is still, somewhat of a frightening experience. It brings to light, the reality of the existence of an all powerful God, and our Savior, the Lord Jesus Christ. I have witnessed that there are those today, still running from the presence of the Lord. Afraid of what might be revealed about them, and what darkness that is inside of them, that they might have to deal with. I have also seen, that if we don't allow Christ and the Spirit of truth, which is the Holy Spirit, to reveal what is inside of us, how will we be delivered from it? It wasn't

so much the show of power that frightened the Israelites, but, that this show of power was acquainted with God. I 'm sure they had witnessed dark clouds and lightening during thunderstorms before while they were in Egypt, but that was just weather, however when it is not just reactions of the flow of currents of hot, and cold streams of moisture, wind, and clouds, but the very nature of a living being; to me, it should have caused a humbling, and sobering effect. One, that in my opinion, should be shared by us today, considering; God has not changed. He is still, all powerful, all knowing, and all present.

In the year 2005,while once again in prayer, I was petitioning the Lord Jesus Christ, for strength, help, and encouragement. I was dealing with some health issues in my body that was causing me a lot of problems continually, keeping me in and out of the hospital emergency room. It was frustrating, to say the least, but never- the- less, It kept me on my knees, praying and seeking the Lord for His help, as well as His deliverance. This was before the miraculous healing

that I received from the Lord Jesus Christ later that year, in the month of June.

During the prayer, I was given a vision by the Holy Spirit, concerning the voice of God and what heaven was preparing for next. In the vision, I was taken up between heaven and earth, it was dark and cloudy. I remember stepping out of the dark, into mid air. There were clouds underneath my feet and clouds over my head, but the place where I was standing, was in between the clouds.

The clouds under me were dark, and the clouds over me were red, and were filled with what looked like fire. The earth was also dark, just like it would look just before day. I could see the sun off in the distance, rising up over the horizon, to the east. The sky under the clouds had began to light up with the colors of red, orange and yellow, just like it would look before the break of day. Over my head, the clouds were layered one upon another, and the sky above them, was a darker red.

As I listened to what I first thought were many voices. I soon learned from listening closer, that it was not many

voices, but just one voice! Layering and layering upon itself! Every time it spoke it was so powerful, that it just boomed with thunder! As I watched, I saw that it was going out all over the earth, like streaks of lightning.

I leaned in closer, to see if I could make out what the voice was saying. I could hear what was being said, I just couldn't remember what was being said. You know how you may hear someone talking around you. You know what they're saying, but as soon as they say it, the memory of what was said, immediately leaves your thoughts, or is hid from you. It reminds me of what Paul said in the book of 2 Corinthians:

"It is not expedient for me doubtless to glory. I will come to visions and revelations of the Lord.

I knew a man in Christ above fourteen years ago, (whether in the body, I cannot tell; or whether out of the body, I cannot tell: God knoweth;) such a one caught up to the third heaven.

And I knew such a man, (whether in the body, or out of the body, I cannot tell: God knoweth;)

How that he was caught up into paradise, and heard unspeakable words, which it is not lawful for a man to utter.

Of such a one will I glory: yet of myself I will not glory, but in mine infirmities."

- 2 Corinthians 12: 1-5, (KJV)

I used to often wonder what Paul meant, when I would read this passage, about, unspeakable words. It was not until I was given this particular vision by the Holy Spirit, that I finally truly understood what he meant. You cannot speak, what you cannot retain in your memory. There are some things the Lord does not fully want to reveal till it is time for them to be revealed. For example; when He told Daniel to seal the book:

"But thou, O Daniel, shut up the words, and seal the book, even to the time of the end: many shall run to and fro, and knowledge shall be increased."

- Daniel 12: 4, (KJV)

When the book of Revelations was given to John on the Isle of Patmos, The Lord Jesus revealed more of what was originally given to Daniel in the Old Testament. Bringing the picture and the understanding of what would be happening in these latter days more into view. Would I liked to have been able to remember what was being said? Yes, but it was not for me to remember, or to repeat, other than what was being given me.

As I was watching this event unfolding before my eyes, still trying to hear what was being said, I noticed that there stood beside me a man. He was tall and dressed in white. I asked him, what are these voices, that are really just one voice, saying? He replied, " This is the voice of the Lord God almighty, He is sending commands throughout the earth!" I asked him, "What are the commands that He sending?" He replied, "Heaven is preparing for two events!" I asked him what two events? He said, Heaven is preparing for the receiving of the saints, and after that, Battle! " I was amazed, and surprised. I was wondering, why the Holy Spirit had

chose me to reveal this too. I was honored, but, I still was somewhat, surprised. I had always thought that these kind of messages were only supposed to come to someone of more important status in God. Someone with the means and ability to effect a lot of people. I felt an urgency in the message. Over the years since, I have shared the message of the vision, verbally, amongst different ones in the Lord, but I hadn't thought to write it down, until now.

Not long after I had become saved, I was going from door to door, witnessing and inviting people to church. I met a young lady who was also a Christian and loved the Lord. I invited her to come to church with me, seeing she only stayed a couple of blocks from me. I told her that when someone comes to pick me up from church, they could swing by and pick her up as well. We became good friends, and often shared testimonies about the goodness of the Lord. She even went with me sometimes, when I would go from door to door. She already was a member of another church, but she still would visit my church on occasion, as well.

I shared with her about the dreams and visions that I had been receiving from the Spirit of the Lord, at that time, this was in 1982. I did not understand why I was having them. I was a very young saint, and I did not understand much back then, such as callings, and gifts of the Spirit. It was all new to me. She told me how that I had been gifted to see visions and dreams pertaining to heaven, and that it was a rare gift. I had shared with her some things I had seen and some of the dreams that I was having. I still wondered, why me? I was not anybody of notoriety, I was just somebody that was just blessed to be saved. The Lord God chooses whom He please to receive His word for His people. I am sure there were many in the Bible, that wondered why or how God chose them, but yet, through their obedience, when He chose them, they were able to help and to bless many people. I do not despise the choosing of the Lord, to the contrary, I am honored. He didn't have to choose me, but He did, and I am thankful and grateful, that He saw something in me, that He could use. I still think back to that day, when thinking about the

different visions and dreams that the Lord has given me since then. It just confirms in me, that God is still in control, and even though things may not look like it sometimes, He is. God has His time table set in which He chooses to move! The Lord knows what He is going to do for His people! God is not swayed by the happenings, and events in this world. He already has His plan of action out there. His spirit is moving all over the world in the hearts of whomever will receive salvation through the Lord Jesus Christ! God is preparing for receiving of His people, the angels and all of heaven. Do we know what we should be doing to get prepared. The time of preparation is nearing an end, the time of action, is about to begin.

> "Behold I come as a thief. Blessed is he that watcheth, and keepeth his garments, lest he walk naked, and they see his shame.

> And he gathered them together into a place called in the Hebrew tongue Armageddon.

And the seventh angel poured out his vial into the air; and there came a great voice out of the temple of heaven, from the throne, saying, It is done.

And there were voices, and thunders, and lightnings; and there was a great earthquake, such as was not since men were upon the earth, so mighty an earthquake, and so great.

And every island fled away, and the mountains were not found."

- Revelations 16:15-18, 20, (KJV)

The commands of God, are going out through the earth, heaven is preparing for the saints of God, and for battle, shouldn't we be preparing for heaven? I am reminded of a passage of scripture, in the Word of God, when Elihu, was speaking to Job, pertaining unto the voice of God:

"At this also my heart trembleth, and is moved out of his place.

Hear attentively the noise of his voice, and the sound that goeth out of His mouth.

He directeth it under the whole heaven, and His lightning unto the ends of the earth.

After it a voice roareth: He thundereth with the voice of His excellency; and He will not stay them when His voice is heard.

God thundereth marvelously with His voice; great things doeth He, which we cannot comprehend."

- Job 37: 1 - 5, (KJV)

It was as if, he was there, when the Holy Spirit revealed this to me, in the vision, when He took me up, between the clouds.

The Windows In Heaven

"Then I beheld all the work of God, that a man cannot find out the work that is done under the sun: because though a man labor to seek it out, yet he shall not find it; yea further; though a wise man think to know it, yet shall he not be able to find it."

- Ecclesiastes 8: 17, (KJV)

How often would we like to look into the future and be able to see what God sees about us. I find, that only the Lord God truly knows our beginning, and our end, as well as all our in between.

In the year 2004, during praying, I was given another a vision by the Holy Spirit. In which I found myself walking in the dark. There were no lights that I could see at the moment. It was pitch black. I wondered why, I was having to walk in the dark, unable to see where I was going. It was overwhelming, it made me nervous. I was starting to feel anxious, and I was in a hurry to get out of it. Continuing to walk forward, I finally saw a light shining from a doorway, a head of me to the right, just little ways further down, what now I could make out as a very, long hallway. Now, the thing that struck me as strange, or unusual about all of this, was that, there was no floor underneath me, that I could see, but yet whatever I was walking on, felt as solid as a rock. I kept looking down to see what I was walking on that felt so hard, but there was nothing to see. Just empty space. I marveled at that, because even though, I could actually feel the solidness under my feet, I couldn't see what was holding me up. In most of the visions, the Holy Spirit gave to me, I could always see where I was standing, and I knew if I was standing on solid ground, or just

suspended in mid air, because the Holy Spirit would always allow me to see where and what I was standing on. This time it was different, I couldn't see anything. I just had to trust, that with every step I took, I would be supported, and able to continue walking forward, even if I didn't know where I was going, or how I was going to get to where I was supposed to be; or even if I was not sure that if I kept walking, that I would have anything, or anyone to stand on. This was a time that, I couldn't afford the luxery of doubt, and confusion. I had to make a choice, to trust God, and to keeping going forward, or sink back into fear, and try to run back. I stopped for a moment, and looked behind me. I couldn't see anything there either, I didn't want to take the chance of becoming lost in the dark, and not being able to find my way out. I started to encourage myself. I told myself, God wouldn't bring me here, if He had no plans of revealing anything to me. I would have to just trust Him, and stand on my knowledge of the kind of God that I know He is. He's a loving God, and a caring Father, whom I know, loves all of His children, and would

never leave them, nor forsake them. This is where I had to remind myself of the many times, that Christ had brought me out of all the dark places, I have traveled to in this life. I knew, I had to have faith, and trust in Him, that He would not let me fall or be lost. I decided to keep walking forward.

I knew the Lord was providing something for me to walk on, because with every step I took, I could feel the firmness under my feet, like the way marble feels when you're standing or walking on it, strong,and solid. My fear was gone, being replaced by confidence.

Ever see yourself stepping out into the emptiness of space, able to walk, as if you were walking on solid ground, and actually feel, something solid under your feet? In the natural, this would be impossible, but through Christ Jesus, I am finding, that there's nothing impossible with God. I guess, I am spending so much time describing this part of the vision, because it reminded me of having that blind faith in God, whereas you submit yourself completely to God, trusting in Him to do just what He said He would do, even if you don't

know how He is going to do it. It reminds of verse in the book of Hebrews:

"Now faith is the substance of things hoped for, the evidence of things not seen."

- Hebrews 11: 1, (KJV)

As I got to the doorway, and looked inside, I noticed that there were three windows in the room, and standing in front of them, but off to the side, was a very tall man. I believed him to be and angel. As far as width is concerned, the room was small. I stepped inside, once again feeling the firmness under my feet, but still not seeing a floor, I could see light coming from the three windows.

The windows sat in the middle of the room, and looked to be taking up the rest of the space from where they sat, to the back wall.

They were angled at a slant, so you would have to look down into them, in order to see through them. They reminded me of the windows that you might would see on the slant of

the roof, that allowed sunlight to shine into the house from up above.

As I moved further into the doorway, the angel motioned with his hand, for me to come in a little closer. Moving a bit slower this time, I entered into the room. I wondered what it was that he wanted me to show me? At first, I was nervous, but my curiosity, got the better of me. As I walked up to the windows, I noticed that each window had a different view, and there were different things going on in each of the windows. I turned to the angel who was now, standing beside me, and asked him what was going on? Why did each window have a different view? At first he did not answer me, he just remained silent, and continued to looking in the windows. I noticed, He was watching the events unfolding in them, just as I was. I recognized, momentarily, some things that was going on in the first window. They were things of the past, old battles, events, and things that I know happened long ago, but for the most part, everything was going by so fast, I couldn't focus in on a certain event. It was like watching the

history of the world go by in a glance! At the same time, the second window was like watching today's news! It revealed events that seemed to be happening all over in the world, in the present. These too, went by in a glance! It reminded me of the passage in the book of Job.- where Elihu was talking about how the Lord sees man:

> "For his eyes are upon the ways of man, He seeth all his goings."
>
> - Job 34:21, (KJV)

To see, all of man's goings, you would have to be able to see, past, present, and future.

I tried desperately to catch some glance of an recent event that I was happening in the world, that I could describe with some detail, but once again everything was moving so fast, I couldn't focus on anything with any remarkable detail. I wanted to catch some present day event in detail, so that I could share it with others, in hope that it would encourage them all the more in the Lord. It is just that they were moving so fast, I couldn't pick up on details, but they were gone before

I could focus on them. It was fascinating to watch, as well as frustrating, seeing as to how I was trying my best to see something in great detail.

The third window, I noticed that there was a lot of fighting, and warring, people running to and fro, there were other events as well. I saw leaders come and leaders go. One second they were up and speaking, the next they were gone and the stream continued on. Once again, the events in this window were all going by very quickly as well. I asked the angel what were these windows. He told me that they were the past, the present and the future. I then asked him, how is it that all these events were happening at the same time, past, present and the future? He replied that there was no past, present, or future with God. Everything was present with God. He sees everything at the same time, and that God was not limited by time. Only man is limited to time.

For the first time, I had a deeper understanding as to what the Bible was saying about Christ, in Hebrews chapter thirteen:

"Jesus Christ the same yesterday, and today, and

for ever."

- Hebrews 13:8, (KJV)

That is why, when the Lord would give the prophets of

old, a word concerning future events, they could speak with

surety of it manifesting just as it was prophesied. Because

even though it was spoken in the past, or the present, for the

future; in the eyes of God, it had already happened. What is

the proof of that you might ask? when you read of some of the

prophesies that were given in the Word of God, though spoken

in the past, or present, were as the prophet was concerned,

about events that were going to happen in the future; as

the word was given, it happened just as it was spoken. One

such example being: Cyrus, the great. He was the Persian

king that conquered Babylon in 539 B.C., and funded the

rebuilding of the city of Jerusalem and the temple, after they

were conquered by Babylon, and the city and the temple were

destroyed. The archeological discovery of the Cyrus Cylinder,

dating from 536 B.C., further verifies the Biblical account of

this event. Isaiah prophesied of King Cyrus being raised up by God as the one whom He would use to perform His will. This prophecy and vision was given to Isaiah years before it actually happened, approximately, 150 years later, to be exact. The prophecy was fulfilled in the book of Ezra. Long after Isaiah was gone:

> "Thus saith the Lord, thy redeemer, and He that formed thee from the womb, I am the Lord that maketh all things; that stretcheth forth the heavens alone; that spreadeth abroad the earth by myself;
>
> That saith of Cyrus, He is my shepherd, and shall perform all my pleasures: even saying to Jerusalem, Thou shalt be built; and to the temple, Thy foundation shall be laid."
>
> - Isaiah 44: 24, 28, (KJV)

Then there are the prophetical visions and prophecies concerning the birth of Christ, that happened just as they were given, to the prophets, thousands of years before. There are the end time prophecies, that we are now witnessing some

of things that were prophesied, unfolding today. Such as the rebirth of the nation of Israel, happening in a day just as was prophesied by Isaiah in the Word of God.

> "Who hath heard such a thing? who hath seen such things? Shall the earth be made to bring forth in one day? or shall a nation be born at once? for as soon as Zion travailed, she brought forth her children."
>
> - Isaiah 66: 8, (KJV)

This happened just as was prophesied, May 14, 1948, the UN agreed to them becoming a state, or nation once again. This happened at midnight on May 14, 1948. Some of the birth pains, or tragedies which they suffered, because of the Holocaust, caused many of the Jewish people from some of all places around the world, or the four corners, so to speak, to want to come together in their own homeland, once again. Things that were spoken thousands of years ago, coming to pass in our generation. There was no way Isaiah, by himself could have foreseen these events, unless they were revealed to him, by an all seeing God. All these things and more, were happening at

the same time before the eyes of God. How wonderful it is, to know that the Lord God is always watching over us, at all times, nothing escaping His loving view. In the Bible, Job comments:

"Doth not He see my ways, and count my steps?"

- Job 31: 4, (KJV)

Job knew that the Lord God was always watching over man. The paths we take, even down to the number of steps that we make, from day to day.

In the Psalm 139, David, when speaking about the omnipresence of the Lord God, writes;

"Whither shall I go from thy spirit? Or whither shall I flee from thy presence?

If I say surely the darkness shall cover me; even the night shall be light about me.

Yea, the darkness hideth not from thee; but the night shineth as day: the darkness and the light are both alike to thee.

- Psalms139: 7, 11-12, (KJV)

For the eyes of the Lord run to and fro throughout the whole earth, to show Himself strong in the behalf of them whose heart is perfect toward Him.

- II Chronicles 16: 9, (KJV).

The eyes of the Lord are in every place, beholding the evil and the good."

- Proverbs 15: 3, (KJV)

I remember trying to lean over the third window that represented the future. While hoping to get a better look at what was happening in the window, immediately, the scene clouded over, whereas, and I wasn't allowed to see anymore. I asked the angel standing in the room, If I could get another look? He replied, No, and that it was not for me to know all that would be happening in the future. He told me, that it was time for me to go back. I felt myself, being pulled backwards out of the room, returning back down the hall, in the dark, from which I had just come. When I opened my eyes, I was back in my own room.

What I learned that day from this particular vision, I will

always take with me. Because it proved to me, how eternal our God really is and the sacrifice that Jesus made to come down to us, to live as a man, with all our problems and limitations, and still maintain His godliness. To feel what we felt, suffer what we suffer. He hungered, He slept, He tired, He had to rest: He felt pain and sorrow. He felt broken heartedness. He cried and wept. He felt the loss of friends. He a worked, he had a profession growing up as a carpenter. As a child growing up in Nazareth, he might have even worked with the sheep, as a shepherd, or in the surrounding vineyards for various vineyard owners. He might have done like some of the other young men of the city of Nazareth, in that day, to help earn money for the family, and waited in the city market place to be hired to work in the nearby fields, as was the custom of the times back then. To give up all that heaven had to offer, for just one minute, would have been more than I could bare, and to think, He gave it all up, to come down to earth, be tortured, whipped, beaten and then crucified on a cross, where He was nailed by His hands and His feet to it.

Heaven, where he felt no pain, suffering, or death! To come to earth, for thirty three years, to give up His life on a cross; so we might have a right to eternal life. No man could have ever foresaw that, given our condition of sin, but praise be the Father, because of His love He sent His word before time, and then sent His Son in time, to redeem, whosoever is willing to be saved, so that we may live with Him for all time.

This vision also taught me, that even though we may, cannot see the future, or even understand the whys of our past and even if we are somewhat stumbling in our present! If we get back on course with Christ, and in Christ! Whatever our past, present or future may be! We can rest assured that God has us in the palm of His hands, just like He allowed me to step out on nothing, but be held up by the power of His Spirit and His will working in my life, I can assured that at all times and we are never out of His sight, or out of His hands.

The Sea of Glass

The year of 2005 brought great spiritual and physical victories for me, and also some great trials as well. I was miraculously healed of cancer, and I was also miraculously healed of fibromyalgia which I was told was in every muscle group in my body! As far as the healing of my body goes, It was a very wonderful year for me. I had been asked to run two revivals that year, in which I got to see Christ bless many saints of God and also witnessed Him do many wonderful things for those of the body of Christ. From the saving of souls to breaking of bondages, and strongholds, to the restoring of different one's

walk with Christ. It is always wonderful to see how Christ blesses and effects every part of our lives. Then there were sorrows too. I am learning, that when the Holy Spirit tells you not to do something, and you do it anyway, thinking you can make a difference in someone's life, you know, those times when you think you know more than God. Not listening, and being disobedient to the will of God, carries a heavy price. Even more so when the Lord has shown you how the thing was going to turn out, step by step, before it even happens, and you go ahead and do it anyway, and of course, it happens exactly as He has shown you. From the dotting of the I, to the crossing of the, T. What can you say, it is disappointing to say the least. When we fail to hear the voice of the Lord, when He is trying to warn us about something. We are not just letting down God, we are letting down our selves.

it is one thing to be prophetical about the ones whom the Lord is using us to speak a word into their lives; but when He talks to us, about us, it's, are you sure Lord? Even when we know that everything inside of us, is telling us, you

know the Lord is right. My mom used to tell me, that a hard head makes a soft behind! That is a true statement. These chastisements, can avoided, if we would listened to the voice of the Lord, when He is talking to us, and trying to guide us out of trouble, or what could be a very negative situation.

There were times during the year that my spirit was so broken, I didn't think I was able to serve the Lord in any capacity, much less, minister in a revival. But these are the times, when I witnessed the Lord move the most in my life. When we are at the point of cannot, Jesus is at the point of yes, we can. As Paul reminds us in Philippians:

> "I can do all things through Christ which strengtheneth me."
>
> - Philippians 4: 13, (KJV)

From my own spiritual healing, to those whom He placed around me. Christ, took my hurt, my pain, as well as my mistakes, and turned them around not only for my good, but others, as well. This is what the Lord God does. He takes your mistakes, and if you are willing to change and be helped by

Him, He will turn them around for the good. It was during these times, when prayer, along with the Word of God becomes our daily bread. When we're seeking Him, for His help, guidance, and wisdom, to help us to overcome the demons that are attacking our faith, and our walk with Christ. When we turn to God, like a loving and protective Father, He gives us the help that we need. Times when we did not think we could do anything, times we almost gave up and quit. Times when we have said to ourselves, It's just too hard Lord, and He reminds us, that we have His strength to lean on. We don't have to go in our strength, we can go in His. That is a wonderful feeling. When you know, that you do not have to go the battle alone. Christ is there to help you stomp on the devil's head.

It was during the month of October, I was fasting and praying getting ready for the revival I was to be ministering over in the month of November. I was praying for a greater anointing to fill my life, and for His strength, to be able to fulfill what He was asking me to do. It was very stressful for me at times. I was going through a difficult time in my

marriage, and at times, it was more than I could bear. I was distressed, and under a lot of pressure. All I could think of, was how could I help someone else, when I needed so much help myself. I was constantly before the Lord in prayer.

Late one night while praying, I had a vision. I saw myself passing through a dark space. After I passed through the momentary darkness,I saw that I was standing on what looked like a wide sea of glass. It was very thick. It looked to be an half of foot thick, and it seemed to stretch as far as the eye could see. it was surrounded by thick clouds.

I quickly noticed that there seemed to be people standing up under the glass, all grouped together. They were all grayish in appearance. They looked like they were made of ash! They seemed to be very angry at my presence, or just angry period. At the front of the sea off in the distance, I could see what looked to be a throne, I couldn't see the face of who it was sitting on it, but everything inside of me, told me, it was the Lord. There were some men standing around it, dressed in robes, each one, had different colored scarf wrapped around

their body and their shoulder. I couldn't see their faces, well either. I was still standing a very far distance away.

I asked the Lord who were these people standing up under the glass and why were they all dressed all gray and were grey themselves. Their skin was the color of ash, that you would find in the fire place after the wood was burned down, and there was nothing left, but the ashes, and why were they so angry. They seemed to back away from me with every step I took toward them, looking down through the glass, trying to see who they were. The glass had a light spectral reflection as the light shined on it. It was just a little cloudy, I believe because of the thickness of the glass. They did not like that I could see them and moved away from me, making growling type noises, with each step I took toward them, as if they wanted me to stay away from them. The closer I came toward them, the louder they became, as if trying to frighten me away, and make me leave them alone. I asked the Lord who were they? He replied, "These are not people, but demons which have just taken the form of people." Then He said, Stomp on their heads! and don't stop till I tell you to!

I started stomping, He said harder! I closed my eyes and began stomping as hard as I could. I heard the Lord say, Harder! Don't stop! I kept stomping! Little did I know, I was moving closer, and closer to the head of the sea of glass, were I saw the throne and the men standing around it. By this time, I was putting all my strength into making sure that I stomped as hard as I could! Then I heard a voice say, Open your eyes, you have made it to the throne!

I opened my eyes, and saw that I was standing at the foot of the throne, in the midst of the men, that I had first seen standing around the throne from a distance. I looked up at the throne, He who I saw sitting on it was clothed in purple and gold. The colors were bright and beautiful. I looked around me, the men, that were standing at the foot of the throne all began to come up around me. I heard the voice of the Lord say to me, "Because I had obeyed Him and did not stop stomping on the demons heads, that I would be able to stomp on their heads all the rest of the days of my life, until I could stand before Him."

I remember being so happy that I had obeyed the Lord and stomped on the demons heads. I felt relieved! and unafraid anymore to do anything that the Lord asked me to do. I knew then that He was going to be with me, and empower me to do whatever He asked me to do. The revival went amazingly to me. As I said earlier, I watched God do some amazing things. Things that I had not seen, since our church, the church I was first saved, used to follow our pastor on revivals, when he was asked to come and minister over the revival. It was amazing. This vision that the Holy Spirit had given me, encouraged me the most, when it came to believing, that no matter what our situation, or circumstance, with God, all things are possible.

When I realized that I was back to myself. I felt the anointing of the Holy Ghost, flowing all through me. I felt, like there was nothing that the Lord wanted me to do, that I could not do, with Him strengthening me and keeping me. With the Lord God as our help and our strength, there is, nothing that we cannot do in Christ. I can imagine what the prophets of old, felt like when the Holy Spirit would come

over them, and bless, and empower them to do great deeds for the Lord. It is a wonderful feeling. It is encouraging as well as empowering to know that the Lord is with us. I needed to see that! It settled in me, that truly it was His will for me to go on, and do what He was asking me to do, and just like that, I know He will empower you too.

> "And He goeth up into a mountain, and calleth unto Him whom He would: and they came unto Him.
>
> And He ordained twelve, that they should be with Him, and that He might send them forth to preach,
>
> And to have power to heal sicknesses, and to cast out devils:"
>
> - Mark 3: 13-15, (KJV)

Jesus is still commissioning workers to go out into the fields, and to lift Him up, for when we lift up the name of Jesus Christ, we put down the forces of darkness! Is it easy work? Not always, But, it's reward out weights the bad!

"And before the throne there was a sea of glass like unto crystal: and in the midst of the throne, and round about the throne, were four beasts full of eyes before and behind.

And the first beast was like a calf, and the second beast like a calf, and the third beast had a face as a man, and the fourth beast was like a flying eagle.

And the four beasts had each of them six wings about him; and they were full of eyes within: and they rest not day and night, saying, Holy, holy, holy, Lord God Almighty, which was, and is, and is to come.

And when those beasts give glory and honor and thanks to Him that sat on the throne, who liveth for ever and ever,

The four and twenty elders fall down before Him that sat on the throne, and worship Him that liveth forever and ever, and cast their crowns before the throne, saying,

Thou art worthy, O Lord, to receive glory and honor and power: for thou hast created all things, and for thy pleasure they are and were created."

- Revelation 4: 6 - 11, (KJV)

CHAPTER EIGHT

The Brass Doors

Most of the time, when we think about passing away, it always seems to fill us with a sense of sadness, fear, and dread. Just to think of one's life ending is a very sobering thought indeed. We immediately think of all the people we are going to miss or things we might have done and not got around to doing, or such like.

We often find ourselves getting caught up in the things of the day. When we do find ourselves staring at the end of this life, we have a tendency to believe that this is the end of it all. Much too often we forget that God has another life planned

for us, that is, if we belong to Him and stay faithful to Him to the end.

> "Now if Christ be preached that He rose from the dead, how say some among you that there is no resurrection of the dead?
>
> But now is Christ risen from the dead, and become the first fruits of them that slept.
>
> For as in Adam all die, even so in Christ shall all be made alive.
>
> Else what shall they do which are baptized for the dead, if the dead rise not at all? why are they then baptized for the dead?"
>
> - 1 Corinthians15 :12, 20, 22, 29, (KJV)

There was a time, when I too, used to think that when we died in this life, that ended it all. Till I got saved, and later, did actually die. I got a chance to see the other side for those who sleep, in Christ. I know a lot of us would like to argue that, those of us who have had this experience, did not really

die, but to those which were present, when it happened, as well as those who experienced it for themselves, it is not a subject of debate, it is a fact. It seems to me that, it's not the dying that is really the question, but, it is what was seen, afterwards. The fact that you were allowed to come back and be able to share what you have seen. Is what our adversary to the cross, doesn't want to be shared! Then there is the ever looming thought that one just might not be prepared to go to heaven. This is why we are given a lifetime to prepare! but there is one thing we need to know, there is a very real heaven, and there is a very real hell. We should be preparing in this life to go to one of them! Hopefully, heaven!

While I was living in Atlanta, Georgia, the Holy Spirit began to once again, give me heavenly visions. One, where He showed me the rapture of the saints, one, where He showed me how we are changed, in the vision, I am now sharing, about the brass doors!

Often when I am laying down, and am feeling relaxed. I find, I can focus more on what I am praying about, at least,

most of the time. This particular time, I had what is known as a night vision, being that I was half awake, and half asleep, but I was still in prayer. In the vision, I remember standing in a hospital corridor. It was somewhat dark. There was a light at the end of the corridor that was coming from another hallway. I saw myself, laying in a hospital bed in the corridor that was dark, up against the wall. That is when, I was no longer watching myself, but I was the one in the bed, dead. It seems I had died of an heart attack, and my body had been pushed outside of the room, and left in the hall way. Strange, I know, I was able to witness, as well as see and experience all this going on at the same time. I watched as I got up and left out of my body. The next thing, I remember seeing, was my spirit or soul, passing through the wall as if, it was not even there! This is where I was no longer watching, but I was a partaker. I could see the structure of the wall from the inside, but that did not prevent me from passing through it, just the same.

When I came through the other side of the wall. I found myself standing in what seemed like a very huge room. The

room was very dark, you could say, pitch black even. There was however one single light! It was shining directly over my head, in front of me. It made a pathway through the darkness of the room. I looked up to see where the light was coming from, but I couldn't make it out. It appeared as if to come out of nowhere, but yet, there it was. I heard a voice, over my head, telling me to follow the path of light and not to be afraid! I started walking, making sure I stayed within the light of the pathway. All around me there was darkness, except on the pathway of light. It felt very cold, andkind of reminded me of the coldness that you would feel in the air, if you were in a cave. It seemed to have a stillness about it. The light, however, felt very warm and comforting to me. It reminded me of a time, once, when I had walked home from the grocery store in the winter. I was living in Ohio then, and my kids were very young. My son was only two, and my daughter was four. I had walked up to the Five Points Plaza, there was a grocery store there at that time. I and my children stayed in an apartment building, a ways from there. The apartments are no longer

there. Sometime after we moved, an electrical fire broke out in the walls of the building, burning up the apartment building, and the apartment building beside it. I am thankful to God, that neither I nor my children were there at that time.

It was freezing outside, but I was determined to get home, so that I could feed my children. There was a lot of snow and ice already on the ground and to make matters even worse, it started to snow again!

As I was walking, the sun began to go down in the sky and so did the temperature. Even though the weatherman had warned about the temperature dropping. I had stayed longer than I had expected to. I wanted to make sure I had enough to feed us until the weather broke, in the next couple of days, when I would be able to come out again.

It was getting colder by the minute! I could feel my hands freezing inside of my gloves! I tried shaking them, to get some feeling back into them. It was a very long walk home from the store. The more I walked through the snow, and the ice; the more I could feel my legs, and my feet, freezing, inside of

my boots, and slowing down. It started to feel like my whole body was trying to stiffen up! As I continued, struggling through the snow, I could feel a sheet of thin ice forming on my face. The temperature was below zero at the time. The weatherman had warned us not to go out in the weather, but I had no choice, there was nothing to feed my children a decent meal with at home, and I wasn't about to let my children go hungry.

I could no longer feel anything in my hands and my feet. Not even when I tried bumping them together, trying to feel something, hoping that they were not frozen or frost bitten. As I was carrying bags of groceries, my hands felt like two blocks of ice. My feet felt like I was walking on stumps! There was no feeling in them at all. I tried stomping my feet on the ground, trying to get some feeling in them. Once again there was nothing! I started to cry, as the thought of possibly, freezing to death, out on the street, in the middle of the night, and not being able to make it home to my children, started coming into my mind! The tears were freezing as fast as they

were falling, leaving streaks of ice on my face. There wasn't even a car on the road, everyone was inside it seemed, but me. I was trying to make my way home, as fast as my, now, slowing more than before legs, could take me.

I started praying, and calling out to Jesus, to please, heat my body up, so I could make it home to my children, and that I knew He could, if he wanted to. I was very frightened at this time, because it was becoming even more darker, and the snow was falling, thicker now.. The street lights had came on, but it was still, very dark in some places, along the way. There was not a car or truck on the road, that I could even flag down to ask if they could give me a ride home out of the weather. I really started crying out to the Lord, as my steps became slower and more of a labor to walk, but what happened next will surprise you!

As I was struggling to make my way through the snow, with the bags of groceries in my arms, I suddenly felt heat rising in my body. Starting at my feet and rising all the way up to my face! In fact, I was heating up so fast in my body, I

started to sweat! I could feel my hands and my feet again. They no longer felt like frozen stumps! It was amazing! It was still snowing, and it was still cold, but I wasn't feeling any of it! In fact, it felt like more like a day in spring, instead of a freezing, cold, day in the winter! I could see the snow still falling, the ice on the ground, still frozen, but I, no longer was! You cannot tell me, that God is not real, and is not, performing miracles! That was a miracle. I was so amazed at what was happening to me. I had to stop and put my groceries down, because it felt like my hands were sweating profusely inside of my gloves, on top of that, the gloves that were previously froze, with little ice crystals forming on them, from the snow, were now, too wet. I had to take them off. My whole body, begin to feel like you would feel, if you were standing in front of a roaring fire in the fireplace! I had to see my hands! When I took off my gloves, my hands were red like fire, and warm. There was no more ice, inside of my gloves, it was melted too. There in the midst of all that snow and ice, I started jumping up and down praising the Lord! I didn't care who might have been

looking out of a window and watching me! I had to give the Lord Jesus the praise! Because He is worthy! He did not let me freeze, He heard my cry! Thankful that I could feel my body again, and I was warm. I picked my groceries up and started back on my way home. Walking fast now, because I could! I wasn't feeling any coldness of the weather, all the rest of the way home! It truly was a miracle! The next service at church, I couldn't wait to share the miracle of how God heated up my body, that night I almost froze, trying to get home from the grocery store. This is just one of the many miracles, that the Lord Jesus Christ performed in my life, perhaps one day I will share them all with you, but that is another story!

As I walked further into the room, I noticed that it was a very large, and wide, place. On the back wall, facing me, were, two very tall metal doors. The path of light, ended at the foot of the doors. As I walked over closer to them, to get a better look, I noticed, that the light, now, was shining on the doors, as if it guiding me to them. I reached out, and put my hands on one of the doors. the metal felt cool to

the touch. They looked to be made of a brass, or a bronze type metal. As I looked up; they seemed to stretch to the ceiling. Even though I could not see the top of the room, because it also, was dark, I just assumed that it had a ceiling, somewhere! The doors were very big and wide, and looked to be very heavy. They had a beautiful, intricate, and ornate, pattern carved into them, much like the carvings, I had seen in previous visions, pertaining to things heavenly. The same beautiful, swirl, brocade, looking pattern. I was standing there thinking, that it must have taken someone a long time, to carve this. It was just beautiful.

I remember looking at them and thinking how really heavy they must be to push! At least, I thought they were. They looked to be about five, or six feet wide, possibly, even wider, I could not tell for sure. I was thinking, there was no way, I would be able push these doors open. I was beginning to feel like I was never going to get out of this room.

Once again, I heard the same voice, that had told me earlier, to follow the path of light, say to me," Push open the

doors." I remember replying back, that the doors were too big, and heavy, and that I was not strong enough to push them open! The voice replied again, "The doors are not heavy, push open the doors!" This time I did not hesitate! I began to push, and to my surprise, the doors weren't heavy at all. They literally swung open at the slightest push. Just like what was told me, in fact, it felt like I was pushing on regular, light weight, wooden doors, Instead of thick, and heavy brass doors!

The strange thing about this, is, that when I obeyed the voice, when it spoke to me, the second time and pushed the doors open; my appearance, changed. I now had long, black, wavy hair, like my mother's. My face was smooth, and seemed to be glowing, and I had this big smile on my face. I noticed, that Instead of the hospital gown, I was wearing before I opened the doors, I was now wearing a long, iridescent, white robe, that flowed with every movement that I made. It was beautiful. As it caught the light, it reflected a rainbow of colors.

I often wondered, what the full significance was of the single light, and the narrow path, that it shined on, the doors,

and why was it so important, that I go through them? While praying for a more clearer, and better, understanding, of all the vision symbolized, this is what was revealed to me: the doors, represented Christ, all who desire, to enter into heaven, must come through the Lord, Jesus Christ, who is the light, the way, and, the only door. -

"Then spake Jesus again unto them, saying, I am the light of the world: he that followeth me shall not walk in darkness, but shall have the light of life.

Jesus saith unto him, I am the way, the truth, and the life: no man cometh unto the Father, but by me.

I am the door: by me if any man enter in, he shall be saved, and shall go in and out, and find pasture.

Enter ye in at the straight gate: for wide is the gate, and broad is the way, that leadeth to destruction, and many there be which go in thereat:

Because strait is the gate, and narrow is the way,

which leadeth unto life, and few there be that find it."

- John 8: 12, 10: 9, 14: 6,

Matthew 7: 13, 14, (KJV)

Because of the light, that shined upon the path, I was blessed, to be able to find my way to the door, and because of obedience, and faith; I was able to go through the doors, and receive the life, I had always desired, but thought, at one time, I would never be able to have. The reason why there was no other light in the room, is because, there is no other way, in which we can enter into heaven. As it says in the Word of God:

"Neither is there salvation in any other: for there is none other name under heaven given among men, whereby we must be saved."

- Acts 3: 13, (KJV)

Why I was told to push open the doors, because it represented the press, or the course of this life, that is set before us, by God. It is a press, because of the daily battles

with our own self doubt, worries, fears, hesitations, disbeliefs, frustrations, and such like, and that of the devil, our adversary, it creates a press, whereas, in order to achieve that which we are seeking from the Lord, we must push against the forces, and powers that be, to stay on the path of true righteousness, faith, and salvation in the Lord Jesus Christ.

The reason why, the doors, were so light, and not heavy, or hard to push open, was because; Christ's burdens are light. What the Lord asks us to do, doesn't give us struggle, the adversary does, and our own selfish ways, but when we listen, and follow Christ, our burdens, do become light. In fact, when we follow, Christ, He relieves the burdens, that we're carrying, as He said, in the Word of God, He gives us rest. -

> "Come unto me, all ye that labor and are heavy laden, and I will give you rest.
>
> Take my yoke upon you, and learn of me; for I am meek and lowly in heart: and ye shall find rest unto your souls.

For my yoke is easy, and my burden is light."

- Matthew 11: 28 - 30, (KJV)

As I walked along, I could feel the joy of the Lord, welling up, inside of me, it was a wonderful feeling, I was so happy to be there. As I looked around, I found myself, standing at the foot of a hill, that was covered in, thick, lush green grass, the kind that is just right for sitting on. As I looked at the hill, I noticed that there were others sitting on the hill in various places, around the side of it. Some in groups of two's, three's, and some in four's, and so on. They all seemed to be enjoying, listening to the person speaking, sitting on a smooth rock, at the top of the hill. As I looked up, to view, who it was; I knew it was the Lord! It was Jesus!

I hurriedly looked for a comfortable spot to sit in, so that I could hear Christ teaching. Ever since the Holy Spirit, so many years ago, when I was first saved, began to teach me the word of God, sitting up to the early hours of the morning, trying to absorb, into my mind, everything He was showing me. I have always desired, to one day, when this life was over,

and we are with Christ, to hear the Lord Jesus teaching, just like those, that were sitting around Him, that day. To be able to hear those inspiring words coming from the Master, that has blessed, and inspired, millions down through the ages, to me, would be a dream come true. Which is why, for the Holy Spirit to give me this particular vision, was just to amazing to me!

As I walked alongside the hill, I observed how bright the light was, that was shining all around us, like a summer's day. It seemed to be emanating from the Lord Jesus, He was the light. Though His face was shadowed, I could see the glory, shining all around Him. It was truly wonderful to see. As I looked around the hill, I could see people, from all over the world sitting, and listening to Christ, hanging on to every word, that was being spoken out of the Savior's mouth. It was awesome! I was so happy to be amongst them, listening to the Savior teaching, It was a desire from the heart, come to pass. Then as I was being pulled back, the scene started to fade into the distance, and it was dark again. When everything cleared,

I was back in my room. I was thinking, why did He bring me back, I was so happy there.

When I think of all this, and what the Spirit of the Lord was revealing to me, I am reminded; just like Christ is the door to salvation, heaven, and life eternal, and only through Him, we may enter in. We have to first, open the doors of our hearts, to Christ, repentance, and forgiveness for our sins, so that He can began, the work of salvation, and redemption, in us. Christ is the door, and the way out of the darkness of this life. He is, the light, and the knowledge of His Word, guides us along this Christian way. This passage came to mind:

> "Behold, I stand at the door, and knock: if any man hear my voice, and open the door, I will come in to him, and will sup with him, and he with me.
>
> To him that overcometh will I grant to sit with me in my throne, even as I also overcame, and am set down with my Father in His throne.

He that hath an ear, let him hear what the Spirit

saith unto the churches."

- Revelation 3:20-22, (KJV)

Just as Christ is our door to true salvation, and only through Him, can this be achieved, So we have to open the door to our hearts to Christ, so He can come in to lead us to, and through, that precious door, which is also Christ, into the Kingdom of heaven, and of God.

John, when talking about the visions that he received, said; I was in the spirit, when He was shown, that which was to come. The Holy Spirit, is still giving people visions and using, whosoever is willing, to be used by God, to get the message of salvation, redemption, forgiveness, and healing out, to His people. Yes, for this moment in time, Christ Jesus, is still knocking at the door of our hearts today, and asking, will we let Him come in? I hesitate to think, if I had not found the courage, to believe the voice, that was telling me to open the door, would I have remained trapped in that dark room, forever? Having the path lit up before me, and to afraid

to open the door. I have found, that very thing that looks impossible for you to do, are the very things Christ wants to show us, that with Him we can do. We can overcome all our fears, doubts, and hesitations, with Christ at the head of our life. If we learn to trust in Him and hear His voice, We can do, what the Lord God, says we can do.

"I can do all things through Christ which strengtheneth me."

- Philippians 4: 13, (KJV)

How are we strengthened? We listen at the voice of Christ. In this vision, I know the Holy Spirit was showing me, what can be, if we, stay on the path of true righteousness, and holiness, and continue to follow Christ, who is the light of this world. It will lead us to the Lord. Where one day, we can sit in the actual presence of the Lord Jesus Christ, and enjoy Him teach, over, and over again, speaking those words of eternal life, to the millions and millions, of saints, from around the world.

CHAPTER NINE

The Catching Away of the Saints

This vision above all the other visions, that the Holy Spirit has given me, confirmed, and established in me, that there is going to be a rapture of the saints of God. The vividness of detail, has never left my memory, since, it was first, given to me. I am sure that this long awaited for event, when the trumpet sounds, will be received with much joy and gladness of heart when it happens, for all those, who have decided to follow Christ.

This particular vision, to me, is the climax of a life, that have endured to the end, fought the good fight, and is now

ready, to live with Christ. It brings to mind the passage of scripture in 2 Timothy:

> "For I am now ready to be offered, and the time of my departure is at hand.
>
> I have fought the good fight, I have finished my course, I have kept the faith:
>
> Henceforth there is laid up for me a crown of righteousness, which the Lord, the righteous judge, shall give me at that day: and not to me only, but unto all them also that love His appearing."
>
> - 2 Timothy 4: 6 - 8, (KJV)

Paul in this letter to Timothy, his son in the gospel, was his last letter to him. Paul was facing, Nero's chopping block, at that time. Having finished his course, or his mission in life, given to him, by Christ, on the road to Damascus; were Christ stopped him, appearing unto him, and thus, changing the course of his life forever. Paul looked forth to the resurrection of the saints of God, understanding that, just as Christ rose

from the grave, now seated at the right hand of God the Father, we too will rise from our slumber, to meet with Christ in the air, and ever live with Him in Glory.

After coming home from work one day, (I was working at the airport at the time),in the year 2009; I don't remember what month, or day it was, just the year. I was very tired, work was very fast paced, and sometimes, very stressful, as well. I had laid down across the bed, trying to relax my nerves, mind, and body. I laid my head back on the pillow, and started to pray, quietly, to the Lord about some things that were pressing in my spirit. I had turned the TV on low, so as not to distract me from prayer, (sometimes, the quiet sounds that were coming from it, helped to relax me, and take my mind off of what was going on around me). I remember closing my eyes momentarily, to focus on what I was praying about; suddenly, it was as if a deep sleep, had come all over me. What I saw next, when I opened my eyes, was just simply, amazing. I remember every detail. I could feel the air around me, the warmth of the day, I was there, I was really there!

I remember looking up at the sky, standing in the midst of a field, it was a beautiful day. I listened, as I heard, what sounded like a trumpet blowing, one single, loud and long note. There were others standing with me in the field. We were all looking up into the sky, where we heard the sound of the trumpet. We were all watching and waiting, as if waiting on someone, or something to appear.

As the trumpet was blowing, I saw the souls of those, that had departed, long ago, rising up out, all around us, from the ground. They looked to be, somewhat transparent, at first, almost like wisps, but, as they rose higher in the sky, their form, became, more solid. They were all dressed in white robes; which also changed, as they rose higher in the sky, becoming more luminous. They reminded me of, beautiful iridescent, and web like, robes. They too, looked to be somewhat, transparent, at first, when looking at them. I watched, as they stretched their arms out,over their heads, they appeared to be, very happy. It was marvelous to see, something like this taking place before my eyes. I could feel the anticipation of the others, as well as

my own, that were standing with me in the field, we were all excited about going up.

There appeared to be very many, without number, rising from all over the earth, from the very young, to the very old, all of them, changing as they rose higher in the sky, taking on a little light of their own. It was beautiful! I watched as the last of them, that rose up out of the ground, had went up, then it was our turn.

It seemed like, we had been waiting a long time. Then the trumpet sounded again, then we which were still standing, started to rise! As we rose, our garments, changed, as well, having the same appearance, as the first. all of them, looking to be somewhat transparent at first. The same as those who rose before us.

I remember, as I rose higher in the sky, about halfway up, I was brought to a stop. I watched, as a long white, fluffy looking cloud floated towards us. The first group, who had rose earlier, were then, drawn into the cloud. The second group, which were we that were standing, started to be drawn

into the light of the sun. This sun, however, wasn't an ordinary sun. It's light was very comforting, soothing, as if it were alive.

I remember being very excited, about being able to rise and go with the others, to meet Jesus in the sky. I felt like I was coming home, as if, I had been away, on a long, long journey, but now, was returning home again.

This experience, helped me to understand, all the more, what Job was saying, in the Bible:

> "For I know that my Redeemer liveth, and that He shall stand at the latter day upon the earth:
>
> And though after my skin worms destroy this body, yet in my flesh shall I see God:
>
> Whom I shall see for myself, and mine eyes shall behold, and not another; though my reins be consumed within me."
>
> - Job 19: 25 - 27, (KJV)

Through repentance, forgiveness, and, the acceptance of the salvation of Jesus Christ in our lives, we can stand at that

latter day, knowing, that we will be reunited with the Father of spirits, who gave us, our spirit, and, our soul.

> "Furthermore we have had fathers of our flesh which corrected us, and we gave them reverence: shall we not much rather be in subjection unto the Father of spirits, and live?
>
> In whose hand is the soul of every living thing, and the breath of all mankind."
>
> - Hebrews 12: 9, Job: 12: 10, (KJV)

It is that part of us, that longs to be with the Father, sharing in sweet communication with Him once again, as we once did, before the fall. I can understand the joy, and the gladness, at the rising, to meet the Lord, and Savior, Jesus Christ, in the air. Truly it will be, a long, and awaited, for event.

I remember, stretching my arms out, over my head; just like the others, I had seen, go before me, reaching out, as I was getting closer to the sun. I saw the cloud, that had those

who had risen first, be drawn, into the sun. Then those of us, that had been standing in the field; were drawn in as well, after the first group went in. Right before, I was to go in, I was stopped in mid air, as if, only being allowed to view this, at the present time. It was marvelous! I saw the sun, began to rise higher in the sky till it was no longer visible to the eyes!

After witnessing something like this, I can understand what Paul meant, when He said:

> "Brethren, I count not myself to have apprehended: but this one thing I do, forgetting those things that are behind, and reaching forth unto those things which are before,
>
> I press toward the mark for the prize of the high calling of God In Christ Jesus."
>
> - Philippians 3: 13-14, (KJV)

Just like the many souls, that I saw, reaching out for the Lord, as they were rising to meet Him in the air, so is our high calling in Christ Jesus, worth reaching for. Christ is

coming, and we will be changed. Paul explains this change, or transformation, in 1 Corinthians, when speaking of the difference, between the body we're sown in, and the body, we're to be raised in:

> "It is sown a natural body; it is raised a spiritual body. There is a natural body, and a spiritual body.
>
> Behold I show you a mystery; We shall not all sleep, but we shall all be changed,
>
> In a moment, in a twinkling of an eye, at the last trump: for the trumpet shall sound, and the dead shall be raised incorruptible, and we shall be changed."
>
> - 1 Corinthians 15: 41-44, 51-52, (KJV)

And so we would not be worried about those who have gone on before us, Paul speaks to this effect:

> "But I would not have you ignorant, brethren, concerning them which are asleep, that ye sorrow not, even as others which have no hope.

For if we believe that Jesus died and rose again, even so them also which sleep in Jesus will God bring with Him."

- 1 Thessalonians 4: 13-14

Why the Lord God choose me, to reveal such wonderful things to, I don't know, but, I am grateful, and truly and thankful to Him, for considering me, and allowing me to see what is to be. I pray that in the sharing of what the Holy Spirit, revealed to me, will encourage you, just as it has encouraged me, to keep pressing towards the mark, that is in Christ Jesus, our Lord, and Savior.

"But God hath chosen the foolish things of the world to confound the wise; and God hath chosen the weak things of the world to confound the things which are mighty;

1 Corinthians 1: 27, (KJV)

These Visions, that the Holy Spirit, along, with some of the outstanding miracles, that the Lord, have performed in

my life, have blessed, and encouraged me, along this journey. It is my prayer, that they will bless you too.

Paul, when speaking of his experiences, spoke about them being used for the furthering of the gospel. Though what he was going through, wasn't pleasant, yet it showed what grace under pressure, can do for those who believe.

> "But I would ye should understand, brethren, that the things which happened unto me have fallen out rather unto the furtherance of the gospel;
>
> According to my earnest expectation and my hope, that in nothing I shall be ashamed, but that with all boldness, as always, so now also Christ shall be magnified in my body, whether it be by life, or by death.
>
> For me to live is Christ, and to die is gain.
>
> For I am in a strait betwixt the two, having a desire to depart, and to be with Christ; which is far better:
>
> Nevertheless to abide in the flesh is more needful for you.

That your rejoicing may be more abundant in Jesus

Christ for me by my coming to you again."

-Philippians 1: 12, 20-21, 23-24, 26, (KJV)

I like Paul, believe to live is Christ! To share the testimonies of what God has done for us in this life, encourages others, to hope, to believe, and to have faith in God. This is why we share, our experiences, and testimonies with the world. Praying that, one day, we will all, get to share in this blessed hope.

My Journey Into Heaven

I used to be very hesitant, about putting into writing, what I saw the day that I collapsed, and died, in the midst of service, being fearful of what might be said about me, but since then, I have learned better. All I know, according to the witnesses, that were there, is that, for twenty five minutes, I was dead, and not breathing. I was told, that my body had turned blue, and had started to stiffen. This happened in the year1990. My son was ten yrs. old, at the time, and my daughter was twelve yrs. old. I had been having some very, rough, and trying times, with dealing with some health issues, stemming

from being injured on the job. The injury set off some medical problems, that I was told, that I should not have had to deal with, until I got in my eighties, God willing. I was told, that the problems that I was having at that time, I would die with, (but, for the grace of God). I was often left, with dizziness, so strong, till it made my head swirl, and there were times, that my muscles would be so weak, till, just moving my arms and legs, was difficult. It felt as if, they just didn't want to respond.

Each day, I had to deal with different levels of pain. Yes, it was trying times, indeed. The only joy, I would get, was when I was in church, and being around my children, laughing with them, or at them, when they would do these funny little stunts, they called, dance time inferno! they would do this little dance, that they saw on TV, while watching cartoons, and it always,made me laugh, till I would just, literally roll off the sofa. they were very funny, when they wanted to be. In 1983, I lost my children, when they were very young, due unto, some unforeseen event, they were gone for eight years, until the Lord brought them back to me. Three years before

their return, I had a vision of them, being brought to me by a man dressed in a white linen robe, with a light blue scarf, around his body, that swung over his left shoulder, while praying at the altar in church. In the vision, I was allowed to hold them in my arms. I could feel the heat of their bodies, as I pressed them to mines, holding them tight, and not wanting to let them go. I told them, how much I missed them, and loved them. I believe to this day, that it was Christ that brought my children to me that day. He told me, that He had to take them back, but in three years, He would bring them back to me, and this time, no one, would be able to take them from me. He did, just as He said. I shared this vision with many of the church members, that were members of the church at that time. It was an extremely difficult, time to go through. It wasn't until, some years later, when my heart, and my mind, was able to receive, God's answer to my struggle, did I understand, my loss. Sometimes, if not all the time, our troubles come back to bite us, when we don't listen to the voice of the Lord, trying to keep us from doing something

that would cause us great pain down the line, and I will leave that alone.

My temporary total disability, had run out, and I had to secure help, and a place to stay immediately, for me and my children. The apartment, where we lived, was only big enough for one, two being the most that it could hold, comfortably. It was very small, and we were in a desperate need a bigger place.

One day, while helping out at the church, which is something I liked to do, because it kept my mind off of what was going on with my health, I had another vision. We were a small church, still growing, and money was tight. A lot of our members were unemployed, or like myself, unable to work a regular job, at the time. We sold dinners on the weekends, to make ends meet. Sometimes our oldest member, an elderly lady, would let us come over and use her kitchen. She lived in a house, right next door to the church.

One Saturday, while at the church, helping out, I had left out of the church, to walk over to her house, It was just a few steps away. We were in a neighborhood, where the houses and

buildings, were very close to each other. Her kitchen, sat in the back of her house, where the back door was. I stepped up on the back step, that led to the kitchen, and suddenly, I was no longer in her kitchen, but I was standing in the living room of another house. I looked to the right, and saw a big dining room! I turned and looked to the back of the living room, and saw stairs, leading upstairs, off from the living room, going up the back wall. I was then pulled outside, where I was able to see the front of the house. It was light green, with a big wooden porch. The house had three bedrooms, just like I needed, for me and my children! I looked at the neighborhood the house was in, and was unfamiliar with the neighborhood, it was in, though. Then just as suddenly, before, it was gone, and I was back standing in the kitchen of the house next to the church. The elderly, church member had walked into the kitchen at that time, and asked me if I was alright? I asked her why did she ask me that? She said I stepped into the kitchen and just stopped. She said I looked, like I was just staring into space. I told her how I had just seen my house. She laughed

and thought I was talking about her house. When I described it to her, and what I had seen. She said to me, well, that surely is not my house. She just kind of chuckled and walked back into the living room.

When I got back to the church, I shared what I had seen with the others working in the kitchen, they kind of chuckled too. I told them, how the Holy Spirit had told me, that in one year, I would be in this house. One them, picked at me, for almost the whole year about it, until, I got my house, one year later, just as the Lord said. She would count off the months that had already passed, and, would ask me when was I going to get my house? Come to find out, the house was down the street, and around the corner from the church. In a neighborhood I had never been in before. The curious thing about that was, the newer building that our church moved into later, sat right on the corner of the other end of the street, that the house sat on. I and my children ended up staying in the house, for nine years. I stayed there just a little while longer, after my children were grown, and gone, and where living somewhere else. Truly

God is good. I just had to stop a moment, and share that testimony, Because it is something that God, in His ultimate mercies, had done for me, and my children, Just to share how much the Lord Jesus Christ loves us, and cares about our well being, and watches out over every aspect of our lives.

Still dealing with my workers compensation case, going back and forth to doctors, having to go, in and out of the emergency room; while trying to cope with what was going on with my health. All, while trying to raise two children; which wasn't easy given the circumstances. I also had to put up with others who didn't understand, why I was going through so much, I didn't understand either. I just knew that I was. I have found that many times, when we are going through some great trial, we often try to justify, what we, or someone else is going through; but if there is, no justification, we are quick to think, that we, or the person, must have done something wrong, and it is just not known, what was done. This isn't, always the case, as Christ proved, in the case of the blind man, and proven by Job, in the Word of God.

Many times I found myself, praying like Job, unto the Lord, when what I was going through, seemed more than I could bear. Asking the Lord to do the same thing for me, that Job did, when he was suffering the most. I understood why Job prayed the way he did, no doubt, feeling, very much alone, in his sufferings.

I find that when you become born again and truly saved, people that once knew you the way you were, don't understand who you have become once you have been truly saved. Friendships that you had in the world before become lost. Even some family relationships are lost as well, when a person becomes, born again. It is because, most of the time, they do not understand what has happened. Job's friends did not understand him, his own wife, did not understand. Job was truly, alone, except for the presence of God. Yes, I understood Job.

This particular Sunday morning we were in the midst of a very anointed worship, and praise service, the Spirit was high, and we were all singing and clapping our hands! Everyone,

were on their feet! Some, patting, and stomping their feet to the beat of the songs! We were having a good time in the Lord! That is when it happened.

I remember as I was singing, I started to feel very flushed, as if an heat wave, had came all over me, and took my breath away, with it. I was struggling to breathe, but I didn't want no one to know what was going on, so, I held my head down, so that no one could see me. We were having too much of a good time in the Lord, and I didn't want to disturb the service. I remember feeling my heart, feeling like it was struggling to beat. Finally, I felt it just give, this one last thump, then there was nothing. I remember feeling this calm, and a peace, just come all over me, at that instance. I thought, I'm dying. I remember looking up at the front of the church where the choir stood, and as I was falling, I was wondering ? Can they see me? Then there was nothing but darkness!

They say death is just a passing from this world to the next. It felt Like I had laid down, and went to sleep, and woke up, somewhere else. There was no more pain, my body felt light,

not heavy at all! I remember feeling so relieved, and at peace. All I could feel was, joy and gladness. There truly was, no sorrow!

> "O Death, Where Is Thy Sting? O Grave, Where Is Thy Victory?"
>
> > - I Corinthians 15: 55, (KJV)

I remember waking up in a field of tall grass. It felt like I had been laying on a bed of cotton, it was so soft and comfortable. I remember getting up, standing to my feet, and looking all around me. It was a beautiful summer like day! There wasn't a cloud in the sky! Just a beautiful blue sky!

I noticed that it was bright, but there was no sun, just beautiful light, shining everywhere. It lit up the whole day! It was warm, and pleasant. The grass seemed to be softly, swaying in the breeze, that seemed to just, sweep across my face, so very gently. It felt good. I remember stretching my hands out to feel the grass as I was walking through it, it felt just like silk. There were a few flowers of different colors, here and there, scattered throughout the field. I remember

looking over to the right and seeing what looked like a small river, running through the field. I walked over towards it. It glistened in the light, as the light reflected off the top of the water, it sparkled like bright shining gold!

I walked over to it. The water was so clear, it looked like a very, clear, crystal. I leaned over, a little further, to look into the water. I saw a pathway underneath the water, of perfectly rounded oval shaped, sandstones! They were all laid out in rows, of perfect order. Each row was a different color of sandstone. There were reds, greens, and, tan, colored sandstones. They looked like they had been placed, and laid there in perfect order, on purpose. The sandstone pathway stretched all the way across the river bed. The width of it, reminded me, of a one lane highway. I remember thinking, how strange it was, to see a pathway of perfectly laid stones, under the water. They were lovely to see. There were no nicks, sharp edges, or scratches, on none of them. They were all perfectly rounded and smooth. As if cut, or sanded that way. It was as if, they were placed there to be walked on! It was beautiful!

The more I stared at the river, the more I wanted to put my hands in it. I kneeled down beside the water, and cupped my hands, so I could pick up the water from the river. To my surprise, it felt like air! It didn't feel like water at all! I couldn't believe it. How could water, not feel like water? It felt like, I had picked up a hand full of flowing light air! I was surprised! I just had to put my face in it. Something I always loved to do as a child. This time, I wanted to put my face in the water. I just loved feeling the coolness of the water on my face, when I was a child. I would always imagine myself deep sea diving and looking at the wonders underneath the sea. I could feel that same excitement coming over me again. I leaned over, and put my face in the water, once again, it had that same, feeling of cool, flowing, air. Air, that flowed and looked like water! I found that I was able to breathe it like air, as well, it was amazing!

I thought how nice it would be, if my whole body were under the water. Just as I was thinking about it in my mind, there I was! Right in the midst of the water, and, underneath

it! It was exciting, to say the least. I found myself floating in the midst of the water, underneath it, and not drowning! I had never learned to swim, even though, I always liked the water. It felt like I was being held up by currents, that were flowing all around me in the water. Once again, I was able to breathe the water, just like air, it felt like air, even though, it looked like water. It was truly amazing, to me!

I remember looking all around me while I was under the water, I noticed that I had on a long wide dress or robe. It floated up around my knees in the water. I noticed, that my physical appearance, had changed as well. I remember thinking, how peaceful and relaxing, it was there, like a quiet calm. I was thinking how this would be a perfect place to get away from things, but I knew I couldn't stay there. I remember thinking how I would like to be back up on land, and just like before, as I was thinking it, there I was, back, standing beside the river. I could feel the light shining, warm on my body again. I turned around to look back over the other side of the river. What I saw next, just totally astounded me, beyond words!

As I looked over the other side of the river, I noticed up above it, I could see, what looked like, the universe, and all of creation, being formed, and going forth, right before my eyes! I saw stars being formed out of what looked like swirling gases, and dust, being swung out into space. As they begin to swirl, faster and faster, they to start to burn with fire. Each one being slung out by what looked like a fiery arm, coming from a large mass of light; which slung each one of them out,into what looked to be, predestinated spots and places in the vast open space. Having arrived there, they stopped, and just continue to burn where they were. As they burned, they became brighter, and brighter, after burning for some time, they then began to slow down, becoming dimmer, until they were no longer burning, at all. As their fire went out, more stars, were being swung out into place, and the process started all over again. I watched, as the universe, began to fill with stars, and various other bodies of lights. It was amazing to see!

I watched as planets were being swung out too. They began as clouds of dust, fragments and gas. As they swirled,

they became tighter, more compact, solid! It was amazing to see. Each of the planets, like the stars, were being placed in specific places in space. Once reaching their destination, they also stopped and remained in place! I could see the face of the planet closest to me, I watched as mountain ridges, and valleys, formed on it. Greenery, atmosphere, clouds, it was awesome! I watched, that as the planet turned, it began to age, the color starting to leave it, becoming more grayish in appearance Finally, dying out and becoming very still! As the planets dyed out, others were being formed, and the process started all over again.

Underneath this viewing of the universe, I could see life on earth coming into being, living, growing older, dying, and life, starting all over again. I saw plants, and trees, starting out as seeds, growing up and out of the ground, becoming full, some bearing fruits, flowers, some just green and full. I watched them, as they begun to grow older, soon bowing over, and laying on the ground, and then becoming part of the earth again. In their place others, began to grow, replacing

those that had fallen. I saw babies in the womb, forming, and growing, coming to birth. I watched as they began as children, then growing into adulthood. I watched as they walked along, and began to age. They started to bowing over. The more they walked, the more they bowed over, until they too were laying on the ground. Their bodies, returning to the earth as a part of it. I was speechless! There were no words to express the majesty of what I had just seen. All I could think of, was why me, how did I merit such an honor to see this. It was magnificent! To watch this happening before my eyes! It was beyond words! All I could do was marvel at the wonder of it all. The ease at which this all was happening! Like it was a ready- made plan. That was just how simply life was being brought into being! It reminded me of what David said in the book of Psalms:

"When I consider thy heavens, the work of thy fingers, the moon and the stars, which thou hast ordained;

What is man, that thou art mindful of him? and the son of man, that thou visitest him?"

-Psalm 8: 3-4, (KJV)

David must have been looking out at the stars one night and just thought about the wonder of it all, and in his praise of the majesty of it all, the Holy Spirit must have given him this Psalm. Oh how wondrous our Lord is. How magnificent to behold! I understood then, when the Bible said,

> "But as it is written, EYE HATH NOT SEEN, NOR EAR HEARD, NEITHER HAVE ENTERED INTO THE HEART OF MAN, THE THINGS WHICH GOD HATH PREPARED FOR THEM THAT LOVE HIM."
>
> -I Corinthians 2: 9, (KJV)

No truer statement has been made concerning what God has in store for those who love, and follow Him. We really don't know. We can only imagine, but truly, we don't know. Until God allows you see for yourself, just a portion of what He has in store, for those who love Him, and are called by His name.

As I looked a little lower, to the shore, I could see trees lining each side of the river, all in a row. As if planted that

way. All of them being somewhat of the same height, but very full and green. I turned, and looked up the river, to see where it was coming from. At the head of the river, I saw a huge throne. It was gold, with beautiful ornate carving s in the wood. I saw the river flowing out from beneath it. Over the top of the throne, I could see stars, like multiple pin points of light, innumerable. They were coming out from the top of it! It was marvelous to see! From each side of the throne, the trees that lined the river, came out!

As I gazed at the throne, I could see a light coming from it. It had a beautiful rosy, creamy hue to it, very pleasant, and comforting to look at. It started to surround me, it felt so good, I just wanted to keep going into it. As I was walking, and the trees that were lining the river on each side, were now on each side of me. Where the river was, now was a street, and I was walking on it. I found myself walking closer, towards the light that sat in the midst of the throne. The closer I got, the more the light grew, until, I could no longer see the throne, just the soft glowing of the light! It had completely

covered the throne, and surrounded me. I could feel myself being totally taken with it! I felt like I was finally going home, like I had been away too long. That is when all of a sudden. The light cleared before me, and I saw my children running towards me. My son was out in front, and my daughter was following, close behind him. That is when, then, I heard the voice of the Lord asked me, "If you die, who will raise your children?" I stopped, I remember saying, "But Lord, I am so tired of suffering. I have had nothing but bad things to happen to me, seemed like all of my life, I just want to be free." It was then that I heard my son shouting, "Momma, momma, don't die I could see the tears running down his face! I could see, the tears on my daughter's face, as well, even though she was silent. I started to cry myself, as I watched my children crying, and my love went out to them. I knew then, that I could not stay, I had to go back. I had waited too long to get them back. I knew that even though I would be returning back to place, whereas I would have more pain filled days and uncertainty about how my life was going to turn out. It did

not matter. I would just have to trust God, to make it alright! I told the Lord, send me back, I was not ready to die. I just got them back. I did not want any other mother raising my children, and that, I wanted to be the only mother to raise my children. I asked Him, to send me back, Lord, I was not ready to die! It was then that I felt myself being drawn back. Everything that I saw in heaven, now began to fade into the light, as I was being drawn back.

The next thing I knew, I was standing in the corner of the sanctuary, watching everybody, wondering what was going on. I could see them all gathered around someone on the floor. As I looked up, towards the back; I saw one of the church members on the stairs that led out of the sanctuary. I noticed, that it was my friend, Sis. Ann., she was telling the pastor, to let her call the ambulance, because I was dead, and had been dead for twenty five minutes! She was telling him, that I was stiff and that rigor mortis had set in, and I was turning blue. She told him, her family is going to think we killed her, pastor please let me call an ambulance! But my

pastor was a praying man, and a man of strong faith, Holy Ghost filled! He believed that Christ could do anything! He replied back to her, Jesus is going to bring her back. To this day, even though he is now with the Lord, I thank God, for his strong faith, trust, and belief in Christ!

I watched as the other members that were standing around whoever it was on the floor, with the pastor being in the middle, praying, everyone of them, calling on the name of Jesus! I looked and saw that all the children had been ushered out of the sanctuary, as the pastor would sometimes do, when praying for someone, concerning a serious matter, and did not want to be distracted. I saw him leaning over the individual on that was on the floor. I couldn't see who it was, because the others were in way, blocking my view. I walked over to get a closer look. That is when I heard my pastor say, Jesus! I felt myself, being pulled closer! He said it again, Jesus! I was pulled closer. By this time, I was standing, between the others. I looked down, and saw who it was that was lying on the floor. It was me! I began wondering, why was I laying on

the floor asleep? Why didn't I get up! The floor was too dusty to be laying on! All I could think of, was that I was going to have a nose full of dust. Strange thing to think of, when you are looking at your own body laying on the floor, strange, I know, but it happened. I heard my pastor say again, this time stronger than before, Jesus! I laid down in my body, feeling compelled to do so I felt like it was time to rejoin my body. It felt like, at the name of Jesus, I had to obey. I saw look of amazement on the faces, of those that had been calling on Jesus, along with the pastor, but they all looked to be happy that I was alive. As the pastor and the different ones where helping me off the floor, He told me, that he thought that they had lost me for a minute, but he refused to give up believing that Jesus would bring me back.

When I got up off the floor I was so glad to see everyone. I quickly began to tell them, how that, I say them praying for me. I went over to my friend, and told her how I saw her on the steps, and what she had said. She acknowledged that it was true, and asked me, how did I know that. She began to

tell me how I was dead, and how that, I wasn't breathing, and that my body had grown stiff. I then told the others where I saw them standing, and what they were doing. Everyone was looking at me with a puzzled look. All of them said to me, they couldn't understand, how I saw them, and what they were doing, seeing as to how, I was laying on the floor, dead, and not breathing! The pastor seemed to be the only one, that did understand what had happened! He told me to thank the Lord God, that He decided to send me back, and not keep me He told me, that he knew that if anyone could bring me back, it would be Jesus! I asked where my children were? One of the members, went upstairs to get them. As soon as my son saw me, he came running towards me! Just like I saw him do in heaven, with my daughter following. My son who is of course, older now, has no memory of the event, my daughter, just remembers me falling, and then someone taking them out of the sanctuary. I am not surprised, my son was only ten at the time, and daughter was only twelve, but I remember clearly my journey into heaven and I know

of some of the beautiful and wondrous things Christ has in store for all those who love and follow Him. Truly eye has not seen, nor ear heard!

I found this passage in the Bible, sometime later, it reminded me of my journey into heaven, and what I saw:

> "And He showed me a pure river of water of life, clear as crystal, proceeding out of the throne of God and of the lamb.
>
> In the midst of the street of it, and on either side of the river, was there the tree of life, which bare twelve manner of fruits, and yielded her fruit every month: and leaves of the tree were for healing of the nations.
>
> And there shall be no night there; and they need no candle, neither light of the sun; for the Lord God giveth them light: and they shall reign for ever and ever."
>
> -Revelation 22: 1-2,5, (KJV)

Am I looking forward to one day, returning to that beautiful place? Some day, when the Lord is ready for me, and says, Well done! I know I will see my beautiful green field again, and breathe in the river, that felt like air!

Hidden Away

Sometimes in life, we have to go through many trials. My father in the gospel, used to call it, "picked out to be picked on". It is not a good feeling, when you are going through something, but It is, when you come out of it. That is really when you can see, the value of it, when you are reflecting back upon it.

> "Many are the afflictions of the righteous: but the
> Lord delivereth him out of them all."
>
> - Psalms 34: 19, (KJV)

The Lord never said we wouldn't go through trials or afflictions, but He did say, He would deliver!

After what had happened to me in, 1990. When I died and the Lord brought me back, so that I could be with my children. I didn't expect, to ever, go through anything like that again, at lease, no time soon. About three years later, while still dealing with some health issues, sometime, during the summer, I can't remember the exact date, unfortunately, I was still, not writing anything down, It just never occurred to me, to do so. My ride had dropped me off in front of the clinic, for a regularly scheduled, Doctor's appointment. I was still not being allowed to travel, or go anywhere at the time by myself, because I was still having problems with dizziness. Which they found out later was due unto my blood pressure vacillating, up and down, suddenly when I would stand up, lay down, walked around, or at times, with any movement on my part. Praise be to God, that now as I am writing this, the Lord has since, delivered me of that too. My doctor's office was in the hospital's Internal Medicine Clinic. I remember

as I was sitting there in the waiting room, I began to feeling, very sick. My head felt very druggy, and heavy. I got up to ask the receptionist how long would it be before I could see my doctor? She told me that there were six other people ahead of me, and that he would be with me, as soon as he can. I told her that I was becoming very dizzy, and I felt like I was going to pass out. She asked me if I wanted a drink of water? I said yes, but I really didn't feel like it was going to help. She told me to just take my seat, and try not to move around, and that the doctor would be with me as soon as possible. I don't think she thought it was as serious, as it was, having to deal with people all day. I went back and sat down, and tried to stay as calm as possible, it didn't help. The dizziness, just continued to grow worse.

By this time, I felt, like my head was literally swooping around, and as I looked around, the room, it took on a kaleidoscope effect! It was becoming harder to focus. I got up again, hoping that if they saw how bad I was feeling, they might move a little faster, on my behalf. Holding onto the

chair, to balance myself, I pulled myself up, and proceeded to the counter, once again. I asked the receptionist, again, how long much longer, would it be before my doctor could see me. I told her, how that, I was experiencing much more dizziness this, than before. She replied to me, that they were moving as fast as they could to get to me. I know I was probably aggravating her, by coming up to the counter for the second time, and no doubt, she might of been thinking, that I was one those pushy patients, trying to take an advantage over the rest of the patients in the room. Having worked as a nursing assistant, before, I could understand her thinking process, by the way, she was handling me, I did not blame her. The pull on my head, however, was becoming intensely, more greater, with each passing minute. She told me to go back to my seat, and try putting my head back between my knees a little longer this time, it just might help.

I went back to my seat, and tried putting my head back between my knees, once again, as the receptionist said. Putting your head between your knees, is standard procedure, when

you are experiencing some dizziness, or light-headedness, but this time, it wasn't working. I was beginning to panic, as the dizziness was coming in waves and waves, each stronger than before. The more I sat there, the more I felt like the floor was trying to come up to meet me. It was frightening. It looked like everything was going round and round. I felt a heaviness come all over my body, like I was carrying lead weights on every part of my body I got up the third time. This time, I was literally, staggering to the counter, as I felt myself losing balance, I leaned over, holding on to the counter. It felt like I was about to drop then. I begged the nurse to let me lay down somewhere, until I could see my doctor. She told me they were preparing a bed for me now, in one of the rooms, to lay down in, until I could see my doctor, and as soon as it was ready, they would come and get me, and to just take a seat. I remember turning around while still holding on to the counter, all I remember seeing, was the floor, quickly, coming up to meet me, then nothing, it was dark.

The next thing I saw; I was standing in front of a big picture

window, the kind that stretches from the floor to the ceiling, in this dark room. There was no light in the room, except for the light that was coming from the window. Over to the left of the window, stood a very tall man, I believed him, to be an angel. He had a silvery white glow about himself. He was looking through the window. As I walked over, a little closer to see what he was looking at, I saw the waiting room where I was. On the floor was my body, and there were doctors all around me, working very quickly, on me. I saw the one, female doctor, placing defibrillator pads on my chest! I heard her shout, clear! I saw the electricity jolt my body, but nothing was happening! As she tried, again, and again, to revive me. Finally, I heard her say, that nothing was happening, and that I still did not have a heartbeat. She then went on to say, that the blood was turning blue in my veins, and rigor mortis was setting in, and that she couldn't move my arms, they had already stiffen.

I could see the look on their faces, nothing was working! As I watched all this going on through the window, I knew

that they weren't going to be able to revive me, because, I wasn't there! I turned to the angel standing beside me, at the window, and asked him, "Why can't they bring me back? Doesn't the Lord want me to live? He very calmly replied, " The Lord has hidden you for Himself." I didn't understand, at that time, why, the Lord God, who had brought me back before, so that I could be with my children, was now, going to just let me die, knowing, that my children were not grown yet. I asked him, "Why has the Lord, hidden me?" He never replied back, but continued, looking through the window. I watched as my doctor, ask the other doctors, that were around my body on the floor, "Are we all agreed on the time of death?" I heard them say, yes, that they were agreed. It was a settling moment for me.

I watched him as he raised his arm and looked at his watch, calling the time of my death. Still not understanding what the Lord was doing, all I could think of, was that it was over, and that the Lord was really going to let me die. Still, I couldn't help thinking, that something was out of time, and

that it was not my time yet to die, but, yet, and still, I also, couldn't help thinking, that I would never see my children again. How very wrong, I was. Once again, it had become dark.

I remember feeling a bumping along. I felt like I was being awakened out of a deep sleep, and a much needed rest, considering, how I was feeling before. For just a slight moment, as, I was waking up, it felt like I was laying on air. Then, I felt my body began to settle, on the bed under me. I knew I was moving, and being pushed somewhere! It was then that I heard a voice, telling me, to open my eyes, so that they knew I was alive! I was hesitant, enjoying the rest. It felt so peaceful while I was asleep, that I almost didn't want, to open my eyes. I thought that I might remain asleep just a few minute longer, at least, until they got me where they were pushing me. But, once again, I heard the voice, tell me to open my eyes, this time, it sounded like a command. I quickly opened my eyes.

Startled, the intern that pushing me, immediately stopped,

looking surprised to see, that I had opened my eyes. He shouted, "Your eyes are open!" I looked at him, wondering, why was that such a surprise to him. It hadn't sunk in mind yet, exactly, what the Lord, had just done for me. Whereas, I was dead, now, once again, through His mercy, I was alive. I asked him, where was he taking me? He said, to the morgue room of the hospital. Then getting in a hurry, he told me that, he would be right back, that he was going to get my doctor. I watched him as he ran around down the hallway, I started to sit up, but then I thought, maybe I better just lay here till they come. I really was enjoying the rest, it felt good. The dizziness, and bad feeling, that I had before, was now, gone, replaced by a feeling, of total refreshment. As my mind cleared, the memory of what the angel said to me in the room, how that, the Lord had hidden me for Himself, came back to me. As I thought about it, I understood. The Lord wanted to bring me back himself, so that no one else could get the glory, and to prove, to all that were there, that there is a God, and He is still on the throne. The miracle, that He performed for me

that day, shook a lot of people, that were there that day in the hospital, that knew and/or, heard of the event. I knew that it had, by the number of people that kept coming in my room, talking to me afterwards. Each one that came in, had a look of amazement on their faces. Some, just came in and just looked at me, and hurriedly left out of the room. It was quite funny to me, to see them look at me, and then quickly turn around and leave. Some, where very excited, asking me questions as to how I was feeling.

Now, the first time this happened, it was before church members, Believers, this second time, it was before, unbelievers, or those that find it hard to believe in an Almighty God. The first time, I believe that God was wanting us to see, that He is still, a miracle working God, and that He can do anything, and to establish us in our faith and trust in Him. This second time, however, I believe He allowed it, so that the world, or the unbeliever could see, that there is, a very real God, and He is still working miracles, and that He is, the Almighty God.

Why the Lord chooses whom He does? Only the Lord

knows that. Why did He choose Job? But I will say this, Job's story has encouraged many a soul, who has ever been under attack from the devil, and have had to suffer great lose, agony, and pain. and has had to endure with those who didn't understand. It was not easy for Job, and it is not easy for us, but his story shows that if you remain faithful to God, even if you don't understand, the whys, or the wherefores of what you are going through. With Christ, you will come out victorious. Job saw God in an even better light, and understanding, after he went through what he did, and God revealed to Him, his power and authority over all creation. He saw that even though, or even if, God allows suffering, it is so that He can reveal to us, that He is God in the midst of suffering, just like He is God, in the midst of our joy. Ready to give us the victory over every circumstance in our lives. Sometimes, we are in need of a more spiritual healing, than we are in need of a physical healing. These healings promote, joy, and confidence, in our Lord, and Savior, Jesus Christ. It proves that we can find joy in the Lord, in the midst of what

may look like a terrible situation, and still love and want to serve Him. Those years, I was suffering with a sickness, that I was told, I would die with, yes, they were difficult, physically, but they did prove to me, that regardless of my condition in life, I could still be of service to my Lord and King, and that I could still enjoy His presence, and that, there is nothing too hard for the Lord. He can, and is more than able, to deliver us from anything. The reason, I said allow, because it is not the Lord, that is causing the afflictions, and the suffering in our lives, it is our adversary, and sometimes, our own mistakes. However, these are the times, that when we turn to the Lord God, we can also receive our greatest miracles, and victories.

When The intern returned, he had my doctor with him. He looked at me, as if he could not believe what he was seeing! He said to the intern, she is alive! He told him, to take me to emergency department. I asked him why did he want me to go to the emergency department, I was feeling better. He told me, that he wanted to have some tests done on me, just to make sure, I was alright. I knew what was going on, so I went

along, they were amazed, at what the Lord had done, and they wanted to know what had happened, because medically speaking, what had happened was a medical impossibility. Impossible for man, that is, but not impossible for God. It reminds me of what the angel Gabrielle, said to Mary, concerning the birth of Jesus Christ:

"With God nothing shall be impossible."

- Luke 1: 37, (KJV)

While in the emergency room, the intern that had pushed me there, came into the room. I asked him, why was practically, everybody that came into my room, asking me, if I had made my will out, and if I died, who did I want them to contact, and if I had made any special arraignments concerning my body. I asked him, because, even though I knew, what God had done for me, I was curious, to see, if anybody else had recognized what had happened to me. The intern replied, Ma'am, don't you know? You died, and you were dead for sixteen minutes. Six doctors worked on you, and could not bring you back, they want to know, why are you alive? That's

why they, keep asking you if you have a will. He went on further to say, that he was taking me to the room where they put the dead, and my eyes just suddenly, opened up. He sighed, and shook his head, as if, he was still in disbelief at what happened, himself. Then he turned and walked out of the room. I started praising the Lord God for His mercy, and thanking Him for allowing me to live, and I know that He did not have to, but He did, and I was thankful.

That following service night I shared the miracle what the Lord God had done for me in the hospital, with the members of my church! It was wonderful to me, to know that God loved me enough, despite my wonderings as to what He was doing, to spare my life once again. It just kept me more, in awe of Him. To know that the miracles I had read about in the Bible, Jesus was still performing them today for His glory! God made our bodies, and He knows how to fix them, and even if He chooses not to, He knows how to give you joy in the midst of sorrow, and any situation or circumstance, you may find yourself in. God is able.

"You made all the delicate, inner parts of my body and knit me together in my mother's womb.

Thank you for making me so wonderfully complex! Your workmanship is marvelous- how well I know it.

You watched me as I was being formed in utter seclusion, as I was woven together in the dark of the womb.

You saw me before I was born. Every day of my life was recorded in you r book. Every moment was laid out before a single day passed."

- Psalm 139: 13-16, (NLT)

I find that this, is what most people stumble at, that we have a creator, a Almighty God, Elohim, and that we are His creation, He created us, and He knows, how to restore us. I thank God, and my Savior, the Lord Jesus Christ for what He did that day. He gave me back my life, and made believers out of some of the workers, at the hospital that day. I am glad that He has blessed me and impressed it within my spirit, to share

what He did for me that day. I pray it will encourage someone else today, to believe in God, and our Lord and Savior Jesus Christ. God is still God, and He still loves and cares for His people, no matter how much the enemy, the devil, is telling you, it isn't so. Don't believe it, trust in God, with all your heart, and know that He loves and cares for you very much. The fact that He sent His Son to die for us, in our place, proves that. In my opinion, none of us have done anything in this life, to say, that we deserve to live, we can desire to live, but because of our sins, past or present, we can't say that we deserve to live, but, for the mercy, and the grace, of our Lord, Jesus Christ, we have been given a chance to live, and to reap eternal life.

CHAPTER TWELVE

The Angel, and The Rope

"For God speaketh once, yea twice, yet man perceiveth it not.

In a dream, in a vision of the night when deep sleep falleth upon men, in slumberings upon the bed;

Then He openeth the ears of men, and sealeth instruction,

That He may withdraw man from his purpose, and hide pride from man."

- Job 33: 14 - 17, (KJV)

Visions and dreams, that are given by the Lord God, are for the purpose of guiding, instructing, revealing of a truth, revealing of future event s, as in reference, to the prophetical.

> "There was a man in the land of Uz, whose name was Job; and that man was perfect and upright, and one that feared God, and eshewed evil."
>
> - Job 1:1, (KJV)

Job was a man that loved the Lord and served him with all his heart. But when Satan decided to test him, to see if he would still serve God, by attacking him, and taking away all that he had, killing his children, his servants, afflicting his body, and turning his wife against him. Even his friends who were supposed to be coming to comfort him, ended up, falsely accuse him, day and night, to further aggravate his sufferings. Truly life became very hard to bare, but Job, still held on to God's hand, even when he didn't understand. Job, suffered from skin worms eating at his body, he suffered from depression, caused by his sufferings, but, as the story goes, it still didn't stop Job from believing in God, or stop him, from wanting to serve him.

In this life, I have found, that sometimes, we are 'picked out' by God, to be 'picked on', so to speak. In other words, sometimes, we may have to go through many trials, and afflictions, but, if God be for you, He is more than the world against you. As Paul taught in the book of Romans, when dealing with the topic, of suffering, had this to say about it.-

> "What shall we then say to these things? If God be for us, who can be against us?
>
> For I am persuaded, that neither death, nor life, nor powers, nor angels, nor principalities, nor powers, nor things present, nor things to come,
>
> Nor height, nor depth, nor any other creature, shall be able to separate us from the love, which is in Christ Jesus our Lord."
>
> - Romans 8: 31, 38-39, (KJV)

Even though Job did not understand why, everything was happening to him, he did not lose his integrity, or charge God foolishly about it. -

"For the thing which I greatly feared is come upon me, and that which I was afraid of is come unto me.

I was not in safety, neither had I rest. neither was I quiet; yet trouble came.

In all this Job sinned not, nor charged God foolishly."

-Job 3: 25-26, 1: 22, (KJV)

Many times we go through troubles without knowing, or understanding why. When you feel that you are living all you know how to serve the Lord, these times of testing, and trial, can seem un- warranted, and even unjust. They can, sometimes, leave us feeling, picked, to be picked on, just like Job did, in the height of his suffering, our emotions, take over, and our vision becomes clouded, as to the true nature of God. God does not cause suffering, but He will sometimes allow it, if He sees that it will work to our good. As is stated in the Word of God:

"And we know that all things work together for the good to them that love God, to them who are the called according to His purpose."

- Romans 8: 28, (KJV)

In the book of Job, God asks Satan, has he considered his servant Job. Then continues to speak of Job's character, where He was concerned. Satan of course steps up, to the challenge.

I remember one Sunday morning while sitting in service, listening to the sermon. I started feeling the muscles in my face, pulling to one side. At the same time, I felt a wave of heat, come all over me. During this time, I was dealing with a great deal of sickness in my body. I remember looking up front, trying to remain calm. I thought that if I just relaxed, the feeling would go away. I remember, seeing, the pastor turn around, at that moment, stop preaching, and started to stare at me. He then ask me, if I was alright? I tried to speak, but my speech, just came out garbled. I felt helpless, and unable to move. Suddenly, I started to feeling very faint. I started falling forward, as if being pulled by over by my own weight.

I seemed to be moving in slow motion, even though, I may have been moving faster, that is what it felt like to me.

The next thing I remember, I was standing in a dark place. On the floor, In front of me, I saw my body curled up, in a fetal position, on my side. I still had on the blue silk dress, I had wore to church that Sunday, I even, the hat that I put on to match, only this time, I felt like I was totally alone. It was as if, this was not supposed to happen. I could feel the coldness of the darkness around me. I couldn't shake the feeling, that this was wrong.

As I looked at my body just lying there, I felt helpless, that there was nothing, I could do or say, to help myself, I was alone. As I stood there watching, in the dark, I wondered, what was going to happen to me next. It was then, that I noticed a light began to shine on my body laying on the floor. I looked up, trying to see where it was coming from. I saw an angel coming down over me, holding onto a gold rope. The angel, himself, shone with a bright golden light! He was holding onto the rope with his right hand, while holding a

torch in his left hand. The torch also, was made of gold, just like the rope. It's light, glowing with a bright flame! The rope, I noticed, looked to be braided with cords, made of golden threads.

I watched, as he came, closer, and closer to me. I then heard a voice, from up above me, say to the angel, come back up! I am not ready for her yet! I then saw the rope turning by itself, as if in obedience to the voice, and go back up, taking,, the angel with it. I stood in amazement, as I watched this taking place before my eyes. I knew then, that this was an untimely incident, and that the enemy, had attempted to take my life again, but the mercies of God, had spared me, once again.

I know this sounds strange, but stranger still is, I am the one that it seemed to keep happening to! I know that the church members, like Job's wife were probably getting tired of seeing me having to go through these things. I know this, because one of them made a comment to me, similar to what Job's wife, did to him. They said to me, you seem to be really

suffering, and really going through, why don't you, just curse God and die, it would at least put you out of your misery! They call themselves, trying to be funny, or make light of the situation, not realizing, what they was saying to me, at the time. They then went on to say, that they was tired of seeing me suffer. Do I know how Job felt? Yes, I do! I was being put to the test! But praise be to God, He brought me through! In 2005, June 17th, during a Benny Hinn, healing crusade in Detroit Michigan, at the Joe Lewis Arena during a 7:30 pm service. I was healed of the sickness that had caused me no end of troubles, and despair, setting off all kinds of health issues, in my body, for 18 years! God delivered me before the world! Just as he promised me He would, five years before! I was thinking, it would be before family, and friends, but God was thinking much more greater. Pastor Hinn's crusades are televised all over the world! What a wonderful God we serve! That date and time, I purposely remembered, because I wanted to have a record of the date and time, when God healed me, in my mind.

I know that we live in a world that wants scientific proof for everything that is done, but some times there are no answers, only faith! Especially when it is the supernatural, miracle working power, of the Holy Spirit. All that we can say is, what the Bible says in Psalms 118. -

"This is the Lord's doing; it is marvelous in our eyes."

-Psalms 118: 23, (KJV)

I regret, not writing the dates down, of when I received my visions, but once again, it was the content, and what was being revealed, that mattered most to me at the time. It is my deepest prayer that whomever reads this can find hope when facing, trying times, bad situations, sickness, and un-welcome circumstances, that as the Word of God, tells us in Psalms 118:

"I shall not die, but live, and declare the works of the Lord."

- Psalms 118: 17, (KJV)

The devil is always, trying to stop the progress of the Lord Jesus Christ, in this world, trying to kill everything he is doing, but our faith in God, like Job, though the trials that he puts us through, may make us weary sometimes, You can rest assured that God will bring us through to the victory, that is found in Jesus Christ.

" As it is written, For thy sake we are killed all the day long; we are accounted as sheep for the slaughter.

Nay, in all these things we are more than conquerors through Him that loved us."

- Romans 8: 36 37, (KJV)

CHAPTER THIRTEEN

The Mountain, and The Valley

In the month of September, in 1980, not long after I was saved, and born again. I had a vision of a mountain, that was split in two. It was in the latter part of the fall, somewhere around the month of November. I was saved during a forty day prayer meet. The meeting would start every night around 7:30 pm, and we would stay on our knees in pray until the power of the Lord would began to fall in the midst of the service. It was an awesome time in the Lord, and it was very rough, and dangerous times as well. Everyone that came to the meeting, was up under, t tremendous attack from the enemy. We stayed

on our knees in prayer, back then. I still do. Some were risking their lives, just to come to church, while others, were going tremendous opposition, just to come and kneel down, and pray! Our pastor was a firm believer in prayer and fasting. In fact we stayed, pretty much on our knees in prayer, most of the time! It made us stronger, and considering what we were all going through at the time, it was needed.. We were a small church, most of us, were still in our early twenties, at the time, but we were faithful to God, and the house of God, valuing the time that we spent in fellowship with the Lord, and each other. We didn't know who, through some form of attack from the enemy, would not be able to come to church, the next time the doors were opened. We were thankful for the prayers that we prayed, and received, as well as the anointed teachings and preaching that was going forth. Being able to be in the midst of the Lord's Spirit, moving so mightily amongst us, was wonderful, strengthening the mind and the soul. Watching, and experiencing, the Spirit of the Lord, move in the midst every service, to young saints, who hadn't

experienced that before, it was more than enough for some of us, to brave winter storms, troubles, and trials, just to come to church! Some of us were threatened with guns, and violence, even being chased by dogs, as we walked to church! We were going through, but when we got to church, we knew Jesus, was going to meet us there! We would pray and call on the name of Jesus, till the power of the Holy Spirit would just fill the room! Oh, but that was when we were blessed to see some of the greatest miracles we had ever seen in our young lives.

> "I will be glad and rejoice in thy mercy: for thou hast considered my trouble; thou hast known my soul in adversities;
>
> And hast not shut me up into the hand of the enemy: thou hast set my feet in a large room."
>
> - Psalm 31: 7, 8, (KJV)

I had been up late, reading and studying my Bible, praying, and having a talk with the Lord about some pressing matters, that was going on in my life at that time. After while, I went

and laid down on the bed for just a moment, to rest my eyes before continuing with my studies. I remember, it was not long before the sun was to come up. I remember, closing my eyes, but I was not asleep, because I wasn't sleepy, just in need of closing my eyes for a moment. I could feel the strain on them, and they were starting to hurt. Immediately, as I closed my eyes, I saw myself being taken over hills, mountains, valleys, rivers, and things. There were two angels, one on each side of me holding me up in the air as we were traveling over the tops of everything. It was night time, and we seemed to be traveling very fast! We soon came up on a mountain that looked to be very big. The mountain was split straight down the middle, in two. There was light coming through the split in the mountain!

As we got closer, we came to the top of the mountain. This is where the angels set me down, still standing beside me. I looked over into the valley, on the other side of the mountain, to see where the light was coming from. There in the valley was a field, full of beautiful flowers, of all colors, scattered throughout the field, and lush green grass. It was all lit up! It

looked to be a bright summers day! There in the middle of the valley was a river that seem to wind its way through the field! It sparkled in the light, very clean and clear, with just a hint of blue sky color in it. The whole scene just made me want to go down there. I started to step off the mountain, the angels stopped me and said, " It was not my time yet to go there." I must admit, at that time, I did not understand what they meant. I thought for a moment, that they just didn't want me to go down there, I know, it was silly, I was still learning!

They took me by the hands, and lifted me up, and we started to go back, over the trees and hills again. I really didn't want to go back into the night again, especially, to what I was dealing with. I didn't understand at that time why they would just bring me to the mountain, allow me to look over, and then want to take me me back through the night, when they could have easily, let me go into the valley where it was all bright. I did not relish the idea of going back into the night. I was still learning about spiritual matters and visions at that time, so things weren't as clear to me then, as they are now, and I

am still learning. It wasn't until later after studying more and searching the Holy Spirit for answers and understanding, did I come to understand the vision. The Lord was giving me a glimpse of the new world, that He is going to recreate after the judgment of this world is past, and He is with us in this earth. It will be a time of great beauty, as the Lord makes everything new again. The river is Christ. He is the life that will be in the midst of the new world. The flowers are in representative of the souls of all the different saints, from around the world, that are going to be there, enjoying the beauty of the Lord. It was not my time yet, because this is yet to happen. How amazing is that. When Christ, who is the life, comes back and stands on the mountain, then these things will began.What I like about the angels being there beside me, it reminded me of Psalms 91, and though, they were taking me back into the night, yet they were protecting, as we traveled. :

> "He shall cover thee with his feathers, and under his
> wings shalt thou trust; his truth shall be thy shield
> and buckler.

Thou shalt not be afraid for the terror by night; nor for the arrow that flieth by day;

Nor for the pestilence that walketh in darkness; nor for the destruction that wasteth at noonday.

A thousand shall fall at thy side, and ten thousand at thy right hand; but it shall not come nigh thee.

Only with thine eyes shalt thou behold and see the reward of the wicked.

Because thou hast made the LORD, which is my refuge, even the Most High, thy habitation;

For he shall give his angels charge over thee, to keep the in all thy ways.

They shall bear thee up in their hands, lest thou dash thy foot against a stone."

- Psalm 91: 4-12, (KJV)

Surely the whole Psalms is a promise from God of His protection for those who love Him. I have found it to be

true. I tried it for myself. Many a day this word of the Lord has saved my life! Literally!! But that is another story! Why would the Lord show me a mountain that split in two? The only answer I could think of was Zechariah.

"Then shall the Lord go forth, and fight against those nations, as when He fought in the day of battle.

And His feet shall stand in that day upon the mount of Olives, which is before Jerusalem on the east, and the mount of Olives shall cleave in the midst thereof toward the east and toward the west, and there shall be a very great valley; and half of the mountain shall remove toward the north, and half of it toward the south.

And ye shall flee to the valley of the mountains; for the valley of the mountains shall reach unto Azal: yea, ye shall flee, like as ye fled from before the earthquake in the days of Uzziah King of Judah: and the Lord my God shall come, and all the saints with thee.

And it shall come to pass in that day, that the light shall not be clear, nor dark:

But it shall be one day which shall be known to the Lord, not day, or night: but it shall come to pass, that at evening time it shall be light.

And it shall be in that day, that living waters shall go out from Jerusalem; half of them toward the former sea, and half of them toward the hinder sea; in summer and in winter shall it be.

And the Lord shall be King over all the earth: in that day shall there be one Lord, and His name one."

- Zechariah 14: 3-9, (KJV)

Upon coming across this in my studying, sometime later, I understood the vision. Yes, this world is going through its troubles and things are being shaken as never before! Though it looks like these are somewhat dark times. Yet things are not completely dark, Jesus is still on the throne, and one day He is coming back for His people, and then we will be coming

back with Him, when he returns to set up His kingdom. At the end of days when the final judgment is passed, we will live in a renewed, and recreated world, able to enjoy the Lord and His holy presence forever. I am grateful, that even as a young saint, the Lord considered me, to reveal to such wonderful things to. I am eternally grateful to my Lord and Savior Jesus Christ, For saving me, and giving me this opportunity to share with you what He is, and has been, in my life, and what He has done, and is continually, doing in my life. May God Bless you, and I hope that you find blessing and inspiration in them, as I have in the remembrance of them, and the sharing of them. In Jesus's mighty name I pray. Amen

Everyone has a purpose in this life, everyone has a calling to do something for the Lord Jesus. If God is calling you to do a work for Him, is it not better to be found doing it. Nothing is a small work in Christ. No matter how we may look at it. It is the fruit that it bears, that tells the story. I hope you find your vision, and, purpose in life, that God has given you.